RABINDRANATH TAGORE

Selected Poems

Translated by WILLIAM RADICE

PENGUIN BOOKS

Dedicated to the Peace Movement
and to E. P. Thompson (1924–1993)

PENGUIN BOOKS

Published by the Penguin Group
Penguin Books Ltd, 80 Strand, London WC2R 0RL, England
Penguin Group (USA) Inc., 375 Hudson Street, New York, New York 10014, USA
Penguin Books Australia Ltd, 250 Camberwell Road, Camberwell, Victoria 3124, Australia
Penguin Books Canada Ltd, 10 Alcorn Avenue, Toronto, Ontario, Canada M4V 3B2
Penguin Books India (P) Ltd, 11 Community Centre, Panchsheel Park, New Delhi – 110 017, India
Penguin Group (NZ), cnr Airborne and Rosedale Roads, Albany, Auckland 1310, New Zealand
Penguin Books (South Africa) (Pty) Ltd, 24 Sturdee Avenue, Rosebank 2196, South Africa

Penguin Books Ltd, Registered Offices: 80 Strand, London WC2R 0RL, England

www.penguin.com

First published in Penguin Books 1985
Reprinted with revisions 1987
Reprinted with revisions 1993
Reprinted with a new Preface and an additional Appendix 1994
Reprinted with a new Preface, Further Reading and corrections in Penguin Classics 2005
7

Printed in England by Clays Ltd, St Ives plc
Set in Linotype Ehrhardt by Syarikat Seng Teik Sdn. Bhd., Malaysia

ISBN-13: 978–0–14–044988–4

as born in 1951 in London. He has pursued a

Contents

Preface to the 2005 Edition

This book is now celebrating its twentieth anniversary, and I present it this time without any *apologia*. In the first edition of 1985 I was nervously presenting my work for the first time, aware of those before me who had fallen short, and wondering if my own attempts to present and translate Rabindranath Tagore would be any more successful. On the whole, the response across the world proved positive – not least among Tagore's ever-watchful compatriots. In the Preface to the 1994 edition, however, I felt obliged to take account of E. P. Thompson's charge that I had unfairly dismissed the work of his father, Edward Thompson. I tried to put matters straight not only in the Preface but in an additional appendix – which can now, I think, along with the 1994 Preface itself, be safely removed.

The 1994 Preface was also an opportunity to mention the expansion of interest in Tagore that had developed since my book was published: the new translations that had appeared not only in English but in other European languages, and musical adaptations such as Param Vir's chamber opera, *Snatched by the Gods*. The expansion has gone on, but this time it is best conveyed by the list of Further Reading. In 1985 it would have been hard to compile such a list without including many older books and translations that even then were no longer in print. But now a list much longer than the one I have supplied could be made up of books currently available. In India, especially, numerous books have appeared, uninhibited by any copyright restrictions. (Copyright in India was extended by a special act of Parliament in 1991, fifty years after Tagore's death, but the extension came to an end in 2001.)

One issue that I discussed in both the 1985 and 1994 Prefaces was whether it was right to go on using 'Tagore', an anglicized form of *Ṭhākur*, or whether we should call the poet – as Bengalis do – 'Rabindranath'. I decided to stick to 'Tagore', writing in 1985: 'I regret this, as "Rabindranath" is a much more beautiful and expressive name than Tagore (it means "Lord of the Sun"), and I respect other writers who have tried to adopt it. But Tagore is convenient.'

Partly because 'Tagore' is widely used in India outside Bengal, as well as all over the world (sometimes with the final 'e' pronounced as a syllable), there seems little chance of its displacement. In fact, the existence of these two names is a useful shorthand for Tagore's Indian and international career (as Tagore) and his specifically Bengali identity as Rabindranath. In lectures and essays I have often depicted the two names as overlapping circles. The two careers developed separately from each other in some ways, yet they also partook of each other. 'Rabindranath' went on informing 'Tagore'; yet the international fame and responsibilities that Rabindranath acquired after he won the Nobel Prize in 1913 also impinged on his Bengali identity.

The critic and scholar Harish Trivedi – whose introduction to a new edition in 1989 of Edward Thompson's *Rabindranath Tagore: Poet and Dramatist* (1948) gave Thompson's pioneering work a new lease of life – has argued that through an ever growing number of new translations we now have a third entity: not the Tagore of his own translations and secondary translations of them, not the Rabindranath of his Bengali works, but the total poet and writer now being presented to non-Bengalis through new translations and books. This is, perhaps, a fulfilment of what Tagore himself came to regret had not been achieved by his own translations. In a letter to William Rothenstein of 26 November 1932 he wrote:

> It was not at all necessary for my own reputation that I should find my place in the history of your literature. It was an accident for which you were also responsible and possibly most of all was Yeats. But yet sometimes I feel almost ashamed that I whose undoubted claim has been recognized by my countrymen to a sovereignty in our own world of letters should not have waited till it was discovered by the outside world in its own true majesty and environment . . .

Every new translation that appears now is a step towards that discovery. There is a long way still to go, but when the present book first appeared I never imagined that it would open a door through which so many others have enthusiastically passed.

In the 1985 Preface I wrote in some detail about the pronunciation of Bengali names, and then in 1994 unhelpfully removed that guidance, leaving readers to sink or swim. The issue *is* rather complicated: Bengali is not pronounced as it is spelt. A transcription that attempts to convey the sound of Bengali names and words weakens their connections with other South Asian languages; yet a system that adopts – as in this book – a 'Sanskritic' system of diacritical marks to indicate the spelling will not help with pronunciation. On the other hand, to pronounce 'Kṛṣṇa' in a standard 'North Indian' way – 'Krishna' – rather than Bengali 'Krishno' is not to go badly wrong. So, on balance, I am content to stick to what I wrote in 1985: 'Anyone wanting to know exactly how to pronounce a word will have to ask a native speaker' – especially as the growth of a Bengali diaspora in the Western world makes it much easier to find a native speaker than it was then.

I have learned over the years that it is a mistake to meddle too much with past books, other than correcting printing errors or obvious factual or translation mistakes. In 1994 I changed the titles of two of the poems. In fact, it is foolhardy to change a title once it has been published, even if it is slightly wrong. Other creative works may be based on that title, and references may be made to it in books of biography or criticism. For this reason, I have decided that 'Snatched by the Gods' and 'Injury' should revert to those titles, imperfect though they may be.

As regards the Introduction, this may well, now, be a period piece. I have removed one statement about Tagore's paintings that was dubious when I wrote it and is certainly untrue now (they are today a source of tremendous pride to their custodians at Santiniketan, not any kind of embarrassment, and are the focus of a highly specialized conservation effort); and one inaccuracy in the list of those who were present when W. B. Yeats read out poems from Tagore's *Gitanjali* at William Rothenstein's house in Hampstead, on 7 July 1912 (Ezra Pound was not present). But readers still seem to find the Introduction helpful as an entrée into Tagore's life and work. So let it stand.

Northumberland, 2005

Further Reading

The standard edition of Tagore's Collected Bengali Works is the *rabīndra-racanābalī* of Visva-Bharati, Calcutta. Vols. 1–26 were first published between 1939 and 1949, with two supplementary volumes in 1940–41; Vol. 27 appeared in 1965, and Vols. 28–30 in 1995–8. Visva-Bharati is also the publisher of volumes of Tagore's letters, his collected songs, separate editions of individual works, and many books relating to Tagore. Now that Tagore is no longer in copyright, other editions of individual works are appearing in India, and collected editions on CD-ROM: *Chirantan Rabindra Rachanaabali* (Kolkata: Celcius Technologies) and *Gitabitan Live* (Tagore's songs, with recordings, Kolkata: ISS Infoway). For many years, the standard edition (though it lacked any information or notes) of Tagore's own English translations was *Collected Poems and Plays*, first published by Macmillan in London in 1936. This has been superseded by a massive and excellent annotated edition, published by the Sahitya Akademi in Delhi and edited by Sisir Kumar Das. Vol. 1 (*Poems*) appeared in 1994, and Vol. 2 (*Plays, Stories, Essays*) and Vol. 3 (*A Miscellany*) in 1996. The stories in Vol. 2 are only those that Tagore translated himself.

The main library and archive for Tagore, and the largest collection of his paintings, is at Rabindra Bhavana, Santiniketan, West Bengal. In London, the Tagore Centre UK has an interesting collection of Tagore books and documents.

The fullest bibliography of Tagore in English is still *Rabindranath Tagore: A Bibliography* by Katherine Henn (The American Theological Library Association, 1985); also useful is Dipali Ghosh, *Translations of Bengali Works into English: A Bibliography* (London and New York: Mansell Publishing Ltd, 1986).

For on-line material about Tagore, go especially to www.visva-bharati.ac.in (an impressive and informative website), and to the Internet journal *Parabaas* at www.parabaas.com.

Please note that Calcutta is now known as Kolkata and has been so cited for works published since 2000.

Works by Tagore

For a useful list that includes older translations, see *Encyclopedia of Literary Translation into English*, 2 vols., ed. Olive Classe (London and Chicago: Fitzroy Dearborn Publishers, 2000).

Final Poems, selected and trans. Wendy Barker and Saranindranath Tagore, preface by Wendy Barker, introduction by Saranindranath Tagore (New York: George Braziller, 2001).

Glimpses of Bengal: Selected Letters, newly trans. after Surendranath Tagore's translation of 1921 by Krishna Dutta and Andrew Robinson and with an introduction by Andrew Robinson (London: Papermac, 1991).

Gora (novel), trans. Sujit Mukherjee, with an introduction by Meenakshi Mukherjee (New Delhi: Sahitya Akademi, 1997).

The Home and the World (novel), trans. Surendranath Tagore (London: Macmillan, 1919); with an introduction by Anita Desai (Harmondsworth: Penguin Books, 1985); new edn with a preface by William Radice (London: Penguin Books, 2005).

I Won't Let You Go: Selected Poems, trans. with an introduction by Ketaki Kushari Dyson (Newcastle upon Tyne: Bloodaxe Books, 1991).

My Reminiscences, Surendranath Tagore's translation of 1912, revised and introduced by Andrew Robinson (London: Papermac, 1991).

Particles, Jottings, Sparks: The Collected Brief Poems, trans. with an introduction by William Radice (New Delhi: HarperCollins, 2000; London: Angel Books, 2001).

The Post Office (play), trans. William Radice, set as a play-within-a-play by Jill Parvin (London: The Tagore Centre UK, 1995).

Quartet (novella), a translation by Kaiser Haq of *caturaṅga* (Oxford: Heinemann, 1993).

Rabindranath Tagore: An Anthology, ed. Krishna Dutta and Andrew Robinson (London: Picador, 1997).

Selected Poems (various translators), ed. Sukanta Chaudhuri, introduction by Sankha Ghosh (New Delhi: Oxford University Press, 2004).

Selected Short Stories, trans. with an introduction by William Radice (Harmondsworth: Penguin Books, 1991, revised 1994, new edn 2005; New Delhi: Penguin India, 1995).

Selected Writings on Literature and Language (various translators), ed. Sisir Kumar Das and Sukanta Chaudhuri (New Delhi: Oxford University Press, 2001).

Show Yourself to My Soul, a translation of *gītāñjali* (the Bengali book of that name, which does not correspond exactly to the selection in Tagore's own English *Gitanjali*) by James Talarovic, foreword by William Radice, introduction by David E. Schlaver (Notre Dame, Indiana: Sorin Books, 2002; translation originally published in 1983 in Dhaka, Bangladesh, by the University Press Ltd).

Three Plays [*raktakarabī, tapatī and arūp ratan*], trans. with an extensive introduction by Ananda Lal (Calcutta: Birla Foundation, 1987; New Delhi: Oxford University Press, 2001).

About Tagore

For fuller bibliographies, see the books by Krishna Dutta and Andrew Robinson.

Chatterjee, Bhabatosh, *Rabindranath Tagore and Modern Sensibility* (New Delhi: Oxford University Press, 1996).

Chaudhuri, Nirad C., *Thy Hand, Great Anarch! India 1921–1952* (London: The Hogarth Press, 1987), especially Book 2, Chapter 5, pp. 595–636: 'Tagore; the lost great man of India'.

Das Gupta, Uma (ed.), *A Difficult Friendship: Letters of Edward Thompson and Rabindranath Tagore 1913–1940* (New Delhi: Oxford University Press, 2003).

Dutta, Krishna and Andrew Robinson, *Rabindranath Tagore: The Myriad-Minded Man* (London: Bloomsbury, 1995; New York: St Martin's Press, 1996).

Dutta, Krishna and Andrew Robinson (eds.), *Selected Letters of Rabindranath Tagore*, with a foreword by Amartya Sen (Cambridge and New York: Cambridge University Press, 1997). A wide-ranging selection, combining English letters with letters translated from Bengali and with extensive notes and commentary; an essay on Tagore and Einstein by Dipankar Home and Andrew Robinson is included in an appendix.

Dyson, Ketaki Kushari, *In Your Blossoming Flower-Garden: Rabindranath Tagore and Victoria Ocampo* (New Delhi: Sahitya Akademi, 1988).

Fraser, Bashabi (ed.), *The Geddes-Tagore Correspondence* (Edinburgh: The Edinburgh Review 109, 2002; Kolkata: Visva-Bharati (*The Tagore-Geddes Correspondence*), 2004).

Hogan, Patrick Colm and Lalita Pandit (eds.), *Rabindranath Tagore: Universality and Tradition* (Cranbury, NJ, London, UK and Mississauga, Ontario: Associated University Presses, 2003). Includes essays on Tagore and nationalism, education, science, Yeats, Satyajit Ray, *Gora* and Jane Austen, Janusz Korczak, etc.

Kripalani, Krishna, *Rabindranath Tagore: A Biography* (London: Oxford University Press, and New York: Grove Press, 1962; revised edn, Calcutta: Visva-Bharati, 1980).

Kundu, Kalyan, Sakti Bhattacharya and Kalyan Sircar (eds.), *Imagining Tagore: Rabindranath Tagore and the British Press (1912–1941)*

(Kolkata: Sahitya Samsad in collaboration with The Tagore Centre UK, 2000).
Lago, Mary M. (ed.), *Imperfect Encounter: Letters of William Rothenstein and Rabindranath Tagore 1911–1941* (Cambridge, Massachusetts: Harvard University Press, 1972).
Lago, Mary and Ronald Warwick (eds.), *Rabindranath Tagore: Perspectives in Time* (London: Macmillan, 1989). Includes essays on Tagore's Western career, his short stories, his educational ideals, Tagore and Elmhirst, Tagore's paintings, Tagore and Western composers, etc.
O'Connell, Kathleen M., *Rabindranath Tagore: The Poet as Educator* (Kolkata: Visva-Bharati, 2002).
Radice, William, *Poetry and Community: Lectures and Essays 1991–2001* (New Delhi: DC Publishers, 2003). Includes essays on translating Tagore, and on Tagore and the Nobel Prize.
Radice, William, 'Rabindranath Tagore' in *Oxford Dictionary of National Biography*, Vol. 53 (Oxford: Oxford University Press, 2004).
Ray, Sibnarayan, *From the Broken Nest to Visva-Bharati: Six Exploratory Essays on Rabindranath* (Kolkata: Renaissance Publishers, 2001).
Robinson, Andrew, *The Art of Rabindranath Tagore*, with a foreword by Satyajit Ray (London: André Deutsch, 1989).
Sahitya Akademi (ed.), *Rabindranath Tagore 1861–1961: A Centenary Volume* (New Delhi: Sahitya Akademi, 1961, reprinted 1986). Introduction by Jawaharlal Nehru; memoirs by several of Tagore's associates; essays on all aspects of Tagore's life and work; essays on Tagore in other lands; bibliography of Tagore's Bengali and English works (with dates); very useful chronicle of his life compiled by Prabhat Kumar Mukherjee (Tagore's biographer in Bengali) and Kshitis Roy.
Thompson, Edward, *Rabindranath Tagore: Poet and Dramatist* (London and New York: Oxford University Press, 1926; second edn 1948; new edn with an introduction by Harish Trivedi, New Delhi: Oxford University Press, 1989).

Chronology

1858 The British Crown takes over the Government of India, following the Mutiny of 1857.
1861 Tagore born in Calcutta, in the family house at Jorasanko.
1873 Goes with his father Debendranath Tagore on a tour of the Western Himalayas.
1875 His mother dies.
1877 Starts to publish regularly in his family's monthly journal, *bhāratī*.
1878 First visit to England.
1880 His book *sandhyā saṅgīt* (Evening Songs) acclaimed by Bankimchandra Chatterjee, the leading writer of the day.
1883 Controversy over Lord Ripon's Ilbert bill, to permit Indian judges to try Englishmen, intensifies antagonism between British and Indians. Tagore marries.
1884 His sister-in-law Kadambari commits suicide.
1885 First Indian National Congress meets at Bombay.
1886 Tagore's daughter Madhurilata (Bela) born.
1888 His son Rathindranath born.
1890 His father puts him in charge of the family estates.
Second, brief visit to England.
Starts to write prolifically for a new family journal, *sādhanā*.
1898 Sedition Bill; arrest of Bal Gangadhar Tilak; Tagore reads his paper *kaṇṭha-rodh* (The Throttled) at a public meeting in Calcutta.
1901 Marriage of his elder daughters Bela and Renuka (Rani).
Inauguration of the Santiniketan School.
1902 His wife dies.
1903 Rani dies.
1904 Satischandra Ray, his assistant at Santiniketan, dies.
1905 *Svadeśī* agitation against Lord Curzon's proposal to partition Bengal, with Tagore playing a leading part.
His father dies.
1907 His younger son Samindra dies.
1908 Thirty-five revolutionary conspirators in Bombay and Bengal arrested.
1909 Indian Councils Act, increasing power of provincial councils, attempts to meet Indian political aspirations.
1910 Bengali *gītāñjali* published.
1912 Third visit to England; first visit to America; publication of the English *Gitanjali*.

1913 Tagore awarded the Nobel Prize for Literature.

1914 230,000 Indian troops join the first winter campaign of the Great War.

1915 Tagore's first meeting with Gandhi.
He receives a knighthood.

1916 Home Rule League formed by Annie Besant and B. G. Tilak.
Tagore goes to Japan and the USA; lectures on *Nationalism* and *Personality*.

1917 E. S. Montagu, Secretary of State, declares the development of self-government in India to be official policy.
Tagore reads his poem 'India's Prayer' at the Indian National Congress in Calcutta.

1918 Rowlatt Act against Sedition provokes Gandhi's first civil disobedience campaign.
Tagore's eldest daughter Bela dies.
German-Indian Conspiracy Trial in San Francisco implicates him: he sends a telegram to President Wilson asking for protection 'against such lying calumny'.

1919 Gen. Reginald Dyer's Amritsar Massacre; Tagore returns his knighthood.

1920 Death of Tilak leaves Gandhi undisputed leader of the nationalist movement. Tagore travels to London, France, Holland, America.

1921 Back to London, France, Switzerland, Germany, Sweden, Germany again, Austria, Czechoslovakia.
After meeting with Gandhi in Calcutta, Tagore detaches himself from the Swaraj (home rule) campaign.
Visva-Bharati, his university at Santiniketan, inaugurated.

1922 Gandhi sentenced to six years imprisonment.
Tagore tours West and South India.

1923 Congress Party under Motilal Nehru and C. R. Das ends its boycott of elections to the legislatures established by the Government of India Act (1919).

1924 Tagore travels to China and Japan.
After only two months at home, sails for South America: stays with Victoria Ocampo in Buenos Aires.

1925 Returns via Italy.
Gandhi visits Santiniketan; Tagore again refuses to be actively involved in Swaraj, or in the charka (spinning) cult.
Bengal Criminal Law Amendment Act crushes new terrorist campaign in Bengal.

1926 Tagore travels to Italy, Switzerland (staying with Romain Rolland at Villeneuve), Austria, England, Norway, Sweden, Denmark, Germany (meets Einstein), Czechoslovakia, Bulgaria, Greece, Egypt.

1927 Extensive tour of South-east Asia.

1928 Starts painting.

1929 To Canada, Japan, Saigon.

1930 To England (via France) to deliver Hibbert Lectures at Manchester College, Oxford (*The Religion of Man*); to Germany, Switzerland, Russia, back to Germany, USA.
Exhibitions of his paintings in Birmingham, London and several European capitals.
Gandhi's 'salt-march' from Ahmedabad to the coast inaugurates new civil disobedience campaign.

1932 Tagore travels (by air) to Iran and Iraq.
His only grandson Nitindra dies.
Gandhi declares fast-unto-death in jail in Poona; later breaks his fast with Tagore at his bedside.

1934–6 Tours of Ceylon and India with a dance-troupe from Santiniketan.

1935 Government of India Act emerges from Round Table Conferences of 1930–32, with all-India Federation and provincial autonomy as its main aims.

1937 Tagore delivers Convocation Address to Calcutta University, in Bengali.
Starts Department of Chinese Studies at Visva-Bharati.
Congress Party ministries formed in most states.
Tagore falls seriously ill in September.

1939 Congress ministries resign on grounds that the British Government has failed to make an acceptable declaration of its war aims.

1940 Tagore's last meeting with Gandhi, at Santiniketan.
Death of C. F. Andrews, Tagore's staunch friend and supporter at Santiniketan.
Oxford University holds special Convocation at Santiniketan to confer Doctorate on Tagore.
Muslim League under Jinnah demands separate state for Muslims.

1941 Tagore dies in Calcutta.

1942 Congress Party calls on Britain to 'quit India' immediately.

1946 Congress forms interim Government under Jawaharlal Nehru.

1947 Viscount Mountbatten announces partition: India and Pakistan become independent dominions.

1948 Assassination of Gandhi.

1950 India is declared a Republic.

Introduction

When someone from the Western world tries to write about some aspect of India, one of his difficulties is that his habits of thought and ways of writing will not necessarily fit the subject he is describing. Brooding on this problem, I was suddenly struck by a verse from the Īśā Upaniṣad. It consists of six propositions, linked by most translators into pairs:

> It stirs and it stirs not; it is far, and likewise near.
> It is inside of all this, and it is outside of all this.
>
> (Max Müller)

> He moves, and he moves not. He is far, and he is near.
> He is within all, and he is outside all.
>
> (Juan Mascaró)

The Upaniṣads, some of which date back to the eighth century B.C., meant more to Rabindranath Tagore than any other literature; and the Īśā Upaniṣad – expounded in detail in the second lecture of *Personality* (1917) – was particularly dear to him. The Īśā Upaniṣad had been a revelation to his father, the religious reformer Debendranath Tagore, who describes in his autobiography how he found the first verse of the text by chance, on a loose page of a Sanskrit book fluttering past him. The verse that struck me is the fifth. It is about the nature of God, Brahman, and it attempts through its contradictions to describe the interplay of world and spirit, eternal and temporal, infinite and finite, transcendent and immanent which Tagore himself defined as the main subject of all his writings. It seemed to me, therefore, that the separate propositions in the verse would serve well as headings for the main sections of this Introduction. I shall be stretching their meaning far beyond what the seer who composed the Īśā Upaniṣad intended; but I know of no better way in which to deal with the complexity and contradictions of Tagore's life and work – a complexity compounded by the fact that this is not a book of his poems in the language in which they were written, but a book of translations.

He moves

Tagore was a child of nineteenth-century Bengal, of Calcutta, a place and a time to which nearly all the main cultural, political and economic features of modern India can be traced. If one were to sum up in a single word all the new ingredients that were added to India by her contact with a Western power, it would be 'progress'. This is not to imply any value-judgement on the merits or otherwise of British imperial rule: it is merely that prior to the British presence, progress as an idea or an ideal did not really exist in India. By the 1830s, however, not only were the inhabitants of Bengal faced by a city, Calcutta, that had progressed from a tiny village on the east bank of the Hooghly to a 'city of palaces', a great commercial centre, capital of all the territories administered by the East India Company; they also found themselves increasingly swept into controversies about progress – educational progress, religious progress, legal and political progress, literary and linguistic progress. The Tagore family was at the centre of this sea-change. Tagore's grandfather, Dwarkanath Tagore, had built up an immense family fortune, a network of agricultural, mining, trading and banking interests controlled through his firm, Carr, Tagore & Co. He came to be known as Prince Dwarkanath, renowned for his lavish way of life. Such a career would not have been possible without the British presence, and appropriately his death in 1846 came not in the land of his birth but in London, during a second visit to England (at a time when there was a strong taboo against Hindus making sea-voyages) in which he came into contact with the English nobility and Queen Victoria. But progress for Dwarkanath was not just commercial progress – he was involved in the foundation of many of Calcutta's major institutions: the Hindu College, which became the centre of English education in Bengal; the Calcutta Medical College; the National Library; the Agricultural and Horticultural Society of India; the Hindu Benevolent Institution; and so on.

Dwarkanath was a friend of Rammohan Roy (1772–1833), pioneer among Indian religious and social reformers; and though he was himself quite traditional in his religious practices, he supported Rammohan's religious reform society, the Brahmo Sabha (later, Brahmo Samaj), against attacks from the orthodox.

The current of religious reform that ran right through nineteenth-century Bengal was what especially attracted Dwarkanath's eldest son Debendranath, who disapproved of his father's worldliness and sometimes clashed with him but who was no less concerned with Improvement, interpreted in a more austere and Victorian way. The family business collapsed after Dwarkanath's death, and Debendranath inherited massive debts which took many years of frugal management to pay off; but landed estates had been left in trust to him and his two brothers and it was into a wealthy family, with a huge house in north Calcutta, that Tagore was born: a family that took it for granted that wealth and influence were to be used for the good of society, and for cultural enrichment.

Dwarkanath had moved, in the direction of material prosperity and public munificence; Debendranath moved, in the direction of inner self-realization and missionary zeal; Rabindranath – fourteenth of the fifteen children that his mother, in best Victorian fashion, bore for her husband – also moved, in a multiplicity of ways that differed from both his father and grandfather but which nevertheless owed something to both. From his father he inherited spiritual aspiration and a desire to do good in the world; from his grandfather he inherited a tremendous zest for life.

Here are some of the ways in which Tagore moved throughout his long life.

He moved in religion, away from the puritanical Brahmo church that his father had created along lines proposed by Rammohan Roy, and away from the Hindu revivalism that was very much in the air by the end of the nineteenth century. Neither Brahmoism nor revivalism left Tagore untouched: his father succeeded in making him Secretary of the Adi Brahmo Samaj for a while, and he composed many songs for it; and his earliest endeavours at Santiniketan – a boarding-school-cum-*āśram* modelled on the ancient Indian *tapovana* (forest hermitage) – were distinctly revivalist in character. But he moved away from both, to religious attitudes that owed something to the personalized devotion of medieval Bengali Vaiṣṇavism, much to the poetry and grandeur of the Upaniṣads, and most to Tagore's sense of his own creativity, a creativity that seemed a counterpart to the creativity of the universe as a whole. 'The Religion of Man' was what he called it; but 'The Poet's Religion', the title he gave to the first lecture in *Creative Unity* (1922), would be a better name, since the religion is inseparable from his artistic theory and practice.

Tagore moved in social, educational and political ideas. His father, religion apart, was conservative by temperament, with no desire to change institutions that had the stamp of legality, decency or honour on them; but Tagore always rebelled against rigid structures. He rebelled against school, to such an extent that from the age of fourteen, and after frequent changes of school, his family in despair consigned him to a haphazard series of tutors at home. When he came to create his own school at Santiniketan, though it went through many changes and compromises, his abiding aim was to break conventional educational moulds: to develop all aspects of a child's personality rather than merely prepare him for exams and professions. He rebelled against the entire educational structure set up by the British, sending his son Rathindranath not to Oxford or Cambridge or the Inns of Court but to the University of Illinois to study agriculture, and founding a university of his own that was entirely independent of British funding or control. He never ceased to attack in his poems, stories, novels, plays and essays all forms of prejudice and bigotry – against women, or non-Hindus, or foreigners (including the British). He moved forward in his political ideals, to such an extent that nationalists were frequently annoyed by his refusal to be a chauvinist: even with Gandhi he differed, dreading the irrationality that was exploited by his civil disobedience campaigns, arguing that national independence meant nothing if it were not preceded by social and cultural renewal from within, fearing the emergence of an Indian nation state that would have those very nationalist, militarist and imperialist features that he deplored in the West. Sometimes his relentless search for new solutions, new patterns of human development, led him astray: he was misled by Mussolini at first, and in his report on Stalinist Russia in 1930, though it was not the glowing paean that some people have claimed it to be, he was not, alas, sufficiently aware of the human cost of the educational and social improvements that he admired there. But he never ceased to search, to think and to question: his faith in man demanded it.

The movement was not merely cerebral, or confined to his experiment at Santiniketan. After his third visit to England in 1912, the publication of the English *Gitanjali*, the Nobel Prize in 1913 and sudden world fame, he moved unremittingly in a physical sense, all round India and all round the world. The list of dates on p. 13 of this book will show the scale of these tours (done by sea and land; only for his last, to Iran and Iraq in 1932, did he use an aeroplane). Their aim was to raise funds for his university, and to say things about the world and its future that he believed were important. They were gruelling, and frequently brought him to the point of nervous collapse – but a restlessness in him drove him on.

This restlessness had always been in Tagore. Before his marriage in 1883 and after it, there had been frequent changes of abode; and at the very end of his life, when ill-health prevented him from travelling, he took to changing his living-place at Santiniketan, even having an experimental cottage built entirely of mud (because he was worried about the frequent fires in the thatched village houses) next to his grand house called Uttarāyaṇ.

In life, so too in his art. Tagore was a perpetual innovator, constantly creating new forms and styles in his poetry; working fundamental changes in Bengali vocal music; introducing novel kinds of drama, opera and ballet; exploring subjects from nursery-rhymes to science in his essays; evolving a unique style in the paintings and drawings that he produced in large quantities from 1928 on; above all, enormously expanding and altering the resources of the Bengali language. In this he was bringing to fruition the efforts of many writers previous to him. The development of Bengal in the nineteenth and twentieth centuries is also the development of its language. In 1800 – virtually no prose; poetry confined to religious subjects and restricted to two monotonous metres. But by 1900 – after the essays of Rammohan Roy and Isvarchandra Vidyasagar (1820–91), the epic poetry of Michael Madhusudan Datta (1824–73), the drama of Dinabandhu Mitra (1829–74), the novels of Bankimchandra Chatterjee (1838–94) and the lyrics of Biharilal Chakravarti (1834–94) – we have Rabindranath Tagore, a writer whose complete works were to run to thirty-two large volumes, covering almost every literary genre. He built on all their achievements, and went further: digging more deeply into Sanskrit (when he wanted a rich and complex diction) than even Madhusudan did; bringing prose closer to natural speech than Bankim had done; inventing a range of lyric metres and verse-forms that no writer before him in any modern Indian language had dreamed of. He was not alone; many other talents emerged during his lifetime. But no one could ignore him, and his achievement remains an almost oppressive legacy, too close still to its inheritors for it to be seen or assessed clearly.

I have tried, in this book, to be true to the spirit of movement in Tagore: not only through a selection that is chronological and which spans almost his whole career, but by trying in the English verse-forms I have used to convey that spirit. The constantly changing verse-forms require equal inventiveness in the translator, and I have tried many things: lines based on syllable or accent as well as metre; verses based on half-rhyme as well as rhyme. Sometimes I have been traditional, just as Tagore was traditional at times; sometimes I have produced forms that I believe are new to English poetry. In my notes I have tried to relate the restlessness and movement in Tagore's poetry – seen in its purest form in the poems from *balākā* (1916) on, in which he used varying line-lengths, spreading out across the page – to his deepest ideas and intuitions: his sense of the *khelā* or play of the universe, of a process at work in Nature and man that involves ceaseless change through time, but which also remains tuned to an underlying and unchanging harmony.

He moves not

Tagore was a radical in the true sense, always trying to get to the root of things: but there were strains of traditionalism in him that separated him from other groups of Bengalis to whom the term 'radical' might more readily be applied. With terrorism he would have nothing to do: his one dip into subversive politics was a short-lived secret society called the Sanjivani Sabha, founded by his elder brother Jyotirindranath in 1876, recalled with amusement in *My Reminiscences*. But there was another very important current in nineteenth-century Bengal that was alien to Tagore – one that had its source in the radical group of students that clustered round a charismatic young Eurasian teacher called Henry Louis Vivian Derozio (1809–31) at Hindu College in the late 1820s. Derozio's ideas can be traced, via his own schoolmasters in Calcutta, to the Scottish Enlightenment, to Hume and Reid and Dugald Stewart. He was perhaps not as revolutionary as some nationalist historians have wished to make out: he was certainly unfairly sacked from Hindu College in 1831. His students moved in various directions – one to the Christian ministry (Krishnamohan Banerji), one to journalism and satirical fiction (Pyarichand Mitra), one to Brahmoism (Ramtanu Lahiri) – but he left behind a legacy of free-thinking, agnosticism and pragmatism that can even be traced through to the socialist politicians who dominate West Bengal today. By the time Tagore was born, 'Young Bengal', as Derozio's group was called, had mellowed, and Hindu College had been absorbed into the Government educational system; but there is a very real temperamental gulf between Tagore and the kind of attitudes that inspired the group's more notorious escapades: their deliberate bating of the orthodox by the eating of beef; their contempt for missionaries; their bibulousness. Tagore was quite a dandy in his early twenties, an aesthete whose dress and demeanour attracted some ridicule; and the diary he wrote of his first visit to England in 1878 – the Brighton balls and musical evenings, the flirtatious séances with the daughters of his London guardians Dr and Mrs Scott – is ample evidence that the grey-bearded, long-robed poet was young once. But drinking parties, or revolt (like his great predecessor the epic poet Michael Madhusudan Datta) against arranged marriage? Never. Seriousness and traditionalism had some hold on him from boyhood.

This traditionalism could sometimes extend to quite surprisingly orthodox practices. Having been married off to a ten-year-old almost illiterate member of the peculiar Tagore family caste (they were Pirali Brahmins, a group that had supposedly lost caste generations ago through smelling – not even eating – some Muslim food), Tagore followed suit by marrying off his daughters Bela and Rani in 1901 when they were only fourteen and twelve respectively. Debendranath also adhered to practices such as the *upanayan* or sacred-thread investiture for Brahmins: Tagore went through it when he was eleven, and his own sons went through it too. But generally of course Brahmoism was anti-orthodox, and the essential cultural tradition to which Tagore belonged went back to Rammohan

Roy. Tagore left the Brahmo church in his twenties; and it would be entirely wrong to describe him as a 'Brahmo writer'. But to Rammohan Roy and his legacy he remained loyal throughout his life. He wrote on him several times: the very last address that he wrote, read out in the Mandir (temple) at Santiniketan in early 1941 when Tagore was too weak to read it himself, was on this great 'Father of Modern India'; and in an important essay of 1925 on 'The Cult of the Charka', a criticism of Gandhi's spinning-cult, he replied painfully to Gandhi's charge that Rammohan Roy was 'a pygmy' compared to some of the other great men of India.

The tenets of Rammohan Roy from which Tagore never moved throughout his life were: contempt for idolatry and externalized, ritualistic religion; a belief that the truth of Hinduism lay in the Vedānta philosophy of the Upaniṣads, with its recognition of only one true God; and a desire to bring the various religions of the world together, to extract their shared and quintessential meaning. Tagore's rationalism – profound and unswerving for all his poetic fervour – was Rammohan's: it inspired in him the same hatred of intolerance and injustice and tyranny, and it also gave him a life-long interest in science. Some historians have identified Rammohan Roy with the 'orientalist' educational policy of the East India company up to 1835, its promotion of Oriental learning in Fort William College – for this policy had its roots in the late eighteenth-century Enlightenment and in particular the work of the pioneering Oriental scholar Sir William Jones. But in fact Rammohan believed that India needed Western science and learning – he wrote a famous letter to the Governor General Lord Amherst in 1823, condemning a Government proposal to establish a Sanskrit College in Calcutta. In his universalism, his belief that India must learn from the West as well as from her own heritage, we see his real debt to the Enlightenment, and the real nature of his influence on Tagore, who saw likewise.

Rammohan formed connections with Unitarianism in India, America and England (where, like Tagore's grandfather Dwarkanath, he died, in Bristol in 1833); and when Tagore was in America for the first time in 1912–13, staying with his son Rathindranath at Urbana, Illinois, it was a Unitarian minister who asked Tagore to give, at various Unitarian chapels, the lectures that he later delivered at Harvard and published as *Sādhanā* (The Realization of Life), 1913. If 'Unitarian' were not a term that has become restricted to a particular sect, it would be a useful word for the tendency in Tagore that was opposite to the 'progress' described in the first section of this Introduction: for just as Tagore's life was a continual progress, a continual moving forward, it was also a search for unity, for a stability of belief and moral principle to give meaning and order to everything he did.

This 'Unitarian' tendency had two complementary directions. On the one hand there was the syncretism in Tagore, a faith in the unity of man and the world that was patterned on his deep religious sense of a harmony underlying all things. This was what inspired the messianic role he took upon himself after he was made world-famous by the Nobel Prize: the defiant lectures against Nationalism in the Japan of 1916; the less-than-happy attempt to preach pan-Asianism in the turbulent China of 1924; the friendships with Romain Rolland (originating in a request from Rolland for Tagore to be a signatory to his 'Declaration of Independence of the Spirit' in 1919) and with Einstein; the noble attempt to create a 'universal Indian' university – Visva-Bharati – that would bring together not only the different cultures and languages of India, but scholars and learning from all over the world. This kind of syncretism goes directly back to Rammohan Roy, and it is what Tagore has left behind in the West as his abiding memory – faint though it is now, and not always advantageous to him, for the world does not suffer idealists gladly. But there was another direction to the Unitarian tendency, and here Tagore was very different from Rammohan.

Rammohan's One God was an abstraction, the pure, impersonal Brahman of the Vedānta. He was a prosaic man, analytical rather than imaginative. Tagore's religion, however, was a poet's religion: the unity of God and his creation was the unity of a creative personality, who revealed himself to Tagore as a personal *jīban-debatā*, a 'life-god'; and just as God governs and penetrates and harmonizes all aspects of an endlessly varied universe, so this *jīban-debatā* governed and penetrated and harmonized Tagore's own varied creative activities. Personality, at the human level, can only be realized through locale, through the immediate culture and language and land to which one belongs. Rammohan was a Bengali by birth, but there was nothing specifically Bengali about him (though he pioneered Bengali discursive prose). Tagore, however, is inseparable from his Bengali background. This was the basic trouble with what the West saw of him: they got the universal message, which because it came to them detached from Tagore's background appeared to many insipid or gutless; they saw the all-Indian, all-world figure, not the Bengali; they read the poetry in English – a language that was being steadily eroded and etiolated by its very universal currency – not in the poet's mother tongue.

Tagore was rooted to Bengal. He travelled all over the world, but no landscape could ever move him more than the flat, dry plain around his beloved Santiniketan. The rivers of East Bengal inspired much of the poetry of his thirties; but it was the drier West Bengal landscape, with its spaciousness of sky and simplicity of earth, that he came to regard as his home. Even the Himalayas – so important to his father, who took Tagore there when he was eleven years old – never meant as much to him. He belonged with the land, the flowers and the trees; the birds; the people – whom he cared for genuinely, not just romantically, combining his educational experiment at Santiniketan with an agricultural experiment at the neighbouring village of Sriniketan; the music, which he enriched immeasurably with his two thousand songs; and above all the language of Bengal. He may have moved to English at a particular phase in his life; but he never moved from Bengali. He insisted that Bengali should be the medium of instruction in Bengal's schools, and wrote several essays and lectures on this theme. When he was invited in February 1937 to deliver the Convocation Address at Calcutta University, he made history by delivering it in Bengali. Back in 1895 he had made a similar stand at the Bengal Provincial Conference, demanding (unsuccessfully) that all business should be conducted in Bengali. His concern for the language went far beyond the literary use he made of it. Near the end of his life, he wrote a technical treatise on the Bengali language, *bāṅglā-bhāṣā paricay* (1938); when the Baṅgiya Sāhitya Pariṣad (Bengali Literary Academy) was founded in 1894, he provided a list of scientific and technical terms.

The Bengali language, the fundamental unifying factor in all Tagore's writing, binding him to one place and one time for all his restless travelling, cannot of course be present in a book of this kind. The difficulty that Western readers will have is that whereas if they read a translation from French, Italian, German or even Russian they are able to relate the text to a preconception of the original language – vague maybe, but real nonetheless – for a modern Indian language there can be no such aid. Sanskrit, after two centuries of Western scholarship, has conveyed its character to at least some foreigners; but the modern Indian languages have been unlearned, unstudied, unappreciated by outsiders. In the early days of the British presence in Bengal, there were enthusiasts. The Baptist missionary William Carey (1761–1843) is revered to this day in Bengal for his pioneering work: he and his colleagues at Serampore and Fort William were among the first writers of Bengali prose. But when Oriental learning ceased to be Government policy in India, and a bureaucracy and educational system based on English established itself after the assumption of the rule of India by the Crown in 1858, the language was barely learnt beyond the practical level, seldom to the level needed for the enjoyment of literature.

One could list some of the characteristics of Bengali: its rich sound patterns, exploited to the full by Tagore; its elegantly economical and regular inflexional system; its abundance of vivid, onomatopoeic words (non-Sanskritic and probably very ancient); its eclecticism of vocabulary – Persian words often giving a colloquial alternative to a Sanskrit word, just as in English there is a choice between a Latin and an Anglo-Saxon word); the freedom with which it can draw on the immense resources of Sanskrit for its higher vocabulary; its subtle and inventive compound verbal expressions. One could also talk of some of its drawbacks: the cumbersome nature of some of its prose, over-Sanskritic in vocabulary, over-influenced by English in syntax; or the facile manner in which it can rhyme so easily in poetry. But what would all this serve? From the point of view of foreigners, in the final analysis Tagore's writings cannot move from the language to which they belong; and the language is not one that many foreigners will probably ever learn.

He is far

Granted that translation, especially of poetry, is ultimately impossible, have foreigners had even the limited access to Tagore's writing that translation can afford? Translations by native speakers have been done steadily over the years, sometimes well – I would single out Sheila Chatterji's translation of Tagore's late book of vers libre, *śyāmalī* (1936, translation published by Visva-Bharati in 1955) as perhaps the best book of verse translation; and some of them have been published outside India (in particular Aurobindo Bose's three books: *A Flight of Swans*, John Murray, 1955; *The Herald of Spring*, 1957; *Wings of Death*, 1960). Edward Thompson, whom I have already mentioned in my Preface, included quite large chunks of translation in his biography of Tagore, and also published a small pamphlet in his own Augustan Books of Poetry series in 1925. An anthology, mainly of short stories, came out in America in 1965 (*The Housewarming and Other Selected Writings*, translated by Mary Lago, Tarun Gupta and Amiya Chakravarti, Signet Classics). But none of these have been sufficient to displace the impression left behind by Tagore's own translations, which are still available, in a volume that gives no information whatever about the original works, as the *Collected Poems and Plays of Rabindranath Tagore*, Macmillan, first edition 1936. This book is not as well known as it was, but it survives sufficiently for many people to have at least glanced through it; and they sometimes express surprise when they learn that Tagore wrote primarily in Bengali.

Tagore started to translate through a sequence of accidents. At the age of fifty, he was suddenly physically and emotionally exhausted. Not only had his literary labours been unremitting; there had been his energetic involvement in the public affairs of Bengal; there had been his school at Santiniketan, inaugurated in 1901; and there had been a shattering series of bereavements – wife, second daughter, father and youngest son. All this threw Tagore in upon himself, producing the austere devotional songs of the Bengali *gītāñjali* (1910); and it is crucial to remember that Tagore's literary entrée to the West came at this particular phase in his art, setting the tone for all that was later expected of him abroad. To revive body and mind, he planned a trip to England (he had been twice before, in 1878 and 1890, but had made no mark then). He needed medical treatment, and he also claimed that he needed to relate his educational experiment to the world outside.

In March 1912 he was due to sail, but suddenly fell too ill to leave. He went to Shelidah, the family estate in north Bengal, to recover; and while he was there – too weak to write anything new – he diverted himself by translating the songs in *gītāñjali*. When he was well enough to sail in May, he went on with the translations on the ship. On arrival in London he went straight to the home of William Rothenstein, who had met Tagore on a painting tour of India in 1910. Rothenstein had already seen a few translations of Tagore's poems done by Ajit Chakravarty, a teacher at Santiniketan, and had been impressed. He asked to see more – Tagore showed him the exercise book he had filled with translations, Rothenstein showed them to Yeats, and on 7 July 1912, Yeats read out the poems at a gathering in Rothenstein's Hampstead home that included Ernest Rhys (who wrote a book about Tagore, published in 1915), Alice Meynell, Arthur Fox Strangways (who played an important part in securing Tagore's profitable contracts with Macmillan) and Charles Freer Andrews (who became one of his most loyal associates at Santiniketan). The whole extraordinary business quickly gathered a momentum of its own, with the India Society edition of *Gitanjali* before the end of the year, rapturously reviewed, quickly followed by the Macmillan edition, and a sudden literary craze powerful enough for Thomas Sturge Moore to make his successful proposal of Tagore's name to the Nobel Prize Committee in 1913.

Tagore's popularity in England did not actually last very long: his lectures on Nationalism (1916) caused offence to a nation at war, and the return of his knighthood after the Jallianwala Bagh massacre in Amritsar in 1919 effectively killed his English reputation. In America – Britain's ally – these acts had also caused offence, and he was coolly received there during his second visit in 1920. His most astonishing successes were in Europe, his tours of 1921, 1926 and 1930. For this, especially the sometimes hysterical acclaim he received in Germany, there may be good historical reason, though no one has yet been able to assess it objectively: and the fame and the charisma had already been established. But the short-lived English fashion remains something of a mystery; as remote and peculiar as the craze for the spurious poems of Ossian in the 1760s.

Were Tagore's translations spurious? They were started in all modesty, and the first book, *Gitanjali*, was the best. Thereafter their increasing inaccuracy and truncatedness owed something to the sheer pressure of work on Tagore, something to the fact that their success gave him inflated confidence in their quality (late in life he looked at them much more wryly: in a letter to Rothenstein in 1932 he regretted that they had been published at all). Short stories were generally farmed out to other people, and were scarcely glanced at by an over-busy Tagore. The plays are a nadir of unfaithfulness (*Sacrifice*, twenty-nine obscure and formless pages in English, is a brilliant, ambitious, cogent five-act drama in Bengali). But leaving the inferior work aside, even *Gitanjali* has not stood the test of time, could not have remained sufficient basis for the survival of a reputation after the formidable, tall, robed and bearded bearer of that reputation had gone from the world scene. The reason for this is not inaccuracy – *Gitanjali* is on the whole reasonably accurate; nor that *Gitanjali* represented only a fraction of Tagore's sixty-odd books of verse (a really fine translation of a single book might revive Tagore's reputation today); nor that it represented the religious rather than the humanistic strain in Tagore (it is false to distinguish the two); nor even that the language of the translations has dated. The simple, most elementary reason – perceived clearly only by Ezra Pound in reviews of Tagore in 1913 in the *Fortnightly Review* and the *New Freewoman* – was that most of the lyrics that Tagore chose to translate are actually *songs*, intimate combinations of words and melody. I shall say more about the songs in the next section of this Introduction. Let me simply say here that I do not believe you can translate songs, and I have not tried to translate songs in this book. Tagore himself said in *Creative Unity* (1922) that a song without its melody is like a butterfly whose wings have been plucked, and in *My Reminiscences* we read of his reluctance to publish books of the words of his songs, for that very reason.

Though he died only sixty years ago, Tagore as he presented himself to the world outside Bengal is far from us today: far because of the dependence of his sudden Western success on a very special set of factors, hard to define; far because his own translations do not really take us close to the scope or fabric of his creative work. The ideals that he preached are far, too – though no more so today than in his own day.

In sober moments, such as the end of his second lecture on Nationalism, he knew that his voice was too feeble, too vulnerable to the charge that he was naïve or unpractical, for it to have any effect on the progress of modern civilization towards (though he died before Hiroshima) what he feared would be self-destruction.

The idealism kept him far from his countrymen too, deeply involved though he was in the life and culture of Bengal. There was a loftiness, a refusal to compromise, that eventually distanced him from the Indian nationalist struggle, though Gandhi and Nehru acknowledged their debt to him to the last, Gandhi calling him 'The Great Sentinel', the conscience of the sub-continent, Nehru (in a letter to Tagore's biographer Krishna Kripalani) describing him, with Gandhi, as one of the two outstanding personalities in the world in the last quarter of a century. The loftiness – which included immense stoicism in the face of more personal bereavements than any man has a right to suffer – was another inheritance from his father Debendranath, who was known as Maharshi or 'great seer'; but Tagore despite his deep religious feeling would not have liked such a title, for running through all his writing, and above all his songs, is not the full self-realization or enlightenment of a mystic or seer, but a passionate human yearning: a sense of the Ideal always being out of reach. His perceptions could bring him joy – in Nature and in children especially – but never the self-satisfaction of the religious fanatic, of one who has 'found the truth'. More often his idealism brought him sorrow, realization that most of his efforts had been futile, that in his beloved school and university at Santiniketan he had, knowingly, tried to fly against the truth (expressed at the end of his third lecture on *Personality*) that institutions, like kingdoms and nations, fade in the air like dreams.

He is near

In this Introduction I am deliberately distancing myself from my material: chapter and verse for Tagore's ideas will be found in the Notes at the end of the book. But the ringing conclusion to the second lecture in *Nationalism* (1916) deserves to be quoted in full:

> I know my voice is too feeble to raise itself above the uproar of this bustling time, and it is easy for any street urchin to fling against me the epithet of 'unpractical'. It will stick to my coat-tail, never to be washed away, effectively excluding me from the consideration of all respectable persons. I know what a risk one runs from the vigorously athletic crowds in being styled an idealist in these days, when thrones have lost their dignity and prophets have become an anachronism, when

the sound that drowns all voices is the noise of the market-place. Yet when, one day, standing on the outskirts of Yokohama town, bristling with its display of modern miscellanies, I watched the sunset in your southern sea, and saw its peace and majesty among your pine-clad hills, – with the great Fujiyama growing faint against the golden horizon, like a god overcome with his own radiance, – the music of eternity welled up through the evening silence, and I felt that the sky and the earth and the lyrics of the dawn and the dayfall are with the poets and idealists, and not with the marketmen robustly contemptous of all sentiment, – that, after the forgetfulness of his own divinity, man will remember again that heaven is always in touch with his world, which can never be abandoned for good to the hounding wolves of the modern era, scenting human blood and howling to the skies.

This passage is utterly characteristic: the passion and dignity of Tagore's idealism; the sense of horror at human evil; a tragic feeling of farness and isolation from the world as it is actually run by professional men; and a profound feeling of nearness to the world of the spirit: all are there. Spiritual reality was never for Tagore an esoteric thing, confined to arcane literature or ritual or any one church or sect. It was immediately and perpetually perceptible in the world and in experience: in the beauty of Nature, in human love, in children. He was a romantic – in a late poem in *naba-jātak* (1940) he self-deprecatingly admits that he is an unrepentant romantic; but if one has no touch whatsoever of romanticism as Tagore defined it one is scarcely human. Tagore expressed his romantic and religious perception most profoundly in his songs: the essential harmony and beauty of the universe (a harmony and beauty that could never be described by science, for all his interest in science) was best conveyed through music. It is vital to understand this. It explains why Tagore – mistakenly, as he must later have realized – tried to translate his songs, or poems that were close to the world of his songs. He felt that his greatest gift was for music, and it was this that he should try to communicate to the outside world.

I have no doubt that he was right in his self-assessment. Ambitious and intelligent though his prose was, daring and original though his drama was, endlessly varied and inventive though his poetry was, Tagore's genius showed itself most naturally and faultlessly in his songs. He often said that his songs would be remembered when all his other works were forgotten, and it is undoubtedly true that in Bengal today it is his songs that are best known. They are not always well or faithfully performed; singers do not always understand the thought and feeling behind the songs; but they are loved. It is in his songs that Tagore is nearest to his people and culture. They appeal to a wide social range; they keep alive in an increasingly urban people a responsiveness to nature and landscape and the seasons, a sense of the divine, an ideal of love, a patriotism that is distinct from chauvinism. The Tagore who with his songs rallied massive processions against Curzon's proposal to partition Bengal in 1905, or who marked the breaking of Gandhi's fast-unto-death in Poona Jail in 1932 by singing a song from *gītāñjali* for him, is no longer here; his intermittent involvement in public life may even be embarrassing to memory; but his songs live on, and transcend by their genius all distrust of his idealism or egoism, all criticism of failings in his other works of art.

I have already said that I do not believe one can translate songs, and none of the poems in this book are songs (Tagore made a song out of lines from 'New Rain', but the original poem is a poem, not a song). Music is the art that is both most specific to a people and a culture (who but Englishmen can understand Anglican anthems?), and the one that can cross national frontiers. I do not think it impossible that Tagore's songs will one day be known and appreciated outside India (they are much easier for a Westerner to follow than the instrumental Indian music that we do now hear quite often); but they will have to be known as songs. Translation of the words will not be enough.

There is a song that Tagore translated in *The Gardener*:

The tame bird was in a cage, the free bird was in the forest.
They met when the time came, it was a decree of fate.
The free bird cries, 'O my love, let us fly to the wood.'
The cage bird whispers, 'Come hither, let us both live in the cage.'
Says the free bird, 'Among bars, where is there room to spread one's wings?'
'Alas,' cries the cage bird, 'I should not know where to sit perched in the sky.'

The free bird cries, 'My darling, sing the songs of the woodlands.'
The cage bird says, 'Sit by my side, I'll teach you the speech of the learned.'
The forest bird cries, 'No, ah no! songs can never be taught.'
The cage bird says, 'Alas for me, I know not the songs of the woodlands.'

Their love is intense with longing, but they never can fly wing to wing.
Through the bars of the cage they look, and vain is their wish to know each other.
They flutter their wings in yearning, and sing, 'Come closer, my love!'
The free bird cries, 'It cannot be, I fear the closed doors of the cage.'
The cage bird whispers, 'Alas, my wings are powerless and dead.'

This translation is unsatisfactory: it is not badly inaccurate, but any English reader will be worried by phrases such as 'My darling', 'the speech of the learned', 'Alas for me'. It also leaves out a whole verse, though the English reader is not to know that. But a more exact or stylistically happy translation would not be the answer.

I could render the first verse as follows:

There was a caged bird in a golden cage, there was a forest bird in the forest.
Somehow the two came together, there was something in the mind of Fate.
The forest bird says, 'Caged bird, friend, let us go off together to the forest.'
The caged bird says, 'Forest bird, come, let us stay alone in the cage.'
The forest bird says, 'No, I will not let myself be fettered.'
The caged bird says, 'Alas, how can I go outside into the forest?'

I could try to polish the translation, make it more natural in English, introduce rhyme or half-rhyme. I could write a lengthy note, relating the song to all Tagore's most characteristic dualities: sky and earth, freedom and restriction, infinite and finite, eternal and mortal, soul and self, God and the world. But none of this would help. Heard in a good performance – by Shantidev Ghosh, doyen of *rabīndra-saṅgīt* (Tagore music) singers at Santiniketan, for example – it is apparent to anyone that the mood, the feeling, the truth of the song are all in the melody. It is an exquisite piece: it expresses in a way that is utterly real but impossible to define both 'nearness' to the world of the spirit (the closeness of the two birds) and 'farness' from it (the bars that separate them). It is haunting, tender, humane, humorous, subtle. For those who belong to Tagore's culture, it keeps him ever near, an abiding, comforting voice.

Tagore is near to his people. Can he ever be near to foreigners, removed from his land and language, deprived of his song?

If I did not believe that there were ways in which Tagore can be near to us, I would not have attempted this book; and these ways can be placed under three main headings: he was a romantic, he was modern, and he was human.

The influence of English poetry on Tagore and other Bengali poets of modern times can be greatly over-emphasized: Bengali critics themselves tend to do so, perhaps because they have often studied English literature before their own. But there is no doubt that the reading and appreciation of English poetry was an important strain in nineteenth-century Bengali culture. Derozio, whom I mentioned earlier, was a good poet after the manner of early Byron or Thomas Campbell; and a later and equally influential teacher at Hindu College – Captain D. L. Richardson – was an excellent critic and a good lyric poet. Richardson published a number of miscellaneous essays and poems (*Literary Leaves*, 1836, *Literary Chit-chat*, 1848, *Literary Recreations*, 1852), and in his time he was the literary leader of the British community in Calcutta – with whom writing verse had long been a popular pastime. They influenced some Bengalis to do the same. The foremost Bengali poet before Tagore, Michael Madhusudan Datta, began his career by writing in English: his poem *The Captive Ladie* (1849) shows the influence of Byron and Moore; other poems, more interestingly, show the influence of Keats. By the time Tagore started writing, Madhusudan had already shown the futility of writing poetry in English, and Tagore never attempted it (he wrote only one original poem in English, *The Child*, written after seeing the Oberammergau Passion Play in 1930). But his youthful contact with English poetry is well attested. He was made to translate *Macbeth* into Bengali by a tutor when he was twelve; his early volume *kaṛi o kamal* (Sharps and Flats, 1886) includes translations of Shelley, Victor Hugo, Mrs Browning, Christina Rossetti, Swinburne, Hood, Aubrey de Vere, Moore and others. Indeed as a young poet he was sometimes called the 'Shelley of Bengal', because of the habit of identifying Bengali writers with English writers (Madhusudan was the 'Milton of Bengal', Bankim was the 'Scott of Bengal', and so on). English poetry meant less and less to Tagore as time went on, but the seeds had been sown. A poem like 'On the Edge of the Sea' is to an English reader a strange mixture of the foreign and the familiar: it is both Indian and Keatsian. English poetic influence (mainly Romantic poetry, major and minor, and Shakespeare) is the point of contact between us and Indian poetry of the last century-and-a-half.

English poetic influence on Tagore seduced Edward Thompson into seeing him as an essentially nineteenth-century poet, a coeval of Tennyson and Swinburne; and Thompson's translations certainly made him seem like that. But this is wrong. Although Tagore started in the nineteenth century, he became a Modern, never detaching his poetry from the times in which he lived, always striving to extend his range and break literary conventions. This was an aspect of the continual progress in him that I have already described.

But there is an important difference between Tagore and the major Moderns of Europe. Joyce, Pound, Stravinsky, Picasso – all have built on Romanticism but at the same time tried to break it up. Subsequent generations of artists have cut their links with it completely. Tagore, however, carried his romanticism intact into the modern world, used it as a sceptre and a torch. Thus to children of the neo-Romanticism of the 1960s, my own era, he is a sympathetic voice. His educational ideals, his anti-materialism, his feminism, his version of the spiritual are all, to my own generation, familiar. In these he is near.

Tagore's idealism sets him apart: it also makes him human. The way to read Tagore is emphatically *not* to sit at his feet, to look to him for wisdom. This is the mistake his contemporary admirers made: it did him no good, made fools of them, and could not last. The way to read Tagore is to see limitations in his faith, vulnerability in his striving. Tagore's whole career as a writer was a progress towards greater and greater honesty. His late poems, most of them put straight down with no metre, no rhyme, no deliberate artifice, should not be read as progress towards greater and greater enlightenment, *mukti*, spiritual fulfilment: read in that way – as wisdom instead of poetry – they will seem feeble and insipid. They are rather an ever more naked self-exposure. A poem such as '*Recovery – 14*', about a pet dog, restates Tagore's Religion of Man: read as such, it will carry no more conviction than the words of an Anglican hymn. Rather, one should sense its implicit suggestion: 'Here I am, a vulnerable and ignorant human being. Here are the beliefs and values on which I have based my life: you can take them or leave them as you please.' If we read it in this way, it becomes moving. Its wisdom is in its ignorance.

Tagore's late poetry becomes less and less poetry, more and more an unadorned human voice. To hear that voice we need to know the man, and that is not easy. There are readable biographies of Tagore, but they do not really break through to the human being in him. There is a nervousness about entering the sanctum, discovering the feet of clay. But I have no doubt that the better we can understand him as a man, the more clearly his very last poems will speak to us.

It is because I do not yet know Tagore well enough that I have not felt able to translate anything from his very last book, *śeṣ lekhā* (Last Writings), or provide the commentary that would be required, the long history in his life and experience of every thought and line of its fifteen short poems. Or perhaps in any case they are untranslatable. Only in its own language can the voice be entirely itself. In the bewilderment, bafflement and incomprehension of his very last poems, Tagore comes nearest to us all; but language keeps him far.

He is within all

Tagore was not the only creative talent in his large family. Debendranath's eldest son Dwijendranath was an eccentric genius, author of a long Bengali poem modelled on the *Faerie Queene*, inventor of shorthand in Bengali (with a manual on it in verse!) and a gifted mathematician; his second son Satyendranath was a scholar as well as the first Indian member of the Indian Civil Service, translating Sanskrit classics and Marathi poetry; his fifth son Jyotirindranath was an accomplished artist in many fields, music especially, and he had a great influence on the education and development of Tagore, who was thirteen years his junior (Jyotirindranath's wife Kadambari was only a little older than Tagore, and they were particularly close: speculation never ceases about her tragic suicide four months after his marriage in 1883). The family was large and talented enough to provide its own cultural fare, and some of Tagore's earliest creations were musical plays performed within the family circle. There was *bālmīki pratibhā* (The Genius of Vālmīki), for example, which cribbed some tunes from Moore's *Irish Melodies*, heard by Tagore on his first visit to England in 1878–80.

This amateur dramatic spirit stayed with Tagore all his life: his later plays, operas and ballets were always performed first by staff and students at Santiniketan (often with Tagore himself taking a part), not on the professional Calcutta stage. I find it useful, when considering Tagore's concept of Personality, to keep his dramatic work in mind. All his work was governed and unified by his own personality: it was as though he was the producer of a complex play lasting his whole life, bringing on different actors, sets, dances (the different genres he cultivated) as he felt inclined. It was a drama that he produced, created – yet remained outside, just as he used to sit on stage during performances of the ballets that he took round India in 1934–6, watching but not participating. In this image we have the paradox of his *jīban-debatā*: his sense on the one hand that his works were endlessly diverse, but on the other hand that they were all part of a unified play; that he was creatively free, always at liberty to try new things, but on the other hand at the mercy of a life-deity, a personality higher than his own, guiding him from outside. The *jīban-debatā* concept accounted for his dual sense of involvement in and detachment from his own creations. That same paradox he felt to be at the heart of the Universe itself; so his own creative personality was but a microcosm of the universal Personality, who was also simultaneously detached and involved; and the diversity and extravagance of his art was but a reflection of the extravagance of Nature itself.

Right from the moment that I conceived this book, I felt that Tagore's concept of *jīban-debatā* would have to direct it. A selection of Tagore's poems could never be done by committee, by trying to decide objectively which were the best or most representative. It would have to start from a vision of unity, and the choice of poems would have to be governed by the laws defining that unity. The structure of the book I therefore conceived in three parts; and these – though I did not at first realize it – would be first the poems up to the Nobel Prize in 1913; then the poems written during his years of travel and world fame; then the poems written after his illness of September 1937, when he could no longer travel. The divisions were unequal in terms of years; a little more equal in terms of books of verse (Tagore produced eleven books in his last four years). But they have a logic to them. With the three-part division established, there would have to be internal principles of selection. These were intuitive, and I find them hard to define, but the most important were contrast, balance, novelty, rhythm. Contrast is the easiest: there would have to be contrasts from one poem to the next, representing the diversity in Tagore. Balance is more difficult: the poems cannot all be entirely different from each other – there will be some that echo others, and the placing of these pairs or trios creates balance. Sometimes, searching for the next poem to translate, I would reject one because it was too near or too far from one that it echoed. Novelty was the criterion that prevented too great a similarity between any two poems: having translated one, I could not do another that was too like it – the selection had to move on, move on, with new forms, new subjects all the time, to be true to the spirit of perpetual progress in Tagore. But it had at the same time to have a cohesiveness that was more than its overall structure or its balance in selection. There had, through all the different types of poem and varieties of verse-form, to be a unity of rhythm.

Rhythm in this sense is impossible to describe. Tagore often referred to the underlying harmony of things in terms of rhythm: he was in no doubt that the rhythms of art – whether musical rhythms, metrical rhythms, structural rhythms or even the rhythm of line and shape that he explored in his paintings – were a reflection of rhythms in Nature and the universe which science could analyse but never communicate. So essential is rhythm to his aesthetic philosophy that I never considered anything other than a verse translation of his poems; for all the agonies and compromises that verse translation imposes, no prose translation could begin to approach Tagore.

But the rhythm we are concerned with is not just universal rhythm: it is the rhythm of Tagore's own individuality, his own personal way of feeling and thinking. Every major artist has his own unique rhythm: it is one of the things that distinguish the major artist from the second-rate. I have tried – I cannot judge whether I have succeeded – to achieve a unity of rhythm in these translations. They are meant to be read aloud. If anyone does so, I hope that he or she will find that there is a connecting and unifying rhythm running through them all. It may not be Tagore's rhythm – how can it be, completely, in another language? But if rhythm is there at all, then I shall have achieved something.

He is outside all

On 24 August 1930, Tagore wrote from Geneva to William Rothenstein, who had been his regular correspondent since 1912. The wry, self-mocking tone of the letter is typical of Tagore's epistolary style; but it also contains a most revealing antithesis:

Very dear friend

To be reconciled to the inevitable with good grace is wisdom, so let me in a spirit of resignation accept the fact that you must have an undisturbed opportunity to produce your pictures while I nourish a desperate hope in my mind to find some rest somewhere in the closely-knit days which hold me captive – and to play truant to all obligations that are compulsory. The rich luxury of leisure is not for me while I am in Europe – I am doomed to be unrelentingly good to humanity and remain harnessed to a cause. The artist in me ever urges me to be naughty and natural – but it requires [a] good deal of courage to be what I truly am. Then again I do not really know myself and dare not play tricks with my nature. So the good for nothing artist must have for his bed-fellow the man of a hundred good intentions.

In Germany my pictures have found a very warm welcome which was far beyond my expectations. Five of them have got their permanent place in [the] Berlin National Gallery, and several invitations have come from other centres for their exhibition. This has a strange analogy with the time which followed the Gitanjali publication – it is sudden and boisterous like a hill stream after a storm and like the same casual flood may disappear with the same emphasis of suddenness. With love

Ever yours
Rabindranath Tagore

In this Introduction I have often identified the 'he' of my quotation from the Īśā Upaniṣad with Tagore himself – a sleight of hand that may arouse suspicions about my personal attitude to Tagore, but which is not, however, at odds with his philosophy or with Indian philosophical tradition generally, which has frequently striven to identify God with man, Brahman with Ātman (soul). But in this final section the sage's intended meaning must stand. It is that God exists outside his creation; in that sense, to those who are part of his creation, he is unreachable.

I have already spoken of Tagore's sense of the 'farness' of his ideal: but that is a feeling that goes hand in hand with his sense of its nearness in the real, observable and perceptible beauty of Nature, human love and children. I am now concerned with something rather different: the feeling that Nature and human creativity lie essentially outside and separate from God; that the Goodness, the Beauty and the Harmony of God may have nothing to do with the autonomous processes of Nature, and that therefore the artist's creativity is likewise amoral, arbitrary, fanciful, whimsical, unreal. This is the suspicion that Tagore voices in his letter to Rothenstein: that the true, natural artist in him was 'naughty', 'good for nothing', essentially separate from the idealist and moralist in him, 'the man of a hundred good intentions'. I have quoted the whole letter, because it was in the paintings that the naughty artist in Tagore was indeed freest, unimpeded and unrestrained by his equally strong moral impulse. This is why the paintings – nearly three thousand of them – are such a puzzle to so many. They are hit-and-miss, amateurish in their technique – but that is not the trouble, for Tagore glorified amateurism in many fields. It is rather their apparent impishness, their revelry in the odd, the grotesque, the meaningless. What have they to do with the author of *Gitanjali* or *The Religion of Man*?

The element in Tagore that found its clearest and most unfettered expression in his paintings was always present in him: it accounts for the equivocal tones in his writing, some of which I have tried to define in my notes to the poems. Tagore's ideal of beauty can be equivocal: in the imagery of the heavenly city of Alakā, taken from Kālidāsa, the poet whom he admired more than any other, with its *birahiṇī* (separated Beloved) condemned to immortality, there is sterility – its very perfection is inhuman and therefore alien. The *jīban-debatā* can be equivocal too: all too often it is *udāsīn*, detached, indifferent to human feeling and concern – Tagore expressed the pain of rejection by an indifferent *jīban-debatā* in countless songs. Nature itself, for all its beauties, can seem *udāsīn* as well: poems such as 'Earth' and 'In the Eyes of a Peacock' present a picture of natural processes aloof from human concerns. Above all Tagore's notion of *khelā*, the endless playfulness of the universe, is equivocal: though it is a source of joy, and is revealed to us in the play of young children, it also has a dark side; it is the vanity and meaninglessness of life, it is *māyā*, the illusion and ignorance to which – according to the cruellest strain in Indian religion and philosophy – we are all, as mortal creatures, perpetually condemned, perpetually cut off as we are from the reality of God, the ideal, the infinite, the eternal.

If the processes of Nature and Art are separate from God, cannot God be dropped from the picture altogether? Should Goodness, Harmony, Unity be dismissed as fictions? I do not know enough to say whether these questions were in Tagore's mind at the end of his life, while the world collapsed into war; but some of his last works seem to hint at them. When I finished my translations, at Santiniketan in the spring of 1982, I chose to stop with a poem in which the naughty artist, rather than the idealist or the moralist, is to the fore. It is an exuberant poem, not I think one that sees no structure at all in the stuff of reality but one which strives, like many works of modern art, to pierce through to a deeper structure that the ordering of our rational mind obscures. But in its vision of language abandoning itself, it comes perilously and awesomely *close* to acceptance of a complete lack of meaning or purpose in the universe: to suspicion that, though there may be laws or rules governing Nature or the mind of man, their status may be as frivolous and arbitrary as the rules of a game; that the whole stupendous structure may rest on a bleak whimsicality. It comes close . . . but I think it stops short. We are brought, as it were, to the edge of a gulf that Tagore could never quite open. He went furthest in his paintings; but in his writing his 'courage to be what I truly am' generally failed him. Had it succeeded, there would have been no poetry, and no song. For though Tagore's Art was sometimes inhibited by his moral and spiritual ideals, it could never have been perfected without them. Poetry is impossible without Love: that is what I hope will emerge more strongly than anything else from the poems that follow.

Gratitude to the Unknown Instructors

What they undertook to do
They brought to pass;
All things hang like a drop of dew
Upon a blade of grass.

(W. B. Yeats)

1882–1913

Brahmā, Viṣṇu, Śiva

In a worldless timeless lightless great emptiness
    Four-faced Brahma broods.
Of a sudden a sea of joy surges through his heart –
    The ur-god opens his eyes.

Speech from four mouths
Speeds to each quarter.
Through infinite dark,
Through limitless sky,
Like a growing sea-storm,
Like hope never sated,
His Word starts to move.

Stirred by joy,   his breathing quickens,
    His eight eyes quiver with flame.
His fire-matted hair   sweeps the horizon,
    Bright as a million suns.

From the towering source of the world
    In a thousand streams
Cascades the primeval blazing fountain,
    Fragmenting silence,
    Splitting its stone heart.

In a universe rampant
With new life exhalant,
With new life exultant,
In a borderless sky
Viṣṇu spreads wide
His four-handed blessing.
He raises his conch
And all things quake
At its booming sound.
The frenzy dies down,
The furnace expires,
The planets douse
Their flames with tears.
The world's Divine Poet
Constructs its history,
From wild cosmic song
Its epic is formed.
Stars in their orbits,
Moon sun and planets –
He binds with his mace

All things to Law,
Imposes the discipline
Of metre and rhyme.

In the Mānasa depths
Viṣṇu watches –
Beauties arise
From the light of lotuses.
Lakṣmī strews smiles –
Clouds show a rainbow,
Gardens show flowers.
The roar of Creation
Resolves into music.
Softness hides rigour,
Forms cover power.

Age after age after age is slave to a mighty rhythm –
At last the world-frame
Tires in its body,
Sleep in its eyes
Slackens its structure,
Diffuses its energy.
From the heart of all matter
Comes the anguished cry –
'Wake, wake, great Śiva,
Our body grows weary
Of its law-fixed path,
Give us new form.
Sing our destruction,
That we gain new life.'

The great god awakes,
His three eyes open,
He surveys all horizons.
He lifts his bow,   his fell *pināka*,
He pounds the world with his tread.
From first things to last   it trembles and shakes
And shudders.
The bonds of nature are ripped.
The sky is rocked by the roar
Of a wave of ecstatic release.
An inferno soars –
The pyre of the universe.

Shattered sun and moon, smashed stars and planets
Rain down from all angles,
A blackness of particles
To be swallowed by flame,
Absorbed in an instant.
At the start of Creation
There was dark without origin,
At the breaking of Creation
There is fire without end.
In an all-pervading sky-engulfing sea of burning
Śiva shuts his three eyes.
He begins his great trance.

Bride

'Day's ending, let's go and fetch water.'
I seem to hear from afar   that old evening call –
But where is the shade and the water?
Where are the steps and the fig-tree?
As I sit alone with my thoughts   I seem to hear
'Day's ending, let's go and fetch water.'

Pitcher at my hip, the winding path –
Nothing but fields to the left   stretching into haze,
To the right the slanting bamboo-grove.
The evening sunlight shines   on the blackness of the pool,
The woods round its edge are sunk in shade.
I let myself idly float   in the pool's deep calm,
The *koel* on the bank has sweetness in its song.
Returning, I suddenly see   above the dark trees,
Painted on the sky, the moon.

The wall, split by the peepul-tree –
I used to run there when I woke.
On autumn mornings the world   glistened with dew,
Clusters of oleanders bloomed.
Two creepers covering the wall   with their flow of green
Were laden with purple flowers.
I sat in my hiding-place   peering through cracks,
My sari trailed on the ground.

Field after field, and on the horizon
A distant village blending with the sky.
Next to me ancient palm-trees stand so densely
Their dark-green foliage merges.
I can see the dam's thin line, its water glinting,
Herd-boys crowd its edge.
The path goes on out of sight, I do not know where –
Who knows through what new places?

Oh this city with its stony body!
Its massive loveless fist has squeezed and crushed
A young girl's feelings, pitilessly.
Where are the boundless fields, the open path,
The birdsong, the trees, the shadows?

There seem to be people all around me,
I can't speak my heart in case they hear me.
Weeping is wasted here, it is stopped by walls,
My weeping always comes back to me.

No one understands why I cry,
They wonder, they want to know the cause.
'Nothing pleases the girl, she ought to be ashamed,
It's always the same with girls from villages.
All these friends and relations to keep her company,
But she sits in a corner and shuts her eyes!'

They point at my body or face,
They argue about how I look –
I feel like a garland-seller, my wares examined,
Tested for quality, coldly.

I loiter alone amidst them all,
Each day hangs so heavily.
People here are like worms crawling between bricks,
There is no love, there is no gaiety.

What of you, mother, where are you?
You can't have forgotten me, surely?
When you sit outside on our roof beneath the new moon
Do you still tell fairy-stories?
Or do you, alone in bed, lie awake at night,
In tears and sickness of heart?
Take flowers to the temple at dawn to offer your prayers
For your exiled daughter's well-being?

Here also the moon rises over the roof,
Its light is at my door and begs for entry.
I feel that it wandered widely   before it found me,
It sought me because it loved me.
I forget myself for a moment,
I rush to fling open the door.
At once the spies all around me   rise like a storm,
Swoop with their cruel authority.

They won't give love, they won't give light.
I feel all the time it would be good to die,
To sink in the lap of the water of the pool,
In its shady darkness, its cool black depths.
Keep on, keep on with your evening call –
'Day's ending, let's go and fetch water.'
When will my evening come?   All playing end?
The cooling water quench all fires?
If anyone knows, tell me when.

Unending Love

I seem to have loved you in numberless forms, numberless times,
In life after life, in age after age forever.
My spell-bound heart has made and re-made the necklace of songs
That you take as a gift, wear round your neck in your many forms
In life after life, in age after age forever.

Whenever I hear old chronicles of love, its age-old pain,
Its ancient tale of being apart or together,
As I stare on and on into the past, in the end you emerge
Clad in the light of a pole-star piercing the darkness of time:
You become an image of what is remembered forever.

You and I have floated here on the stream that brings from the fount
At the heart of time love of one for another.
We have played alongside millions of lovers, shared in the same
Shy sweetness of meeting, the same distressful tears of farewell –
Old love, but in shapes that renew and renew forever.

Today it is heaped at your feet, it has found its end in you,
The love of all man's days both past and forever:
Universal joy, universal sorrow, universal life,
The memories of all loves merging with this one love of ours –
And the songs of every poet past and forever.

Ah, supreme poet, that first, hallowed day
Of Āṣāṛh on which, in some unknown year, you wrote
Your *Meghadūta*! Your stanzas are themselves
Like dark-layered sonorous clouds, heaping the misery
Of all separated lovers throughout the world
Into thunderous music.

Who can say what thickness of cloud that day,
What festiveness of lightning, what wildness of wind
Shook with their roar the turrets of Ujjayinī?
As the thunderclouds clashed, their booming released
In a single day the heart-held grief of thousands of years
Of pining. Long-repressed tears,
Breaking time's bonds, seem to have poured down
In torrents that day and drenched your noble stanzas.

Did every exile in the world that day
Raise his head, clasp his hands, face his beloved's home
And sing to the clouds one and the same
Song of yearning? Did each lover ask a fresh, unfettered cloud
To carry on its wings a tearful message of love
To the distant window where his beloved
Lay wretched on the ground with clothes disordered
And hair unplaited and weeping eyes?
Did your music, O poet, carry all their songs
As you journeyed in your poem through land after land
Over many days and nights
Towards the lonely object of your love?
Compare the Ganges in full monsoon flood,
Absorbing streams from every side till all become one in the sea.
Compare the vapour that mountains,
Prisoners of their own stone, send forth in Āṣāṛh:
Jealous of the freedom with which clouds pass above them,
They breathe it from a thousand caverns:
It rises fast as desire, unites over the peaks
And becomes in the end a great mass dominating the sky.

Since that day, countless first days
Of the cooling rainy season have passed.
Every year has given new life to your poem
By showering it with fresh rain,
By spreading cool shade, by echoing once again
With the sound of gathered clouds, by filling streams
With waves that rush like your rain-swelled verse.

All this time, companionless people have sat in loveless rooms
Through the long, rain-weary, starless evenings of Āṣāṛh.
In faint lamplight, they have slowly read aloud that verse
And drowned their own loneliness.
Their voices come to me from your poem;
They sound in my ear like waves on the sea-shore.

In the easternmost part of India,
In verdurous Bengal, I sit.
Here too the poet Jayadeva watched on a rainy day
The blue-green shadows of distant *tamāl*-trees,
The density of a sky in full cloud.

Today is a dark day, the rain is incessant,
The wind ferocious – treetops rise
Like arms at its attack; their swishing is a cry.
Lightning darts through the clouds, ripping them,
Dotting the sky with sharp, crooked smiles.

In a gloomy closed room I sit alone
And read the *Meghadūta*. My mind leaves the room,
Travels on a free-moving cloud, flies far and wide.
There is the Āmrakūṭa mountain,
There is the clear and slender Revā river,
Tumbling over stones in the Vindhya foothills;
There, along the banks of the Vetravatī,
Hiding in the shade of green, ripe-fruited *jambu*-trees,
Are the villages of Daśārṇa, their fences streaming
With *ketakī*-flowers, their paths lined with great forest-trees
Whose overhanging branches are alive with the twitter of village-birds
Building their nests in the rain.
There is that unknown stream along whose jasmine-wooded banks
Forest-girls idly wander:
Lotuses at their ears wilt from the heat of their cheeks
And are desperate for the shade of the cloud.
See how the village-wives stare up at the sky:
Simple women – no coyness in their gaze
As the cloud's thick blue shadow falls on their dark blue eyes!
See how the Siddha women languishing on a cloud-blue rock
Revel in the cloud's looming coolness; but at the sudden onset of its storm
Cower, rush back to their caves
Clutching their clothes and crying, 'Help,
Help, it'll blow the mountains down!'
There is Avantī and the Nirvindhyā river;
There is Ujjayinī, gazing at her own great shadow in the Śiprā river.

It is midnight, and the doves in her towers
Sleep away love's urges: but women, restless with desire,
Go out into the broad dark streets to await their trysts
While lightning pricks through the gloom.
There is Kurukṣetra, in the land of Brahmāvarta!
There is the peak of Kanakhala, where the wild youthful foam of the Ganges
Played with Śiva's hair, laughed at his consort's frown
As it touched his moon-crest.

My heart travels thus, like a cloud, from land to land
Until it floats at last into Alakā –
Heavenly, longed-for city
Where pines that most loved of loves,
That paragon of beauty. Who but you, O poet,
Revealer of eternal worlds fit for Lakṣmī to dally in,
Could take me there? To the woods of undying spring-flowers
Forever moonlit, to the golden-lotus-lake,
To the sapphire rock, to its crowning jewel-studded palace
Where, submerged in overwhelming riches,
That bereft and lonely Being weeps her lament?
Through the open window she can be seen –
Wasted in body, lying on her bed like a sliver of moon
Sunk low in the eastern sky.
Poet, your spell has released
Tight bonds of pain in this heart of mine.
I too have entered that heaven of yearning
Where, amidst limitless beauties,
Alone and awake, that adored one spends her unending night.

The vision goes. I watch the rain again
Pouring steadily all around.
The darkness thickens; the solitariness of night approaches.
Far across the plain, the wind moans aimlessly.
I am sleepless half the night, asking –
Who has cursed us like this? Why this gulf?
Why do we aim so high only to weep when thwarted?
Why does love not find its true path?
It is something not of the body that takes us there,
To the bed of pining by the Mānasa lake,
To the sunless, jewel-lit, evening land
Beyond all the rivers and mountains of this world.

The Golden Boat

Clouds rumbling in the sky; teeming rain.
I sit on the river-bank, sad and alone.
The sheaves lie gathered,   harvest has ended,
The river is swollen and fierce in its flow.
As we cut the paddy it started to rain

One small paddy-field, no one but me –
Flood-waters twisting and swirling everywhere.
Trees on the far bank   smear shadows like ink
On a village painted on deep morning grey.
On this side a paddy-field, no one but me.

Who is this, steering close to the shore,
Singing? I feel that she is someone I know.
The sails are filled wide,   she gazes ahead,
Waves break helplessly against the boat each side.
I watch and feel I have seen her face before.

Oh to what foreign land do you sail?
Come to the bank and moor your boat for a while.
Go where you want to,   give where you care to,
But come to the bank a moment, show your smile –
Take away my golden paddy when you sail.

Take it, take as much as you can load.
Is there more? No, none, I have put it aboard.
My intense labour   here by the river –
I have parted with it all, layer upon layer:
Now take me as well, be kind, take me aboard.

No room, no room, the boat is too small.
Loaded with my gold paddy, the boat is full.
Across the rain-sky   clouds heave to and fro,
On the bare river-bank, I remain alone –
What I had has gone: the golden boat took all.

Broken Song

Kāśināth the new young singer fills the hall with sound:
The seven notes dance in his throat like seven tame birds.
His voice is a sharp sword slicing and thrusting everywhere,
It darts like lightning – no knowing where it will go when.

He sets deadly traps for himself, then cuts them away:
The courtiers listen in amazement, give frequent gasps of praise.
Only the old king Pratāp Rāy sits like wood, unmoved.
Baraj Lāl is the only singer he likes, all others leave him cold.
From childhood he has spent so long listening to him sing –
Rāg Kāfi during *holi*, cloud-songs during the rains,
Songs for Durgā at dawn in autumn, songs to bid her farewell –
His heart swelled when he heard them and his eyes swam with tears.
And on days when friends gathered and filled the hall
There were cowherds' songs of Kṛṣṇa, in rāgs Bhūpālī and Mūltān.

So many nights of wedding-festivity have passed in that royal house:
Servants dressed in red, hundreds of lamps alight:
The bridegroom sitting shyly in his finery and jewels,
Young friends teasing him and whispering in his ear:
Before him, singing rāg Śahānā, sits Baraj Lāl.
The king's heart is full of all those days and songs.
When he hears some other singer, he feels no chord inside,
No sudden magical awakening of memories of the past.
When Pratāp Rāy watches Kāśīnāth he just sees his wagging head:
Tune after tune after tune, but none with any echo in the heart.

Kāśīnāth asks for a rest and the singing stops for a space.
Pratāp Rāy smilingly turns his eyes to Baraj Lāl.
He puts his mouth to his ear and says, 'Dear *ustād*,
Give us a song as songs ought to be, this is no song at all.
It's all tricks and games, like a cat hunting a bird.
We used to hear songs in the old days, today they have no idea.'

Old Baraj Lāl, white-haired, white turban on his head,
Bows to the assembled courtiers and slowly takes his seat.
He takes the tānpurā in his wasted, heavily veined hand
And with lowered head and closed eyes begins rāg Yaman-kalyāṇ.
His quavering voice is swallowed by the enormous hall,
It is like a tiny bird in a storm, unable to fly for all it tries.
Pratāp Rāy, sitting to the left, encourages him again and again:
'Superb, bravo!' he says in his ear, 'sing out loud.'

The courtiers are inattentive. some whisper amongst themselves,
Some of them yawn, some doze, some go off to their rooms;
Some of them call to servants, 'Bring the hookah, bring some *pān*.'
Some fan themselves furiously and complain of the heat.
They cannot keep still for a minute, they shuffle or walk about –
The hall was quiet before, but every sort of noise has grown.
The old man's singing is swamped, like a frail boat in a typhoon:
Only his shaky fingering of the tānpurā shows it is there.

Music that should rise on its own joy from the depths of the heart
Is crushed by heedless clamour, like a fountain under a stone.
The song and Baraj Lāl's feelings go separate ways,
But he sings for all he is worth, to keep up the honour of his king.

One of the verses of the song has somehow slipped from his mind.
He quickly goes back, tries to get it right this time.
Again he forgets, it is lost, he shakes his head at the shame;
He starts the song at the beginning – again he has to stop.
His hand trembles doubly as he prays to his teacher's name.
His voice quakes with distress, like a lamp guttering in a breeze.
He abandons the words of the song and tries to salvage the tune,
But suddenly his wide-mouthed singing breaks into loud cries.
The intricate melody goes to the winds, the rhythm is swept away –
Tears snap the thread of the song, cascade like pearls.
In shame he rests his head on the old tānpurā in his lap –
He has failed to remember a song: he weeps as he did as a child.
With brimming eyes king Pratāp Rāy tenderly touches his friend:
'Come, let us go from here,' he says with kindness and love.
They leave that festive hall with its hundreds of blinding lights.
The two old friends go outside, holding each other's hands.

Baraj says with hands clasped, 'Master, our days are gone.
New men have come now, new styles and customs in the world.
The court we kept is deserted – only the two of us are left.
Don't ask anyone to listen to me now, I beg you at your feet, my lord.
The singer alone does not make a song, there has to be someone who hears:
One man opens his throat to sing, the other sings in his mind.
Only when waves fall on the shore do they make a harmonious sound;
Only when breezes shake the woods do we hear a rustling in the leaves.
Only from a marriage of two forces does music arise in the world.
Where there is no love, where listeners are dumb, there never can be song.'

A Half-acre of Land

I had forfeited all my land except for one half-acre.
The landlord said, 'Upen, I'll buy it, you must hand it over.'
I said, 'You're rich, you've endless land, can't you see
That all I've got is a patch on which to die?'
'Old man,' he sneered, 'you know I've made a garden;

If I have your half-acre its length and breadth will be even.
You'll have to sell.' Then I said with my hands on my heart
And tears in my eyes, 'Don't take my only plot!
It's more than gold – for seven generations my family
Has owned it: must I sell my own mother through poverty?'
He was silent for a while as his eyes grew red with fury.
'All right, we'll see,' he said, smiling cruelly.

Six weeks later I had left and was out on the road;
Everything was sold, debt claimed through a fraudulent deed.
For those want most, alas, who already have plenty:
The rich *zamindār* steals the beggar-man's property.
I decided God did not now intend me for worldliness:
In exchange for my land he had given me the universe.
I became disciple to a *sādhu* – I roamed the world:
Many and pleasing were the sights and places I beheld.
But nowhere on mountain or sea, in desert or city could I wander
Without thinking, day and night, of that half-acre.
Roads, markets, fields – over fifteen years went past;
But finally my homesickness grew too great to resist.

I bow, I bow to my beautiful motherland Bengal!
To your river-banks, to your winds that cool and console;
Your plains, whose dust the sky bends down to kiss;
Your shrouded villages, that are nests of shade and peace;
Your leafy mango-woods, where the herd-boys play;
Your deep ponds, loving and cool as the midnight sky;
Your sweet-hearted women returning home with water;
I tremble in my soul and weep when I call you Mother.
Two days later at noon I entered my native village:
The pottery to the right, to the left the festival carriage;
Past temple, market-place, granary, on I came
Till thirsty and tired, at last I arrived at my home.

But shame on you, shame on you, shameless, fallen half-acre!
What mother gives herself freely to a chance seducer?
Do you not remember the days when you nursed me humbly
With fruits and herbs and flowers held in your sari?
For whom are these lavish garments, these languorous airs?
These coloured leaves stitched in your sari, this head of flowers?
For you I have wandered, homeless, world-weary, pining,
Whereas you, you witch, have sat here idling and laughing.
How a wealthy man's love has turned your head! How wholly
You have changed – all signs of the past have gone completely.
You cared for me before, you fed me, your bounty was abundant.
You were a goddess; now, for all your wiles, you are a servant.

As I paced with my heart in two I looked round and saw
There was still, near the wall, the same old mango-tree.
I sat at its foot and soothed my pain with tears,
And memories rose in my mind of childhood days:
How after a storm that had kept me awake one night
I had dashed out at dawn to gather all the fallen fruit;
Memories of playing truant in the sweet, still noon –
Alas to think those days can never return.
Suddenly a sharp gust of wind shook the branches above me
And two ripe mangoes fell to the ground beside me.
I mused: my mother still knows her son, maybe.
I took that gift of love, reverently touched my brow.

Then the gardener appeared from somewhere, like a messenger of death –
A topknotted Oṛiyā, abusing me for all he was worth.
I said, 'I gave away everything with scarcely a murmur,
And now when I claim two mangoes there is all this uproar.'
He didn't know me, he led me with a stick at his shoulders;
The landlord, rod in hand, was fishing with his retainers.
When he heard what had happened he roared, 'I'll kill him.'
In each vile thing he said his retainers exceeded him.
I said, 'Two mangoes are all I beg of you, master.'
He sneered, 'He dresses as a *sādhu* but he's a pukka robber.'
I wept, but I laughed as well at the irony of life –
For he was now the great *sādhu*, and I was the thief.

Day's End

Day's end has come, the world is darkening –
    It is too late for further sailing.
On the bank, a girl,   I ask her with a smile,
    'On whose foreign shore am I landing?'
She leaves without a word,   her head bowed,
    Her full water-jar overflowing.
        These steps shall be my mooring.

On the forest's thick canopy shade is falling,
    I find the sight of this country pleasing.
Nothing stirs or moves,   neither water nor leaves,
    Birds throughout the forest are sleeping.
All I can hear   is bracelet on jar

Down the empty path, sadly tinkling.
I find this gold-lit country pleasing.

A golden trident of Śiva glitters,
A distant temple-lantern glimmers.
A marble road gleams in the shade,
It is sprinkled with fallen *bakul*-flowers.
Rows of roofs lurk amidst groves,
At the sight, my traveller's heart quivers.
A distant temple-lantern glimmers.

From the king's far palace the breeze brings a melody,
It floats through the sky, a song in rāg Pūrvī.
The fading scene draws me on –
I feel a strange detached melancholy.
Travel and exile lose their appeal,
Impossible hopes no longer call me.
The sky resounds with rāg Pūrvī.

On the forest, on the palace, night is descending –
It is too late for further sailing.
All that I need is a place for my head,
And I'll end this life of buying and selling.
As she winds her way she keeps her eyes low,
The girl with the jar at her hip, overflowing.
These steps shall be my mooring.

On the Edge of the Sea

The fierce pinching cold of a winter night, crickets chattering,
The city asleep, nobody moving in the house, lamps out.
I was sunk in deep comfortable slumber, limbs stretched at ease,
My bedding enfolding me with soothing warmth like a lover.
It was then that I heard someone calling my name from outside –
My sleep was suddenly broken and I sat up in terror.
The sound struck me to the core like a piercing sharpened arrow –
Sweat broke out on my forehead and my body turned to gooseflesh.
I threw off the covers, left my bed, scarcely clad as I was –
With heart thudding I opened the door and stood looking outside.
From the burning-ground by the river came the howl of jackals,
From above me the shriek of some night-bird passing overhead.
Before the door I saw a woman sitting on a black horse,
Veiled, utterly motionless like an image in a picture.

Another horse stood beside them, with its tail touching the earth,
Its body dark grey as if made of smoke from the burning-ground.
No movement at all in the horse, but it eyed me sideways –
I was quaking and trembling all over my body with dread.
In the yellowish sky the half-moon looked frosted and weary,
The old and leafless fig-tree near me was shivering with cold.
Then the veiled woman raised her hand and beckoned me silently –
As if under a spell, in a trance, I mounted the grey horse.

The horse set off like lightning, I could only look back briefly –
My house seemed unreal and tenuous like a puff of vapour.
Horror and anguish were squeezing my heart, I felt tears rising,
But some harsh power in my throat kept pressing them down again.
On each side of the road stood lines of houses with doors shut fast –
I thought of the men and women inside them in their warm beds.
The empty road seemed painted on a land without life or sound –
At the gateway of the palace two watchmen were slumped in sleep.
No noise at all except now and then dogs distantly barking,
Or the boom of the bell in the palace-tower striking the hours.

Road without end, night without end, places never seen before –
It was like an amazing dream, there was no meaning in it.
I cannot remember what I saw, everything was confused –
The horses galloped on and on like arrows aimed at nowhere.
Their hoofs made no noise as they fell and they raised no trail of dust,
There seemed no solid ground anywhere, only lines across mist.
Sometimes we passed places that were familiar for a moment –
But instantly the road would swerve off again I knew not where.
I felt I saw clouds, I felt I saw birds, and tender green leaves,
But I could not distinguish clearly anything that I saw.
Were they palaces on one side of me, or huge roots of trees,
Or were they only my mind's fantasies forming in the sky?
Sometimes I noticed the woman again, caught sight of her veil –
Her cruel silent manner as she rode brought panic to my heart.
In my fear I forgot the names of all gods, my tongue was tied –
The wind roared in my ears and the horses galloped and galloped.

The moon descended beneath the horizon before night's end,
But in the sleepy eyes of the east there was a bloodshot glow.
The horses drew up on an empty sandy beach by the sea,
In the black rocks in front of us I saw the mouth of a cave.
I heard no noise of waves from the sea, no dawn-birds were singing,
There was no delicate morning breeze wafting the scent of woods.
The veiled woman alighted from her horse and I did the same –
I followed her through the darkly yawning entrance of the cave.
Inside was a magnificent carved chamber with rock pillars,

There were tiers of brilliant lanterns swinging on golden chains.
The stone walls of the chamber had been carved into images –
Marvellous birds and women, leaves and creepers intertwining.
In the middle hung a canopy with pearl-studded tassels –
Beneath it was a jewelled bed spread with immaculate linen.
Incense was rising from censers on either side of the bed,
At the corners were wonderful statues of women on lions.
There were no people, no guards, I saw no attendants or maids.
The height of the cavern magnified the slightest sound vastly.
The woman sat down softly on the bed, her face still covered –
With her finger she signalled me to come and sit beside her.
I was freezing all over and my heart was quaking wildly –
Fear had begun to play a terrifying tune in my veins.
Suddenly there were flutes and vīṇās sounding all around us,
Showers of flower-dust were cascading down on to our heads,
The rows of suspended lanterns flared into double brightness –
I heard the woman laugh behind her veil, a sweet high-pitched laugh.
It echoed and resounded in that huge and empty chamber –
It jolted my heart anew and I clasped my hands and pleaded,
'I am but a guest from another place, please do not mock me –
Who are you, why are you cruel and silent, where have you brought me?'

Immediately the woman struck the ground with a golden stick
And clouds and clouds of smoky incense darkened the carved chamber.
There arose a tumult of conches and ululating cries –
An ancient Brahmin entered with ritual grasses in his hand.
An escort of forest-women had formed two lines behind him –
Some carried garlands, some fans, some vessels of holy water.
The Brahmin seated himself and the women stood in silence
While he made calculations on the ground with a piece of chalk,
Silently drawing wheels and circles and a network of lines.
When he had finished he announced that the time was auspicious.
Then the veiled woman got up from the bed with her head held low,
I too rose and stood beside her as if driven by magic.
The unspeaking forest-women made a circle around us,
They showered grains of puffed rice and flower-petals on our heads.
The priest gave us both his blessing and went on reciting mantras –
I could not follow anything he said, I waited spellbound.
My unknown bride pledged herself to me mutely and I shuddered,
My hand was turned to ice by the touch of her warm supple hand.
The old Brahmin left slowly followed by the women in lines –
They carried the ritual objects on their heads or on their hips.
Only one of them, lamp in hand, stayed to show us where to go.
Together we walked behind her, none of us speaking a word.
We passed through a succession of long dark halls that frightened me,

Suddenly I realized that a door had opened before us –
How can I describe the overwhelming room that we entered?
Its variety of coloured lights, flowers of every kind,
Garments laid out for us, studded with gold and silver and gems.
On a jewelled dais was a bed, flower-strewn as in a dream.
My bride seated herself on the bed with her feet on a stool.
I said, 'I see all of this, but I still have not seen your face.'

Hundreds of bantering voices began to laugh from all sides,
They exploded around us like hundreds of bursting fountains.
Slowly, very slowly the veiled woman lifted up her arms
And raised her veil, smiling a sweet smile at me but not speaking.
When I saw her face I fell at her feet in astonishment –
Tearfully I cried, 'You, even here, my *jīban-debatā*!'
In that beautiful face, in that smile and those nectar-filled eyes
Was the daemon who forever tricks me, makes me laugh and weep.
The daemon whose constant games are the pains and joys of my life
Had revealed its familiar face once again, in this unknown world.
I kissed the woman's pure soft lotus-feet in grief and wonder –
I could no longer restrain what I suffered and my tears streamed.
A flute began to play beautiful music that pierced my heart.
In that huge and deserted palace the woman laughed and laughed.

Love's Question

And is this all true,
My ever-loving friend?
That the lightning-flash of the light in my eyes
Makes the clouds in your heart explode and blaze,
Is this true?
That my sweet lips are red as a blushing new bride,
My ever-loving friend,
Is this true?

That a tree of paradise flowers within me,
That my footsteps ring like viṇās beneath me,
Is this true?
That the night sheds drops of dew at the sight of me,
That the dawn surrounds me with light from delight in me,
Is this true?
That the touch of my hot cheek intoxicates the breeze,
My ever-loving friend,
Is this true?

That daylight hides in the dark of my hair,
That my arms hold life and death in their power,
Is this true?
That the earth can be wrapped in the end of my sari,
That my voice makes the world fall silent to hear me,
Is this true?
That the universe is nothing but me and what loves me,
My ever-loving friend,
Is this true?

That for me alone your love has been waiting
Through worlds and ages awake and wandering,
Is this true?
That my voice, eyes, lips have brought you relief,
In a trice, from the cycle of life after life,
Is this true?
That you read on my soft forehead infinite Truth,
My ever-loving friend,
Is this true?

Snatched by the Gods

The news has gradually spread round the villages –
The Brahmin Maitra is going on a pilgrimage
To the mouth of the Ganges to bathe. A party
Of travelling-companions has assembled – old
And young, men and women; his two
Boats are ready at the landing-stage.

Mokṣadā, too, is eager for merit –
She pleads, 'Dear grandfather, let me come with you.'
Her plaintive young widow's eyes cannot see reason;
She entreats him, she is hard to resist. 'There is no
More room,' says Maitra. 'I implore you at your feet,'
She replies, weeping – 'I can find space
For myself somewhere, in a corner.' The Brahmin's
Mind softens, but he still hesitates
And asks, 'But what of your little boy?'
'Rākhāl?' says Mokṣadā, 'he can stay
With his aunt. After he was born I was ill
For a long time with puerperal fever, they despaired
Of my life; Annadā took my baby

And suckled him along with her own – she gave him
Such love that ever since then the boy
Has preferred his aunt's lap to mine. He is so
Naughty, he listens to no one – if you try
And tell him off his aunt comes
And draws him to her breast and weeps and cuddles him.
He will be happier with her than with me.'

Maitra gives in. Mokṣadā immediately
Hurries to get ready – packs her things,
Pays respects to her elders, floods
Her friends with tearful goodbyes. She returns
To the landing-stage – but whom does she see there?
Rākhāl, sitting calmly and happily
On board the boat – he has run there ahead of her.
'What are you doing here?' she cries. He answers,
'I'm going to the sea.' 'You're going to the sea?'
Says his mother, 'You naughty, naughty boy,
Come down at once.' His look is determined,
He says again, 'I'm going to the sea.'
She grabs his arm, but the more she pulls
The more he clings to the boat. In the end
Maitra smiles, says tenderly, 'Let him be,
He can come along.' His mother flares up –
'All right, then, come,' she snaps,
'The sea can have you!' The moment those words
Reach her own ears, her heart cries out,
Repentance runs through it like an arrow; she clenches
Her eyes and murmurs, 'God, God';
She takes her son in her arms, covers him
With loving caresses, blesses him, prays for him.
Maitra draws her aside and whispers,
'For shame, you must never say such things.'
Suddenly Annadā rushes up – people
Have told her that Rākhāl has been allowed
To go with the boats. 'My darling,' she cries,
'Where are you going?' 'I'm going to the sea,'
Says Rākhāl cheerfully, 'but I'll come back again,
Aunt Annadā.' Nearly mad, she shouts to Maitra,
'But who will control him, he is such a mischievous
Boy, my Rākhāl! From the day he was born
He has never been away from his aunt for long –
Where are you taking him? Give him back!'
'Aunt Annadā,' says Rākhāl, 'I'm going to the sea,
But I'll come back again.' The Brahmin says kindly,

Soothingly, 'So long as Rākhāl is with me
You need not fear for him, Annadā. It is winter,
The rivers are calm, there are many other
Pilgrims going – there is no danger
At all. The trip will take two months –
I shall bring your Rākhāl back to you.'

At the auspicious time and with prayers
To Durgā, the boats set sail. Tearful
Womenfolk stay behind on the shore.
The village by the Cūrṇī river seems tearful
Too, with its wintry morning dew.

*

The pilgrimage is over and the pilgrims are returning.
Maitra's boat is moored to the bank,
Waiting for the afternoon tide. Rākhāl,
Curiosity satisfied, whimpers with homesick
Longing for his aunt's lap. His heart
Is weary of endless expanses of water.
Sleek and glossy, dark and curving
And cruel and mean and spiteful water,
How like a thousand-headed snake it seems,
So full of deceit, greedy tongues darting,
Hoods rearing, mouths foaming as it hisses and roars
And eternally lusts for the children of Earth!
O Earth, how speechlessly loving you are,
How stable, how certain, how ancient; how smilingly,
Greenly, softly tolerant of all
Upheavals; wherever we are, your invisible
Arms embrace us all, day and night,
Draw us with such huge and rapturous force
Towards your calm, horizon-touching breast!

Every few moments the restless little boy
Comes up to the Brahmin and asks anxiously,
'Grandfather, when will the tide come?'

Suddenly the still waters stir,
Awaking both banks with hope of departure.
The prow of the boat swings round, the cables
Creak as the current pulls; gurgling,
Singing, the sea enters the river
Like a victory-chariot – the tide has come.
The boatman says his prayers and unleashes
The boat on to the northward-racing stream.
Rākhāl comes up to the Brahmin and asks,
'How many days will it take us to get home?'

With four miles gone and the sun still not set
The wind has started to blow more strongly
From the north. At the mouth of the Rūpnārāyaṇ river,
Where a sandbank narrows the channel, a fierce
Seething battle breaks out between the scurrying
Tide and the north wind. 'Get the boat to the shore,'
Cry the passengers repeatedly – but where is the shore?
Everywhere, whipped-up water claps
With a thousand hands its own mad death-dance:
It jeers at the sky in the furious uprush
Of its foam. On one side are glimpses of the distant
Blue line of the woods on the bank; on the other,
Ravenous, gluttonous, murderous waters
Swell in insolent rebellion against the calm
Setting sun. The rudder is useless
As the boat spins and tumbles like a drunkard.
The men and women aboard tremble
And flounder as icy terror mixes
With the piercing winter wind. Some are dumb
With fear; others yell and wail and weep
For their dear ones. Maitra, ashen-faced,
Shuts his eyes and mutters prayers.
Rākhāl hides his face in his mother's breast
And shivers mutely. Desperate now,
The boatman calls out to everyone, 'Someone
Among you has cheated the gods, has not
Given what is owing – hence these waves,
This unseasonal typhoon. I tell you, make good
Your promise now – you must not play games
With angry gods.' The passengers throw money,
Clothes, everything they have into the water,
Recking nothing. But the water surges higher,
Starts to gush into the boat. The boatman
Shouts again, 'I warn you now,
Who is keeping back what belongs to the gods?'

The Brahmin suddenly points to Mokṣadā
And cries, 'This woman is the one, she made
Her own son over to the gods and now
She tries to steal him back.' 'Throw him overboard,'
Scream the passengers with one voice, heartless
In their terror. 'O grandfather,' cries Mokṣadā,
'Spare him, spare him.' With all her heart
And might she squeezes Rākhāl to her breast.

'Am I your saviour?' barks Maitra, his voice
Rising in reproach and bitterness. 'You stupidly
Thoughtlessly gave your own son
To the gods in your anger, and now you expect me
To save him! Pay the gods your debt –
All these people will drown if you break
Your word.' 'I am a foolish, ignorant
Woman,' says Mokṣadā: 'O God, O reader
Of our inmost thoughts, is what I say
In the heat of anger my true word?
Did you not see how far from the truth
It was, O Lord? Do you only listen
To what our mouths say? Do you not hear
The true message of a mother's heart?'

But as they speak the boatman and oarsmen
Roughly tear Rākhāl from his mother's clasp.
Maitra turns his face away, shuts his eyes,
Blocks his ears, grits his teeth.
A sharp cry sears his heart like a whiplash
Of lightning, stings like a scorpion – 'Aunt Annadā,
Aunt Annadā, Aunt Annadā!' That helpless, hopeless
Drowning cry stabs Maitra's tightly
Shut ears like a spike of fire. 'Stop!'
He bursts out, 'Save him, save him, save him!'
For an instant he stares at Mokṣadā lying senseless
At his feet; then he turns to the water. The boy's
Agonized eyes show briefly among the frothing
Waves as he splutters 'Aunt Annadā' for the last
Time before the black depths claim him. Only
His frail fist sticks up once in a final
Pathetic grasp at the sky's protection,
But it slips away again, defeated. The Brahmin,
Gasping 'I shall bring you back', leaps
Into the water. He is seen no more. The sun sets.

New Rain

It dances today, my heart, like a peacock it dances, it dances.
        It sports a mosaic of passions
        Like a peacock's tail,
It soars to the sky with delight, it quests, O wildly
It dances today, my heart, like a peacock it dances.

Storm-clouds roll through the sky, vaunting their thunder, their thunder.
Rice-plants bend and sway
As the water rushes,
Frogs croak, doves huddle and tremble in their nests, O proudly
Storm-clouds roll through the sky, vaunting their thunder.

Rain-clouds wet my eyes with their blue collyrium, collyrium.
I spread out my joy on the shaded
New woodland grass,
My soul and *kadamba*-trees blossom together, O coolly
Rain-clouds wet my eyes with their blue collyrium.

Who wanders high on the palace-tower, hair unravelled, unravelled –
Pulling her cloud-blue sari
Close to her breast?
Who gambols in the shock and flame of the lightning, O who is it
High on the tower today with hair unravelled?

Who sits in the reeds by the river in pure green garments, green garments?
Her water-pot drifts from the bank
As she scans the horizon,
Longing, distractedly chewing fresh jasmine, O who is it
Sitting in the reeds by the river in pure green garments?

Who swings on that *bakul*-tree branch today in the wilderness, wilderness –
Scattering clusters of blooms,
Sari-hem flying,
Hair unplaited and blown in her eyes? O to and fro
High and low swinging, who swings on that branch in the wilderness?

Who moors her boat where *ketakī*-trees are flowering, flowering?
She has gathered moss in the loose
Fold of her sari,
Her tearful rain-songs capture my heart, O who is it
Moored to the bank where *ketakī*-trees are flowering?

It dances today, my heart, like a peacock it dances, it dances.
The woods vibrate with cicadas,
Rain soaks leaves,
The river roars nearer and nearer the village, O wildly
It dances today, my heart, like a peacock it dances.

The Hero

Say we made a journey, mother,
Roaming far and wide together –
  You would have a palanquin,
  Doors kept open just a chink,
  I would ride a red horse, clip
Clop-clip along beside you, lifting
  Clouds of red dust with my clatter.

Now, suppose it's getting darker,
Suddenly we're blocked by water –
  What a place, how bleak and wild,
  Not a man or beast in sight.
  You take fright, feel in your mind
We're lost. I tell you, 'Don't be frightened,
  Look, we'll take that dried-up river.'

What a thorny, thistly region –
All the cattle have been taken
  Under cover for the night.
  How the path we're taking winds,
  Darkness makes it hard to find –
Then suddenly I hear you crying,
  'Near the water, what's that lantern?'

Next thing shouts and yells surround us,
Figures closing in upon us –
  All four bearers fall away,
  Quake in bushes; you remain
  Crouched in fear, reciting names
Of gods, while I keep calmly saying,
  'I am here, no one shall harm us.'

Just imagine, *lāṭhi*-wielding
Long-haired desperate villains wearing
  Jabā-flowers behind their ears –
  'Stay right there,' I shout, 'keep clear!
  See this sword? I'll chop you, pierce
Each man who comes one footstep nearer.'
  Still they come, leaping and yelling.

You say, 'No, Oh don't go near them!'
I say, 'Sit tight, I can take them,
  Watch –' I spur my horse, at once
  Swords and bucklers clash and thud –
  Mother, you would faint at such

A fight! Some flee; the rest I scupper
Somehow: run them through, behead them.

You think they have surely killed me,
All those hefty men against me,
Till I roll up, smeared with blood,
Pouring sweat – 'The battle's done,
Come outside,' I call. You rush
And hug me, kiss me. 'What a lucky
Thing,' you say, 'that you were with me.'

Life is such a boring matter,
Why are the exciting stories never
True? How this one would amaze
Neighbours, brothers – what? such great
Strength in one so small? My fame
Would spread, with everybody saying,
'What luck he was with his mother!'

Death-wedding

Why do you speak so softly, Death, Death,
Creep upon me, watch me so stealthily?
This is not how a lover should behave.
When evening flowers droop upon their tired
Stems, when cattle are brought in from the fields
After a whole day's grazing, you, Death,
Death, approach me with such gentle steps,
Settle yourself immovably by my side.
I cannot understand the things you say.

Alas, will this be how you will take me, Death,
Death? Like a thief, laying heavy sleep
On my eyes as you descend to my heart?
Will you thus let your tread be a slow beat
In my sleep-numbed blood, your jingling ankle-bells
A drowsy rumble in my ear? Will you, Death,
Death, wrap me, finally, in your cold
Arms and carry me away while I dream?
I do not know why you thus come and go.

Tell me, is this the way you wed, Death,
Death? Unceremonially, with no
Weight of sacrament or blessing or prayer?
Will you come with your massy tawny hair
Unkempt, unbound into a bright coil-crown?
Will no one bear your victory-flag before
Or after; will no torches glow like red
Eyes along the river, Death, Death?
Will earth not quake in terror at your step?

When fierce-eyed Śiva came to take his bride,
Remember all the pomp and trappings, Death,
Death: the flapping tiger-skins he wore;
His roaring bull; the serpents hissing round
His hair; the bom-bom sound as he slapped his cheeks;
The necklace of skulls swinging round his neck;
The sudden raucous music as he blew
His horn to announce his coming – was this not
A better way of wedding, Death, Death?

And as that deathly wedding-party's din
Grew nearer, Death, Death, tears of joy
Filled Gaurī's eyes and the garments at her breast
Quivered; her left eye fluttered and her heart
Pounded; her body quailed with thrilled delight
And her mind ran away with itself, Death, Death;
Her mother wailed and smote her head at the thought
Of receiving so wild a groom; and in his mind
Her father agreed calamity had struck.

Why must you always come like a thief, Death,
Death, always silently, at night's end,
Leaving only tears? Come to me festively,
Make the whole night ring with your triumph, blow
Your victory-conch, dress me in blood-red robes,
Grasp me by the hand and sweep me away!
Pay no heed to what others may think, Death,
Death, for I shall of my own free will
Resort to you if you but take me gloriously.

If I am immersed in work in my room
When you arrive, Death, Death, then break
My work, thrust my unreadiness aside.
If I am sleeping, sinking all desires
In the dreamy pleasure of my bed, or if I lie
With apathy gripping my heart and my eyes

Flickering between sleep and waking, fill
Your conch with your destructive breath and blow,
Death, Death, and I shall run to you.

I shall go to where your boat is moored,
Death, Death, to the sea where the wind rolls
Darkness towards me from infinity.
I may see black clouds massing in the far
North-east corner of the sky; fiery snakes
Of lightning may rear up with their hoods raised,
But I shall not flinch in unfounded fear –
I shall pass silently, unswervingly
Across that red storm-sea, Death, Death.

Arrival

Our work was over for the day, and now the light was fading;
We did not think that anyone would come before the morning.
    All the houses round about
    Dark and shuttered for the night –
One or two amongst us said, 'The King of Night is coming.'
We just laughed at them and said, 'No one will come till morning.'

And when on outer doors we seemed to hear a knocking noise,
We told ourselves, 'That's only the wind, they rattle when it blows.'
    Lamps snuffed out throughout the house,
    Time for rest and peacefulness –
One or two amongst us said, 'His heralds are at the doors.'
We just laughed and said, 'The wind rattles them when it blows.'

And when at dead of night we heard a strange approaching clangour,
We thought, sleep-fuddled as we were, it was only distant thunder.
    Earth beneath us live and trembling,
    Stirring as if it too were waking –
One or two were saying, 'Hear how the wheels of his chariot clatter.'
Sleepily we said, 'No no, that's only distant thunder.'

And when with night still dark there rose a drumming loud and near,
Somebody called to all, 'Wake up, wake up, delay no more!'
    Everyone shaking now with fright,
    Arms wrapped close across each heart –
Somebody cried in our ears, 'O see his royal standard rear!'
At last we started up and said, 'We must delay no more.'

O where are the lights, the garlands, where are the signs of
celebration?
Where is the throne? The King has come, we made no preparation!
Alas what shame, what destiny,
No court, no robes, no finery –
Somebody cried in our ears, 'O vain, O vain this lamentation:
With empty hands, in barren rooms, offer your celebration.'

Fling wide the doors and let him in to the lowly conch's boom;
In deepest dark the King of Night has come with wind and storm.
Thunder crashing across the skies,
Lightning setting the clouds ablaze –
Drag your tattered blankets, let the yard be spread with them:
The King of Grief and Night has come to our land with wind and
storm.

Highest Price

'Who will buy me, who will buy me, rid me of my cares?'
Thus I shout and thus I wander through my nights and days;
And with each day that passes
My basket presses
Upon my head more heavily.
People come and go: some laugh; some watch me tearfully.

At noon I make my way along the king's great stone-paved road,
And soon he comes in his chariot, sword in hand, crown on his head.
'I'll buy by force,' he says
And grabs me, tries
To drag me off. I wriggle free
With ease; the king climbs into his golden chariot and rides away.

In small back lanes I wander past bolted and shuttered doors.
A door opens; an old man with a money-bag appears.
He examines what I have
And says, 'I'll give
You gold.' He returns again and again,
Empties his purse. With far-off thoughts I carry my basket on.

At evening over the richly blossoming forest moonbeams fall.
Near to the base of a *bakul*-tree I meet a beautiful girl.
She edges close: 'My smile
Will make you sell,'
She says. Her smile soon turns to weeping.
Slowly, softly she moves away into the woodland gloaming.

Along the sea shore the sun shines, the sea breaks and rolls.
A child is on the sandy beach: he sits playing with shells.
He seems to know me; he says,
'I'll buy your cares
For nothing.' Suddenly I am released
From my heavy load; his playful face has won me free of cost.

1914–1936

The Conch

How can we bear to see your conch lying there in the dirt?
The tragedy of it cuts off air and blocks out light.
    Warriors, rise, brandish your banners!
    Singers, get up and sing! Doers,
    Charge into action! Do not falter!
How can we let your inspiring conch stare up at us from the dirt?

I came to the prayer-room with an offering of flowers neatly laid out,
Longing to end my long day's labours with heavenly quiet.
    I thought this time my heart's lacerations
    Would heal; I thought my ablutions
    Would purge me – till I saw the degradation
Of your great conch lying on the path, lying in the dirt.

What am I doing with this prayer-lamp, what do I mean by this prayer?
Must I drop my flowers of peace – weave scarlet garlands of war?
    I hoped for a calm end to my struggles;
    I thought my debts had been paid, my battles
    Won, and now I could thankfully settle
In your lap: but suddenly your mute conch seemed to sound in my ear.

O change me, touch me with youth, alchemize me! Let fiery melody
Blaze and twirl in my breast, life-fire leap into ecstasy!
    Let night's ribs crack; let skies,
    As they fill with dawning enlightenment, raise
    Terror in remotest dark. From today
I shall fight to seize and carry aloft your conch of victory.

Now I know I can no more close my eyes in slumber.
Now I know that monsoon showers of arrows must batter
    My heart. Some people will rush to my side;
    Others will weep and sigh in dread;
    Horrifying nightmares will rock the beds
Of sleeping hearers: but today your conch will joyously thunder.

When I looked to you for rest I received nothing but shame;
But dress me for battle now, let armour cover each limb.
    Let new obstructions chafe and challenge me;
    I shall take all blows and hurts unflinchingly;
    My heart shall drum redress for your injuries;
I shall give all my strength, win back your conch and make it BOOM.

Shah-Jahan

You knew, Emperor of India, Shah-Jahan,
That life, youth, wealth, renown
All float away down the stream of time.
Your only dream
Was to preserve forever your heart's pain.
The harsh thunder of imperial power
Would fade into sleep
Like a sunset's crimson splendour,
But it was your hope
That at least a single, eternally-heaved sigh would stay
To grieve the sky.
Though emeralds, rubies, pearls are all
But as the glitter of a rainbow tricking out empty air
And must pass away,
Yet still one solitary tear
Would hang on the cheek of time
In the form
Of this white and gleaming Taj Mahal.

O human heart,
You have no time
To look back at anyone again,
No time.
You are driven by life's quick spate
On and on from landing to landing,
Loading cargo here,
Unloading there.
In your garden, the south wind's murmurs
May enchant spring *mādhabī*-creepers
Into suddenly filling your quivering lap with flowers –
Their petals are scattered in the dust come twilight.
You have no time –
You raise from the dew of another night
New blossom in your groves, new jasmine
To dress with tearful gladness the votive tray
Of a later season.
O human heart,
All that you gather is thrown
To the edge of the path by the end of each night and day.
You have no time to look back again,
No time, no time.

Thus, Emperor, you wished,
Fearing your own heart's forgetfulness,
To conquer time's heart
Through beauty.
How wonderful the deathless clothing
With which you invested
Formless death – how it was garlanded!
You could not maintain
Your grief forever, and so you enmeshed
Your restless weeping
In bonds of silent perpetuity.
The names you softly
Whispered to your love
On moonlit nights in secret chambers live on
Here
As whispers in the ear of eternity.
The poignant gentleness of love
Flowered into the beauty of serene stone.

Poet-Emperor,
This is your heart's picture,
Your new *Meghadūta*,
Soaring with marvellous, unprecedented melody and line
Towards the unseen plane
On which your loverless beloved
And the first glow of sunrise
And the last sigh of sunset
And the disembodied beauty of moonlit *cāmeli*-flower
And the gateway on the edge of language
That turns away man's wistful gaze again and again
Are all blended.
This beauty is your messenger,
Skirting time's sentries
To carry the wordless message:
'I have not forgotten you, my love, I have not forgotten you.'

You are gone, now, Emperor –
Your empire has dissolved like a dream,
Your throne is shattered,
Your armies, whose marching
Shook the earth,
Today have no more weight than the windblown dust on the Delhi road.

Your singers no longer sing for you;
Your musicians no longer mingle their tunes

With the lapping Jumna.
The jingle of the anklets of your women
Has died from your palaces:
The night sky moans
With the throb
Of crickets in their crumbling corners.
But your tireless, incorruptible messenger,
Spurning imperial growth and decline,
Spurning the rise and fall of life and death,
Utters
Through the ages
The same, continuous message of eternal mourning:
'I have not forgotten you, my love, I have not forgotten you.'

Lies! Lies! Who says you have not forgotten?
Who says you have not thrown open
The cage that holds memory?
That even today your heart wards off
The ever-falling darkness
Of history?
That even today it has not escaped by the liberating path
Of forgetfulness?
Tombs remain forever with the dust of this earth:
It is death
That they carefully preserve in a casing of memory.
But who can hold life?
The stars claim it: they call it to the sky,
Invite it to new worlds, to the light
Of new dawns.
It breaks
The knot of memory and runs
Free along universal tracks.
Emperor, no earthly empire could ever keep you:
Not even the whole
Ocean-resounding natural world could supply you.
And so
When your life's *commedia* was complete
You kicked this world away
Like a used clay vessel.
You are greater than your fame: more and more of it is thrown
From your soul's chariot
As it journeys on:
Your relics lie here, but you are gone.
The love that could not move or carry forward,
The love that blocked its own road

With its own grand throne
Could adhere to you no more than the dust of a road on your feet
For all its intimate sweetness –
And thus
You returned it to the dust behind you,
And grief's seed,
Blown by your heart's feeling,
Was shed from the garland of your life.
You travelled on afar:
The deathless plant that grew
From that seed to meet the sky
Speaks to us now with sombre melody –
'Stare no matter how distantly,
That traveller is no longer here, no longer here.
His beloved kept him not,
His realms released him,
Neither sea nor mountain could bar him.
Today his chariot
Travels at the beck of the night
To the song of the stars
Towards the gate of dawn.
I remain here weighted with memory:
He is free of burdens; he is no longer here.'

Gift

O my love, what gift of mine
Shall I give you this dawn?
A morning song?
But morning does not last long –
The heat of the sun
Wilts it like a flower
And songs that tire
Are done.

O friend, when you come to my gate
At dusk
What is it you ask?
What shall I bring you?
A light?

A lamp from a secret corner of my silent house?
But will you want to take it with you
Down the crowded street?
Alas,
The wind will blow it out.

Whatever gifts are in my power to give you,
Be they flowers,
Be they gems for your neck,
How can they please you
If in time they must surely wither,
Crack,
Lose lustre?
All that my hands can place in yours
Will slip through your fingers
And fall forgotten to the dust
To turn into dust.

Rather,
When you have leisure,
Wander idly through my garden in spring
And let an unknown, hidden flower's scent startle you
Into sudden wondering –
Let that displaced moment
Be my gift.
Or if, as you peer your way down a shady avenue,
Suddenly, spilled
From the thick gathered tresses of evening
A single shivering fleck of sunset-light stops you,
Turns your daydreams to gold,
Let that light be an innocent
Gift.

Truest treasure is fleeting;
It sparkles for a moment, then goes.
It does not tell its name; its tune
Stops us in our tracks, its dance disappears
At the toss of an anklet.
I know no way to it –
No hand, nor word can reach it.
Friend, whatever you take of it,
On your own,
Without asking, without knowing, let that
Be yours.
Anything I can give you is trifling –
Be it a flower, or a song.

Deception

Binu was twenty-three when illness struck her.
Doctors and drugs
Became a greater torment than the illness itself;
Different-labelled bottles, different-shaped pill-boxes piled up.
After a year and a half of treatment her bones stuck out:
Then they said, 'Give her a change of air.'
So it was that Binu took her first train-journey,
Left her parents-in-law's house for the first time since marriage.

The restrictions, the airless sequestration of the joint family
Had forced so broken a rhythm on our life together:
Our meetings furtive,
Our days a patchwork of snatched words and abortive smiles.
Today suddenly Earth seemed to be raising the whole light of the sky
To welcome us afresh as man and wife;
The expression in Binu's illness-enlarged eyes
Was like a bride's first unveiled look again, in a new world.

When beggars along the railway-track
Wailed at us for alms,
Binu would dig into her box for coins,
Wrap them in paper,
Fling them freely.
How could her happiness bear its own weight
But by making everyone happy?
It was as if we had left behind our broken domestic moorings
To sail away down a river of permanent love:
Binu's mood and charity
Could not but fill the journey with universal grace.
The thought seemed to burst again and again in her mind:
'Today my husband cares only for me;
There is no one else anywhere,
No husband's relatives before, behind or around me –'
The relief of it thrilled her bodily.

At Bilāspur station we had to change trains;
We got down hurriedly.
Six hours to fill in the waiting-room:
They seemed an age to me,
But Binu said, 'Why? It's good to wait.'
There seemed no limit to her delight.
The journey was a flute that made her want to dance:
Waiting, moving were made one by her happiness.
She opened the door of the waiting-room and said,

'Look, look at those horse-carts passing –
And can you see? That calf over there, how shiny and plump it is,
What deep love in its mother's eyes!
And next to that steep-sided pond over there,
That little fenced-in house under *śiśu*-trees,
Near the railway-line,
Is it the station-master's? What a lovely place to live.'

I spread out a bed-roll in the waiting-room.
'Binu,' I said, 'have a rest now. Lie down and sleep.'
I pulled a chair on to the platform
And began to read an English novel I had bought.
Goods trains passed; passenger trains –
About three hours went by.
Suddenly I heard Binu call from just inside the waiting-room,
'Can you come? I want to tell you something.'

There was a Hindusthānī woman inside the room:
She looked me in the eyes,
Bowed, withdrew to the platform where she stood clutching a pillar.
Binu said, 'She's called Rukmiṇī.
She lives in that row of huts by the well over there;
Her husband is a station coolie.
Some years ago
There was trouble where they lived:
The *zamindār* was a tyrant – they had to flee.
They used to have seven *bighā*s of land, I forget the name of their village,
It was by a river somewhere – '
I interrupted her, said with a smile,
'The train will be here before you've finished Rukmiṇī's life-story.
Come on, it won't hurt to cut it short.'
'Yes it will,' said Binu angrily, glaring, frowning –
'Why should I cut it short?
You're not hurrying to get to the office – what's the fuss?
You can listen to it right through.'
So much for my English novel. Instead I listened in full
To the lengthy story of a railway coolie.
The nub was at the end, an expensive one:
The coolie's daughter was being married; they needed
Bracelets, bangles, armlets for the dowry.
They'd cut it right down, but they'd have to spend twenty-five rupees.
It was such a worry:
Rukminī was terribly cast down by it.
Could I not,

Just this once,
Relieve Rukmiṇī of the worry?
Before we got on the train, I must give her
The whole twenty-five rupees.

What an absurd business!
Whoever heard of such a thing?
The woman was probably a sweeper or something equally disgusting,
Cleaning out the waiting-room daily –
To think of giving twenty-five rupees to her!
I'd quickly go bankrupt if I gave away money like that.
'All right, I understand,' I said. 'But I find
I only have a hundred-rupee note –
No way of changing it.'
'They'll change it for you at the ticket-office,' said Binu.
I answered, 'All right, I'll see what I can do.'
I called the woman, took her aside,
And then I tore into her:
'I'll make sure you lose your job!
Going around duping passengers? I'll soon put a stop to it.'
When she burst into tears and clung to my feet
I gave her two rupees and had done with her.

The temple-light went dark, went out.
At the end of two months I was on my way home.
When I got down once again at Bilāspur to change trains,
I was alone.
In her final moments Binu had taken the dust of my feet and said,
'Whatever else in my life I shall forget,
These last two months will be marked on my brow forever –
Like the everlasting vermilion in the parting of Lakṣmī's hair.
These two months have filled my soul with nectar:
That is what I remember as I bid you farewell.'

O all-seeing God,
If only I could tell Binu today
That I am guilty of a dreadful omission from that two-month offering –
A debt of twenty-five rupees.
Even if I could give a hundred thousand rupees to Rukmiṇī today
They could never fill that lack.
Binu never knew I had pressed deceivingly into her hands
The two months that she took away with her.

At Bilāspur I inquired of everyone,
'Where is Rukmiṇī?'
They reacted blankly:

Who was Rukmiṇī? No one knew.
I racked my brains: 'The wife of Jhamru the coolie,' I remembered.
And then they answered, 'They're no longer here.'
'Where can I find them?' I asked.
'Why should anyone know that?' said the station-master, getting annoyed.
The ticket-clerk smirked and said, 'They went off a month ago
To Darjeeling or Khasrubāg
Or maybe Ārākān.'
When I tried to ask if anyone knew their address,
I was brushed away angrily: what business of theirs was the coolie's address?

How could I explain? What seemed so trivial to them that day
Was for me direst necessity:
To find the one person able to rid me of my burden of deceit.
'These two months have filled my soul with nectar.'
How shall I bear the memory of Binu's last words?
I remain here a debtor;
My lie will stay with me always.

Grandfather's Holiday

Blue sky, paddy fields, grandchild's play,
Deep ponds, diving-stage, child's holiday;
Tree shade, barn corners, catch-me-if-you-dare,
Undergrowth, *pārul*-bushes, life without care.
Green paddy all a-quiver, hopeful as a child,
Child prancing, river dancing, waves running wild.

Bespectacled grandfather old man am I,
Trapped in my work like a spiderwebbed fly.
Your games are my games, my proxy holiday,
Your laugh the sweetest music I shall ever play.
Your joy is mine, my mischief in your eyes,
Your delight the country where my freedom lies.

Autumn sailing in, now, steered by your play,
Bringing white *śiuli*-flowers to grace your holiday.
Pleasure of the chilly air tingling me at night,
Blown from Himālaya on the breeze of your delight.
Dawn in Āśvin, flower-forcing roseate sun,
Dressed in the colours of a grandchild's fun.

Flooding of my study with your leaps and your capers,
Work gone, books flying, avalanche of papers.
Arms round my neck, in my lap bounce thump –
Hurricane of freedom in my heart as you jump.
Who has taught you, how he does it, I shall never know –
You're the one who teaches me to let myself go.

Palm-tree

Palm-tree: single-legged giant,
topping the other trees,
peering at the firmament –
It longs to pierce the black cloud-ceiling
and fly away, away,
if only it had wings.

The tree seems to express its wish
in the tossing of its head:
its fronds heave and swish –
It thinks, Maybe my leaves are feathers,
and nothing stops me now
from rising on their flutter.

All day the fronds on the windblown tree
soar and flap and shudder
as though it thinks it can fly,
As though it wanders in the skies,
travelling who knows where,
wheeling past the stars –

And then as soon as the wind dies down,
the fronds subside, subside:
the mind of the tree returns
To earth, recalls that earth is its mother:
and then it likes once more
its earthly corner.

The Wakening of Śiva

My past days bulging with the sap of the turbulence of youth –
O master of cyclic Time, are you indifferent to them now,
        O tranced ascetic?
Have they with *kiṃśuk* blossoms on gusty Caitra nights
Blown away, have they floated uncared-for off into infinite sky?
Have they on rafts of slim white rainless post-monsoon cloud
Drifted at the whim of arbitrary winds to moor on oblivion
        Through harsh neglect?

Those days that once so colourfully decked your matted yellow locks
With white and red and blue and yellow flowers –
        Are they all forgotten?
In the end they laughingly stole your beggar's tabor and horn
And gave you flute and anklets; they filled your drinking-bowl
With potent distillations of the heavy scents of spring;
They drowned the dense inertia of your trance
        In an upsurge of sweetness.

Your trance collapsed then, vanished into the air, whirling with the speed
Of a dry leaf towards the snowy deserts of the north,
        The songless Himālaya.
The days transformed your meditation, translated your mantras into scents
Of flowers borne by the jesting, fancy-free, southern spring-breeze.
Those mantras gave oleanders, *kāñcan*, *sẽuti* riotous life;
Those mantras lit the forest with new leaves, sparked its groves
        Into blue-green flame.

The rushing flood-waters of spring ended your austerities;
You listened now with rapture to the music of Gaṅgā's flowing tears
        Tangled in your hair.
Your wealth revived, its splendour sprang up afresh;
The wonder in your heart overflowed with its own extravagance.
You discovered in yourself your proper, generous beauty;
Joyously you took in your hands the gleaming nectar-cup
        That the world hungers for.

Wildly you roamed through the woods with your pulsing dances,
To whose rhythm and tempo I constantly matched my tunes –
        Dancing beside you.
In my eyes there were dreams of paradise, moonlit by your brow;
The ever-renewing force of your *līlā* filled my heart.
I saw it in smiles, at its point of escape into the heart of beauty;
I saw it in shyness, at its point of hesitant switching to delight;
        I felt the Flux of Form.

The brimming vessel of those days, have you since spilt its fullness?
Have you rubbed out their curlicued pattern, their lip-print
Of passionate red?
Were you careless with their tear-swelled torrent of unsung songs,
Did you let them lie forgotten in broken jars in your courtyard?
Did your dance of destruction pound them into dust?
Does the moan of the sterile hot south-west wind signify the death
Of your former days?

No, no, they are with you still: you have merely hidden them away
In the absolute night of your yoga, absorbed them into silence
To guard them secretly.
Gaṅgā, meshed in your hair, is at present surreptitious in her flow;
The shackles of your sleep have blanked the moon on your forehead.
What deceit there is in your *līlā*, to disguise you so miserably!
As far as the eye sees, the darkness whispers, 'They are gone,
Those days are gone.'

You are Time's herdsman: in the evening of an era you sound your horn,
And past days rush like cattle to the safety of your byre,
Eager for its calm.
Across the deserted plains of the universe marsh-fires flicker;
Cobras of lightning dart their hoods through epoch-ending clouds.
Separate moments converge into darkness, disconsolate, crushed,
Their energy sucked into the bonds of your deep unbreathing trance,
Their motion annihilated.

But I know that after its long night your trance will reach
Explosive conclusion when Flux sweeps you into its dance again,
Into its stream of delight.
The suppressed days of youth will be freed, to emerge
As eager promptings of delicious passion; rebellious youth
Will be a warrior displaying again and again how he can smash
Fossilized discipline; and I shall prepare his lion-throne,
His victorious welcome.

For I am Indra's messenger: I come to break your penance,
O Śiva, fearsome ascetic; I am heaven's conspiracy against you.
Age after age I come,
A poet, to your hermitage. I fill my basket with garlands of victory;
Irrepressible conquest shouts through the plangent rhythms of my verse.
By the force that drives my feelings, roses open;
By the impulse of ecstatic discovery that opens new leaves,
I hurl forth my songs.

O bark-clad anchorite, I know all your deceptions.
Your bark is illusory armour: you joyfully anticipate defeat
At the hands of beauty.
You may burn up Kāma again and again with your fire,
But you always restore him to doubly blazing life;
And because I fill and refill his quiver
With passion, I am come with my snares of music, a poet,
Into the lap of earth.

I know, I know, though you seem aloof, in reality you long
For the agonized insistent pleas of your beloved to wake you suddenly
Into new ardour.
You hold yourself apart, sunk in seemingly impenetrable trance
Because you want her to weep the fiery tears of separation.
But the wonderful images of your union with Umā on breaking your trance –
I see them through all ages, play them on my vīṇā in your consort's rāga,
For I am a poet.

Your attendants, life-hating lovers of burning-grounds, do not know me:
They cackle with the devilish rancour of the mean in spirit
When they see what I am.
But in the months of spring, when the time is auspicious for your nuptials
And sweet-smiling modesty blooms in Umā's cheeks,
Then call your poet to the route of your wedding procession,
Let him join the seven sages who accompany you with trays
Of festive garlands.

Śiva, the eyes of your ghoulish attendants will redden with fury
When they see your resplendent body dressed in scarlet wedding-robes,
Bright as the dawn.
You shall cast off your necklace of skulls, bury it in *mādhabī*-creepers;
You shall rub off the ash on your forehead, replace it with pollen.
Umā will smile buoyantly, glance at me sideways:
Her smile will inspire my flute, raise songs of the triumph of beauty
In my poet's heart.

Guest

Lady, you have filled these exile days of mine
With sweetness, made a foreign traveller your own
As easily as these unfamiliar stars, quietly,
Coolly smiling from heaven, have likewise given me
Welcome. When I stood at this window and stared
At the southern sky, a message seemed to slide
Into my soul from the harmony of the stars,
A solemn music that said, 'We know you are ours –
Guest of our light from the day you passed
From darkness into the world, always our guest.'
Lady, your kindness is a star, the same solemn tune
In your glance seems to say, 'I know you are mine.'
I do not know your language, but I hear your melody:
'Poet, guest of my love, my guest eternally.'

In Praise of Trees

O Tree, life-founder, you heard the sun
Summon you from the dark womb of earth
At your life's first wakening; your height
Raised from rhythmless rock the first
Hymn to the light; you brought feeling to harsh,
Impassive desert.

Thus, in the sky,
By mixed magic, blue with green, you flung
The song of the world's spirit at heaven
And the tribe of stars. Facing the unknown,
You flew with fearless pride the victory
Banner of the life-force that passes
Again and again through death's gateway
To follow an endless pilgrim-road
Through time, through changing resting-places,
In ever new mortal vehicles.
Earth's reverie snapped at your noiseless
Challenge: excitedly she recalled
Her daring departure from heaven –
A daughter of God leaving its bright
Splendour, ashy-pale, dressed in humble
Ochre-coloured garments, to partake

Of the joy of heaven fragmented
Into time and place, to receive it
More deeply now that she would often
Pierce it with stabs of grief.

O valiant
Child of the earth, you declared a war
To liberate her from that fortress
Of desert. The war was incessant –
You crossed ocean-waves to establish,
With resolute faith, green seats of power
On bare, inaccessible islands;
You bewitched dust, scaled peaks, wrote on stone
In leafy characters your battle
Tales; you spread your code over trackless
Wastes.

Sky, earth, sea were expressionless
Once, lacking the festival magic
Of the seasons. Your branches offered
Music its first shelter, made the songs
In which the restless wind – colouring
With kaleidoscopic melody
Her invisible body, edging
Her shawl with prismatic tune – first knew
Herself. You were first to describe
On earth's clay canvas, by absorbing
Plastic power from the sun, a living
Image of beauty. You processed light's
Hidden wealth to give colour to light.
When celestial dancing-nymphs shook
Their bracelets in the clouds, shattering
Those misty cups to rain down freshening
Nectar, you filled therewith your vessels
Of leaf and flower to clothe the earth
With perpetual youth.

O profound,
Silent tree, by restraining valour
With patience, you revealed creative
Power in its peaceful form. Thus we come
To your shade to learn the art of peace,
To hear the word of silence; weighed down
With anxiety, we come to rest
In your tranquil blue-green shade, to take
Into our souls life rich, life ever

Juvenescent, life true to earth, life
Omni-victorious. I am certain
My thoughts have borne me to your essence –
Where the same fire as the sun's ritual
Fire of creation quietly assumes
In you cool green form. O sun-drinker,
The fire with which – by milking hundreds
Of centuries of days of sunlight –
You have filled your core, man has received
As your gift, making him world-mighty,
Greatly honoured, rival to the gods:
His shining strength, kindled by your flame,
Is the wonder of the universe
As it cuts through daunting obstacles.
Man, whose life is in you, who is soothed
By your cool shade, strengthened by your power,
Adorned by your garland – O tree, friend
Of man, dazed by your leafy flutesong
I speak today for him as I make
  This verse-homage,
As I dedicate this offering
    To you.

Last Honey

End of the year, of spring; wind, renouncing the world, leaves
  The empty harvested fields with a farewell call to the bees –

  Come, come; Caitra is going, shedding her leaves;
Earth spreads out her robe for summer languor beneath the trees;
But *sajne*-tresses dangle and mango-blossoms are not all shed,
  And edging the woods *ākanda* lays its welcoming bed.
  Come, come; in the drought there'll be nothing of these
But the dance of their withered wraiths in the barren night, so come, bees.

I hear the song of the closing year like a flute in the rustling leaves,
So smear your wings with pollen's chronicle before its fragrance flees.
  Take all you can from flowers that summer heat will strew;
  Cram the old year's honey into the hives of the new.
  Come, come; do not delay, new year bees –
Look what a wealth of parting gifts has been laid on the year as she leaves.

The fierce, destructive heat of Baiśākh will quickly seize
The *dolan-cā̃pā* buds that tremble now in the Caitra breeze.
Finish all that they have to give, let nothing stay;
As the season ends let everything go in an orgy of giving away.
Come, thieves of hidden honey; come now, bees –
The year has chosen to marry death and wants to give all as she leaves.

Sea-maiden

Wet with sea-water, with loose dripping hair
You sat on the rocky shore.
Your flowing yellow skirt
Rolled and curved round your feet.
The tender dawn
Wrote in glistening gold on your naked breasts and unadorned skin.
With a *makara*-crested crown on my brow,
Holding in my right hand bow and arrow
I stood majestically
And said, 'I have come from a far country.'

Starting from your stone seat in alarm,
You cried, 'Why have you come?'
I said, 'Do not be afraid:
I have come to pick pūjā-offerings in your flowering wood.'
You came with me, smiling your favour;
We picked jasmine and *jātī* and *cā̃pā*-flower.
We dressed a basket with flowers; we sat together
And jointly worshipped dancing Śiva.
Dawn-mist vanished; the light that flooded the sky
Showed Pārvatī smiling as she caught her husband's eye.

When over the mountains appeared the evening star,
You sat alone indoors.
Blue silk girdled your waist; on your head, a *mālatī*-chaplet;
Round each of your wrists a bracelet.
I played my flute as I drew near;
'I come as your guest,' I said at your door.
You lit your lamp in dread and alarm,
Stared at me, said, 'Why have you come?'
I said, 'Do not fear me:

I have come to dress you in my finery.'
You smiled; I placed
A necklace of golden crescents across your breast.
I circled your bound-up hair with my own
Makara-crown.
Your companions lit lamps and marvelled;
The jewels on your body sparkled.
You sweetened and disturbed the spring night;
Your anklets jingled as you danced to my beat.
The full moon smiled; Śiva and Pārvatī,
Light and shade, played in the waters of the sea.

I did not notice the ending of the day;
I found myself floating again in my boat on a twilit sea.
Suddenly the wind was against me:
Waves reared, a storm blew up fiercely.
Salt-water filled my boat,
And it sank with its cargo of jewels in the dark night.

Again but broken in fortune I came to wait at your door,
In stained rags, no splendour.
Opening the door of the Śiva temple I saw
That our basket of flowers still lay there.
I saw, lit by the restless festivity
Of the surging mêlée
Of moonlight dancing in the sea,
My patterns still painted on your meek lowered brow,
My necklace still on your breast.
Unobserved I saw, expressed
In your gestures and form,
The pitch and beats of my drum;
In your limbs the swing
Of my tālas delighting, singing, oscillating.

Hear my prayer, beautiful maiden;
Come before me with your lamp again.
This time I am no longer *makara*-crowned;
I no longer have bow and arrow in my hand;
Neither have I brought a basket for the gathering of flowers
In your wood by the sea where the south wind blows.
My vīṇā is all I have with me.
Look at me, see whether you recognize me.

Question

God, again and again through the ages you have sent messengers
To this pitiless world:
They have said, 'Forgive everyone', they have said, 'Love one another –
Rid your hearts of evil.'
They are revered and remembered, yet still in these dark days
We turn them away with hollow greetings, from outside the doors of our houses.

And meanwhile I see secretive hatred murdering the helpless
Under cover of night;
And Justice weeping silently and furtively at power misused,
No hope of redress.
I see young men working themselves into a frenzy,
In agony dashing their heads against stone to no avail.

My voice is choked today; I have no music in my flute:
Black moonless night
Has imprisoned my world, plunged it into nightmare. And this is why,
With tears in my eyes, I ask:
Those who have poisoned your air, those who have extinguished your light,
Can it be that you have forgiven them? Can it be that you love them?

Flute-music

Kinu the milkman's alley.
A ground-floor room in a two-storeyed house,
Slap on the road, windows barred.
Decaying walls, crumbling to dust in places
Or stained with damp.
Stuck on the door,
A picture of Gaṇeśa, Bringer of Success,
From the end of a bale of cloth.
Another creature apart from me lives in my room
For the same rent:
A lizard.
There's one difference between him and me:
He doesn't go hungry.

I get twenty-five rupees a month
As junior clerk in a trading office.
I'm fed at the Dattas' house
For coaching their boy.
At dusk I go to Sealdah station,
Spend the evening there
To save the cost of light.
Engines chuffing,
Whistles shrieking,
Passengers scurrying,
Coolies shouting.
I stay till half past ten,
Then back to my dark, silent, lonely room.

A village on the Dhaleśvarī river, that's where my aunt's people live.
Her brother-in-law's daughter –
She was due to marry my unfortunate self, everything was fixed.
The moment was indeed auspicious for her, no doubt of that –
For I ran away.
The girl was saved from me,
And I from her.
She did not come to this room, but she's in and out of my mind all the time:
Dacca sari, vermilion on her forehead.

Pouring rain.
My tram costs go up,
But often as not my pay gets cut for lateness.
Along the alley,
Mango skins and stones, jack-fruit pulp,
Fish-gills, dead kittens
And God knows what other rubbish
Pile up and rot.
My umbrella is like my depleted pay –
Full of holes.
My sopping office clothes ooze
Like a pious Vaiṣṇava.
Monsoon darkness
Sticks in my damp room
Like an animal caught in a trap,
Lifeless and numb.
Day and night I feel strapped bodily
On to a half-dead world.

At the corner of the alley lives Kāntabābu –
Long hair carefully parted,

Large eyes,
Cultivated tastes.
He fancies himself on the cornet:
The sound of it comes in gusts
On the foul breeze of the alley –
Sometimes in the middle of the night,
Sometimes in the early morning twilight,
Sometimes in the afternoon
When sun and shadows glitter.
Suddenly this evening
He starts to play runs in Sindhu-Bārõyā rāg,
And the whole sky rings
With eternal pangs of separation.
At once the alley is a lie,
False and vile as the ravings of a drunkard,
And I feel that nothing distinguishes Haripada the clerk
From the Emperor Akbar.
Torn umbrella and royal parasol merge,
Rise on the sad music of a flute
Towards one heaven.

The music is true
Where, in the everlasting twilight-hour of my wedding,
The Dhaleśvarī river flows,
Its banks deeply shaded by *tamāl*-trees,
And she who waits in the courtyard
Is dressed in a Dacca sari, vermilion on her forehead.

Unyielding

When I called you in your garden
Mango blooms were rich in fragrance –
Why did you remain so distant,
Keep your door so tightly fastened?
Blossoms grew to ripe fruit-clusters –
You rejected my cupped handfuls,
Closed your eyes to perfectness.

In the fierce harsh storms of Baiśākh
Golden ripened fruit fell tumbling –
'Dust,' I said, 'defiles such offerings:
Let your hands be heaven to them.'
Still you showed no friendliness.

Lampless were your doors at evening,
Pitch-black as I played my vīṇā.
How the starlight twanged my heartstrings!
How I set my vīṇā dancing!
You showed no responsiveness.

Sad birds twittered sleeplessly,
Calling, calling lost companions.
Gone the right time for our union –
Low the moon while still you brooded,
Sunk in lonely pensiveness.

Who can understand another!
Heart cannot restrain its passion.
I had hoped that some remaining
Tear-soaked memories would sway you,
Stir your feet to lightsomeness.

Moon fell at the feet of morning,
Loosened from night's fading necklace.
While you slept, O did my vīṇā
Lull you with its heartache? Did you
Dream at least of happiness?

Earth

Accept my homage, Earth, as I make my last obeisance of the day,
Bowed at the altar of the setting sun.

You are mighty, and knowable only by the mighty;
You counterpoise charm and severity;
Compounded of male and female
You sway human life with unbearable conflict.
The cup that your right hand fills with nectar
Is smashed by your left;
Your playground rings with your mocking laughter.
You make heroism hard to attain;
You make excellence costly;
You are not merciful to those who deserve mercy.
Ceaseless warfare is hidden in your plants:
Their crops and fruits are victory-wreaths won from struggle.
Land and sea are your cruel battlefields –
Life proclaims its triumph in the face of death.

Civilization rests its foundation upon your cruelty:
Ruin is the penalty exacted for any shortcoming.

In the first chapter of your history Demons were supreme –
Harsh, barbaric, brutish;
Their clumsy thick fingers lacked art;
With clubs and mallets in hand they rioted over sea and mountain.
Their fire and smoke churned sky into nightmare;
They controlled the inanimate world;
They had blind hatred of Life.

Gods came next; by their spells they subdued the Demons –
The insolence of Matter was crushed.
Mother Earth spread out her green mantle;
On the eastern peaks stood Dawn;
On the western sea-shore Evening descended,
Dispensing peace from her chalice.

The shackled Demons were humbled;
But primal barbarity has kept its grip on your history.
It can suddenly invade order with anarchy –
From the dark recesses of your being
It can suddenly emerge like a snake.
Its madness is in your blood.
The spells of the Gods resound through sky and air and forest,
Sung solemnly day and night, high and low;
But from regions under your surface
Sometimes half-tame Demons raise their serpent-hoods –
They goad you into wounding your own creatures,
Into ruining your own creation.

At your footstool mounted on evil as well as good,
To your vast and terrifying beauty,
I offer today my scarred life's homage.
I touch your huge buried store of life and death,
Feel it throughout my body and mind.
The corpses of numberless generations of men lie heaped in your dust:
I too shall add a few fistfuls, the final measure of my joys and pains:
Add them to that name-absorbing, shape-absorbing, fame-absorbing
Silent pile of dust.

Earth, clamped into rock or flitting into the clouds;
Rapt in meditation in the silence of a ring of mountains
Or noisy with the roar of sleepless sea-waves;
You are beauty and abundance, terror and famine.
On the one hand, acres of crops, bent with ripeness,
Brushed free of dew each morning by delicate sunbeams –

With sunset, too, sending through their rippling greenness
Joy, joy;
On the other, in your dry, barren, sickly deserts
The dance of ghosts amid strewn animal-bones.

I have watched your Baiśākh-storms swoop like black hawks
Ripping the horizon with lightning-beaks:
The whole sky roars like a rampant lion,
Lashing tail whipping up trees
Till they crash to the ground in despair;
Thatched roofs break loose,
Race before the wind like convicts from their chains.

But I have known, in Phālgun, the warm south breeze
Spread all the rhapsodies and soliloquies of love
In its scent of mango-blossom;
Seen the foaming wine of heaven overflow from the moon's goblet;
Heard coppices suddenly submit to wind's importunity
And burst into breathless rustling.

You are gentle and fierce, ancient and renewing;
You emerged from the sacrificial fire of primal creation
Immeasurably long ago.
Your cyclic pilgrimage is littered with meaningless remnants of history;
You abandon your creations without regret; strew them layer upon layer,
Forgotten.

Guardian of Life, you nurture us
In little cages of fragmented time,
Boundaries to all our games, limits to all renown.

Today I stand before you without illusion:
I do not ask at your door for immortality
For the many days and nights I have spent weaving you garlands.
But if I have given true value
To my small seat in a tiny segment of one of the eras
That open and close like blinks in the millions of years
Of your solar round;
If I have won from the trials of life a scrap of success;
Then mark my brow with a sign made from your clay –
To be rubbed out in time by the night
In which all signs fade into the final unknown.

O aloof, ruthless Earth,
Before I am utterly forgotten
Let me place my homage at your feet.

Africa

When, in that turbid first age,
The Creator, displeased with himself,
Destroyed his new creations again and again;
In those days of his shaking and shaking his head in irritation
The angry sea
Snatched you from the breast of Mother Asia,
Africa –
Consigned you to the guard of immense trees,
To a fastness dimly lit.
There in your hidden leisure
You collected impenetrable secrets,
Learnt the arcane languages of water and earth and sky;
Nature's invisible magic
Worked spells in your unconscious mind.
You ridiculed Horror
By making your own appearance hideous;
You cowed Fear
By heightening your menacing grandeur,
By dancing to the drumbeats of chaos.

Alas, shadowy Africa,
Under your black veil
Your human aspect remained unknown,
Blurred by the murk of contempt.
Others came with iron manacles,
With clutches sharper than the claws of your own wild wolves:
Slavers came,
With an arrogance more benighted than your own dark jungles.
Civilization's barbarous greed
Flaunted its naked inhumanity.
You wailed wordlessly, muddied the soil of your steamy jungles
With blood and tears;
The hobnailed boots of your violators
Stuck gouts of that stinking mud
Forever on your stained history.

Meanwhile across the sea in their native parishes
Temple-bells summoned your conquerors to prayer,
Morning and evening, in the name of a loving god.
Mothers dandled babies in their laps;
Poets raised hymns to beauty.

Today as the air of the West thickens,
Constricted by imminent evening storm;
As animals emerge from secret lairs
And proclaim by their ominous howls the closing of the day;
Come, poet of the end of the age,
Stand in the dying light of advancing nightfall
At the door of despoiled Africa
And say, 'Forgive, forgive – '
In the midst of murderous insanity,
May these be your civilization's last, virtuous words.

1937–1941

The Borderland – 9

I saw, in the twilight of flagging consciousness,
My body floating down an ink-black stream
With its mass of feelings, with its varied emotion,
With its many-coloured life-long store of memories,
With its flutesong. And as it drifted on and on
Its outlines dimmed; and among familiar tree-shaded
Villages on the banks, the sounds of evening
Worship grew faint, doors were closed, lamps
Were covered, boats were moored to the ghāṭs. Crossings
From either side of the stream stopped; night thickened;
From the forest-branches fading birdsong offered
Self-sacrifice to a huge silence.
Dark formlessness settled over all diversity
Of land and water. As shadow, as particles, my body
Fused with endless night. I came to rest
At the altar of the stars. Alone, amazed, I stared
Upwards with hands clasped and said: 'Sun, you have removed
Your rays: show now your loveliest, kindliest form
That I may see the Person who dwells in me as in you.'

The Borderland – 10

King of Death, your fatal messenger came to me
Suddenly from your durbar. He took me to your vast courtyard.
My eyes saw darkness; I did not see the invisible light
In the depths and layers of your darkness, the light
That is the source of the universe; my vision
Was clouded by my own darkness. That a great hymn
To light should swell from the inmost cavern of my being
And reach to the realm of light at the edge of creation –
That was why you sent for me. I sang,
Aiming in my melody to bring to the theatre of physical
Existence the poetic glory of the spirit.
But my vīṇā could not play the music of destruction,
Could not compose a rāga of silent wrath;
My heart could not engender a serene image of the terrible.
And so you sent me back. The day will come
When my poetry, silently falling like a ripened fruit
From the weight of its fullness of joy,
Shall be offered up to eternity. And then at last
I shall pay you in full, finish my journey, meet your call.

Leaving Home

One in the morning – waking in a flurry,
Fresh sleep ruptured. The clock by his pillow
Had roused him brusquely with its harsh alarm.
His time in the house was finished.
Now, in the cold of Aghrāṇ,
At the call of merciless duty,
He must leave family, go to an alien land.
All that was discardable for now
Would remain behind:
The rickety divan with its grimy bedspread;
The broken-armed easy-chair;
In the bedroom,
Balanced on a leaning tepoy
A spattered old mirror;
In a corner, a wooden cupboard
Stuffed with worm-eaten ledger-books;
Stacked against the walls,
Piles of outdated almanacs.
In a niche, a tray of withered, abandoned pūjā-flowers:
All of this there in the feeble lamplight,
Wrapped in shadow, motionless, meaningless.

The taxi brashly honked its presence at the door.
The deeply sleeping town
Stayed aloof.
The distant police-station-bell rang three-and-a-half.
Gazing up at the sky,
Sighing deeply,
He invoked divine protection for his long journey.
Then he padlocked the door of his house.
Dragging his unwilling body,
He moved forward, paused –
Above him, bats' wings
Swept across the black emptiness of the sky
Like shadowy spectres of the cruel fate
That was leading his life into uncertainty.
By the temple, the aged banyan-tree
Had been swallowed by the night as by a snake.
By the bank round the newly-dug tank
Where labourers' dwellings had sprung up
Roofed with date-palm leaves, faint lights flickered.
Near them, the scattered bricks of a tumbledown kiln.

Images of life, outlines blurred
By the ink-wash of night –
Farmers busy all day in the fields cutting paddy;
Girls gossiping, arms round each other's necks;
Boys, released from school,
Scampering raucously;
A sack-laden ox cajoled and shoved to morning market;
Herd-boys floating across to fields on the other side of the river
By clinging to the necks of buffalo –
The ever-familiar play of life as the taxi rushed the traveller
Through the dark, but before its dawn arousal.

As he sped past a weed-filled pond
The scent of its water
Evoked the cool, tender embrace of many days and nights.
But on went the car by the winding route
To the station:
Rows of houses on either side –
People inside them comfortably sleeping.
Through gaps between the trees in the dark mango-groves
The morning-star could be glimpsed,
Honouring the brow of silence
With the mark of infinity.
On the traveller went,
Alone among sleeping thousands,
While the car that hastened him echoed far and wide
Down the empty streets,
Callous in its sound.

In the Eyes of a Peacock

The terrace where I sit is screened
From the springtime dawn sunshine.
What a boon to have leisure –
No pressing tasks crowding in upon me yet;
No hordes of people pestering me,
Trampling over my time.
I sit and write:
The sweetness of a free morning collects in my pen-nib
Like the juice that drips from a slit in a date-palm.

Our peacock has come to sit on the railing next to me,
Tail spread downwards.
He finds safe refuge with me –
No unkind keeper comes to him here with shackles.
Outside, unripe mangoes dangle from branches;
Lemon trees are loaded with lemons;
A single *kuṛci*-tree seems surprised
By its excess of flowers.
The peacock bends his head to this side and that
With unthinking natural restlessness.
His detached stare
Pays not the slightest attention to the marks in my note-book.
If the letters were insects he would look:
He would not then regard a poet as utterly useless.
I smile at the peacock's solemn indifference,
Observe my writing through his eyes;
And indeed the same aloofness
Is in the entire blue sky,
In every leaf of the tree that is hung with green mangoes,
In the buzzing of the wild bee-hive in our tamarind-tree.
I reflect that in ancient Mohenjodaro,
On a similarly idle late Caitra morning,
A poet must have written poems,
And universal nature took no account whatsoever.
The peacock is still to be found in the balance-sheet of life,
And green mangoes still hang from branches;
Their value in the gamut of nature from blue sky to green woods
Will not diminish at all.
But the poet of Mohenjodaro is completely excluded
From the wayside grass, from the dark night's fireflies.

I expand my consciousness
Into endless time and vast earth;
I absorb the huge detachment of nature's own meditations
Into my own mind;
I regard the letters in my note-book
As autumnal flocks of insects –
I conclude that if I were to tear out the pages today
I would merely be advancing the ultimate cremation awaiting them
anyway.

Suddenly I hear a voice –
'Grandfather, are you writing?'
Someone else has come – not a peacock this time
But Sunayanī, as she is called in the house,

But whom I call Śunāyanī because she listens so well.
She has the right to hear my poems before anyone else.
I reply, 'This won't appeal to your sensitive ears:
It's *vers libre.*'
A wave of furrows plays across her forehead –
'I'll put up with it,' she says,
Then adds a little flattery:
'Prose, when *you* recite it,
Can take on the colour of poetry.'
And she throws her arms round my neck and hugs me.
I quip, 'Are you trying to transfer some of that poetic colour
From my throat into your arms?'
She answers, 'That's not how a poet should talk:
I'm the one who passes the touch of poetry into *your* voice:
I may even have awoken song.'

I listen in silence, too happy to reply.
I say to myself – The aloofness of nature
Is constant, like a mountain it looks down loftily
From numberless accumulated years.
But my Śunāyanī,
Morning star,
Can lightly and suddenly scale its immensity;
And time's great disregard surrenders to that instant.

Poet of Mohenjodaro, your evening star
Has passed through its setting
To surmount again the crest of morning
Here in my life.

New Birth

New deliverer –
The new age eagerly looks
To the path of your coming.
What message have you brought
To the world? In the mortal arena
What seat has been prepared for you?
What new form of address
Have you brought to be used
In the worship of God in Man? What song of heaven
Have you heard before coming?

What great weapon for the fighting of evil
Have you placed in the quiver, bound to the waist
Of the young warrior?
Will you, perhaps, where a tide of blood besmirches your path,
Where there is malice and discord,
Construct a dam of peace,
A place of meeting and pilgrimage?
Who can say if there is written on your forehead
The invisible mark
Of the triumph of some great striving?
Today we search for your unwritten name:
You seem to be just off the stage,
Like an imminent star of morning.
Infants bring again and again
A message of reassurance –
They seem to promise deliverance, light, dawn.

Flying Man

Satanic machine, you enable man to fly.
Land and sea had fallen to his power:
All that was left was the sky.

God has given as a gift a bird's two wings.
From the flash of feathery line and colour
Spiritual joy springs.

Birds are companions to the clouds: blue space
And great winds and brightly-coloured birds
Are all of the same race.

The rhythms in the life and play of birds belong
To the wind; from the sky's music comes
Their energy and song.

Thus each dawn throughout the forests of the earth
Light, when it wakes, unites with birdsong
In one harmonious birth.

In the great peace beneath the immense sky,
The dancing wings of birds quiver
Like wavelets rippling by.

Age after age through birds the life-spirit speaks:
It is carried by birds along tracks of air
To far-flung forests and peaks.

Today what do we see? And what is its meaning?
The banner of arrogance has taken wing,
Proud and overweening.

This thing has not been blessed by the life-divinity.
The sun disowns it, neither does the moon
Feel any affinity.

In the brutal roaring of an aeroplane we hear
Incompatibility with sky,
Destruction of atmosphere.

High among the clouds, in the heavens, its din
Adds new blasphemous grating laughter
To man's catalogue of sin.

I feel the age we live in is drawing to a close –
Upheavals threaten, gather the pace
Of a storm that nothing slows.

Hatred and envy swell to violent conflagration:
Panic spreads down from the skies,
From their growing devastation.

If nowhere in the sky is there left a space
For gods to be seated, then, Indra,
Thunderer, may you place

At the end of this history your direst instruction:
A last full stop written in the fire
Of furious total destruction.

Hear the prayer of an earth that is stricken with pain:
In the green woods, O may the birds
Sing supreme again.

Railway Station

I come to the station morning and evening,
I love to watch the coming and going –
Hubbub of passengers pressing for tickets,

Down-trains boarded, up-trains boarded,
Ebb and flow like an estuarine river.
Some people sitting there ever since morning,
Other people missing their train by a minute.

Day – Night – clanking and rumbling,
Trainloads of people thundering forth.
Changing direction at every moment,
Eastwards, westwards, rapid as storms.

The essence of all these moving pictures
Brings to my mind the image of language,
Forever forming, forever unforming,
Continuous coming, continuous going.
Crowds can fill the stage in an instant –
The guard's flag waves the train's departure
And suddenly everyone disappears somewhere.
The hurry disguises their joys and sorrows,
Masks the pressure of gains and losses.

Bho – Bho – blows the whistle,
Ruled by the clock's division of time.
No one can bear to wait for a second,
Some get aboard, some stay behind.

Succeeding, failing, boarding or remaining,
Nothing but picture after picture.
Whatever catches the eye for a moment
Is erased the next moment after.
A whimsical game, a self-forgetting
Ever-dissolving sequence –
Each canvas ripped, its shreds discarded
To pile up along the roadside,
Detritus lifted hither and thither
By tired hot summer breezes.
'Hold back, hold back,' rings out the clamour
Of passengers left stranded –
Next thing they have also vanished,
Chasing, running, wailing.

Clang – Clang – sounds the tocsin,
Time for good-bye, off goes the train.
Passengers leaning out of the windows,
Waving until they are whisked away.

The world is merely the work of a painter,
This is the truth I have accepted –

Not made by a craftsman, beaten and moulded,
Not a thing the hand can grip hold of,
But an insubstantial visual sequence.
Age follows age, never losing momentum,
A stream of forming and passing pictures.
Alone in the midst of the to-ing and fro-ing
I watch the constant flux of the station.

One – brush – the picture is painted,
Another brush blacks it out again.
Who are those coming from one direction?
Who are those floating the other way?

Freedom-bound

Frown and bolt the door and glare
With disapproving eyes,
Behold my outcaste love, the scourge
Of all proprieties.
To sit where orthodoxy rules
Is not her wish at all –
Maybe I shall seat her on
A grubby patchwork shawl.
The upright villagers, who like
To buy and sell all day,
Do not notice one whose dress
Is drab and dusty-grey.
So keen on outward show, the form
Beneath can pass them by –
Come, my darling, let there be
None but you and I.
When suddenly you left your house
To love along the way,
You brought from somewhere lotus honey
In your pot of clay.
You came because you heard I like
Love simple, unadorned –
An earthen jar is not a thing
My hands have ever scorned.
No bells upon your ankles, so
No purpose in a dance –

Your blood has all the rhythms
    That are needed to entrance.
You are ashamed to be ashamed
    By lack of ornament –
No amount of dust can spoil
    Your plain habiliment.
Herd-boys crowd around you, street-dogs
    Follow by your side –
Gipsy-like upon your pony
    Easily you ride.
You cross the stream with dripping sari
    Tucked up to your knees –
My duty to the straight and narrow
    Flies at sights like these.
You take your basket to the fields
    For herbs on market-day –
You fill your hem with peas for donkeys
    Loose beside the way.
Rainy days do not deter you –
    Mud caked to your toes
And *kacu*-leaf upon your head,
    On your journey goes.
I find you when and where I choose,
    Whenever it pleases me –
No fuss or preparation: tell me,
    Who will know but we?
Throwing caution to the winds,
    Spurned by all around,
Come, my outcaste love, O let us
    Travel, freedom-bound.

Yakṣa

No pause in the passage of the Yakṣa's yearning on towards Alakā,
    Borne by impatient winds,
Following the hazy horizon's rain-racked beckoning
    From mountain to mountain,
    Forest to forest.
A careering crane's-wing-flap of joy, tuned to the music
Of the heart-rending sighs of the shadow-cast rains,
    Flies to ever-far heaven
    Along with his longing;
A high beauty forever accompanies his deep pain.

A huge separation dwells at the heart of onward time
That tries door after future door,
Life after future life
In an endless attempt to close its distance from perfection.
The world is its poem, a rolling sonorous poem
In which a remote presage of joy annotates vast sorrow.
O blessed Yakṣa –
The fire of creation is in his yearning.

Where silently his beloved waits, watching the minutes,
The long days move.
Her room is closed: no road to look out on –
Her hope,
Worn out by waiting, lies in the dust.
The poet has given her pining no language,
Her love no pilgrimage –
For her, the unspeaking Yakṣa city
Is a meaningless prison of riches.
Permanent flowers, eternal moonlight –
Mortal existence knows no grief as great as this:
Never to awake from dreams.
God has granted that the Yakṣa may pound her door with yearning.
He longs to sweep his beloved
Away on the surging stream of his heart,
Away from the motionless mounts of heaven
Into the light of this many-coloured, shadow-dappled mortal world.

Last Tryst

Ink-black clouds banked in the north-east:
The force of the coming storm latent in the forest,
Waiting as quietly as the bats hanging
In the branches. Darkness blanketing
Dense leaves that are still and silent
As a crouching tiger intent
On its prey. Flocks of crows
Suddenly aloft in a craze
Of fear, like tattered
Shreds of darkness littered
Over the void of a cosmos
Broken into chaos.

Where have you come from today in the guise
Of a storm, your unbound hair scented with past wild flowers?
In my youth you came once before on another
Day, first messenger
Of the freshly shining Spring.
You brought the first flowering
Jasmine of Āṣāṛh, you were indescribably lovely.
You blossomed in my heart,
In my boundless wonder: I do not know from what
Radiant world unseen
You came into the light of vision.
You meet me today by a path no less mysterious.
How potent your face
Appears in the brief lightning-flame!
How novel its expressions seem!

Is the path by which you come today
The same as I knew before?
I see
Sometimes its faint outline;
Sometimes not the slightest hint or glimmer can be seen.
You have brought in your basket flowers recalled or forgotten,
But others I have never hitherto known;
And in your fragrance you carry
The message of a season new to me.
A deathly-dark suffusion
Obscures its coming revelation.
O honour me
With its garland, place it around my neck in this dimly
Starlit palace of silence. Let this our last
Tryst
Carry me into the infinite night
Beyond all earthly limit;
Let it make me one
With the not known.

Injury

The sinking sun extends its late afternoon glow.
The wind has dozed away.
An ox-cart laden with paddy-straw bound
For far-off Nadiyā market crawls across the empty open land,
Calf following, tied on behind.

Over towards the Rājbaṃśī quarter Banamālī Pandit's
Eldest son sits
On the edge of a tank, fishing all day.
From overhead comes the cry
Of wild duck making their way
From the dried-up river's
Sandbanks towards the Black Lake in search of snails.

Along the side of newly-cut sugar-cane
Fields, in the fresh air of trees washed by rain,
Through the wet grass,
Two friends pass
Slowly, serenely –
They came on a holiday,
Suddenly bumped into each other in the village.
One of them is newly married – the delight
Of their conversation seems to have no limit.
All around, in the maze
Of winding paths in the wood, *bhā̃ṭi*-flowers
Have come into bloom,
Their scent dispensing the balm
Of Caitra. From the *jārul*-trees nearby
A *koel*-bird strains its voice in dull, demented melody.

A telegram comes:
'Finland pounded by Soviet bombs.'

The Sick-bed – 6

O my day-break sparrow –
In my last moments of sleepiness,
While there is still some darkness,
Here you are tapping on the window-pane,
Asking for news
And then dancing and twittering
Just as your whim takes you.
Your pluckily bobbing tail
Cocks a snook at all restrictions.
When magpie-robins chirrup at dawn,
Poets tip them.
When a hidden *koel*-bird hoots all day
Its same unvarying fifth,
So high is its rating

It gets the applause of Kālidāsa
Ahead of all other birds.
You couldn't care less –
You never keep to the scale –
To enter Kālidāsa's room
And chatter
And mess up his metres
Amuses you greatly.
Whenever you perch on a pillar
At the court of King Vikramāditya
And bards spout,
What are their songs to you?
You are closer to the poet's mistress:
You happily join in her round-the-clock prattle.
You do not dance
Under contract from the Spring –
You strut
Any old how, no discipline at all.
You do not turn up politely
At woodland singing-contests;
You gossip with the light in broad vernacular –
Its meaning
Is not in the dictionary –
Only your own throbbing little chest
Knows it.
Slanting your neck to right or left,
How you play about –
So busy all day for no apparent reason,
Scrabbling at the ground,
Bathing in the dust –
You are so unkempt
The dirt doesn't show on you, worry you at all.
You build your nest in the corner of the ceiling
Of even a king's chamber,
You are so utterly brazen.

Whenever I spend painful, sleepless nights,
I always look forward
To your first tap-tap at my door.
The brave, nimble, simple
Life's message that you bring –
Give it to me,
That the sunlight by which all creatures dwell
May call me,
O my day-break sparrow.

The Sick-bed – 21

When I woke up this morning
There was a rose in my flower-vase:
The question came to me –
The power that brought you through cyclic time
To final beauty,
Dodging at every turn
The torment of ugly incompleteness,
Is it blind, is it abstracted,
Does it, like a world-denying *sannyāsī*,
Make no distinction between beauty and the opposite of beauty?
Is it merely rational,
Merely physical,
Lacking in sensibility?
There are some who argue
That grace and ugliness take equal seats
At the court of Creation,
That neither is refused entry
By the guards.
As a poet I cannot enter such arguments –
I can only gaze at the universe
In its full, true form,
At the millions of stars in the sky
Carrying their huge harmonious beauty –
Never breaking their rhythm
Or losing their tune,
Never deranged
And never stumbling –
I can only gaze and see, in the sky,
The spreading layers
Of a vast, radiant, petalled rose.

Recovery – 10

Lazily afloat on time's stream,
My mind turns to the sky.
As I cross its empty expanses
Shadowy pictures form in my eyes
Of the many ages of the long past
And the many peoples

That have hurtled forward,
Confident of victory.
The Pāṭhāns came, greedy for empire;
And the Moghuls,
Brandishing victory-banners,
The wheels of their conquering chariots
Raising webs of dust.
I look at the sky –
No sign of them now today:
Through the ages
The light of sunrise and sunset
Continues to redden the sky's pure blue
At dawn and dusk.
Then others came,
Along tracks of iron
In fire-breathing vehicles –
The mighty British,
Scattering their power
Beneath the same sky.
I know that time will flow along their road too,
Float off somewhere the land-encircling web of their empire.
I know their merchandise-bearing soldiers
Will not make the slightest impression
On planetary paths.

But the earth when I look at it
Makes me aware
Of the hubbub of a huge concourse
Of ordinary people
Led along many paths and in various groups
By man's common urges,
From age to age, through life and death.
They go on pulling at oars,
Guiding the rudder,
Sowing seeds in the fields.
Cutting ripe paddy.
They work –
In cities and in fields.
Imperial canopies collapse,
Battle-drums stop,
Victory-pillars, like idiots, forget what their own words mean;
Battle-crazed eyes and blood-smeared weapons
Live on only in children's stories,
Their menace veiled.
But people work –

Here and in other regions,
Bengal, Bihar, Orissa,
By rivers and shores,
Punjab, Bombay, Gujurat –
Filling the passage of their lives with a rumbling and thundering
Woven by day and by night –
The sonorous rhythm
Of Life's liturgy in all its pain and elation,
Gloom and light.
Over the ruins of hundreds of empires,
The people work.

Recovery – 14

Every day in the early morning this faithful dog
Sits quietly beside my chair
For as long as I do not acknowledge his presence
By the touch of my hand.
The moment he receives this small recognition,
Waves of happiness leap through his body.
In the inarticulate animal world
Only this creature
Has pierced through good and bad and seen
Complete man,
Has seen him for whom
Life may be joyfully given,
That object of a free outpouring of love
Whose consciousness points the way
To the realm of infinite consciousness.
When I see that dumb heart
Revealing its own humility
Through total self-surrender,
I feel unequal to the worth
His simple perception has found in the nature of man.
The wistful anxiety in his mute gaze
Understands something he cannot explain:
It directs me to the true meaning of man in the universe.

On My Birthday – 20

Today I imagine the words of countless
Languages to be suddenly fetterless –
After long incarceration
In the fortress of grammar, suddenly up in rebellion,
Maddened by the stamp-stamping
Of unmitigated regimented drilling.
They have jumped the constraints of sentence
To seek free expression in a world rid of intelligence,
Snapping the chains of sense in sarcasm
And ridicule of literary decorum.
Liberated thus, their queer
Postures and cries appeal only to the ear.
They say, 'We who were born of the gusty tuning
Of the earth's first outbreathing
Came into our own as soon as the blood's beat
Impelled man's mindless vitality to break into dance in his throat.
We swelled his infant voice with the babble
Of the world's first poem, the original prattle
Of existence. We are kin to the wild torrents
That pour from the mountains to announce
The month of Śrābaṇ: we bring to human habitations
Nature's incantations – '
The festive sound of leaves rustling in forests,
The sound that measures the rhythm of approaching tempests,
The great night-ending sound of day-break –
From these sound-fields man has captured words, curbed them like a breakneck
Stallion in complex webs of order
To enable him to pass on his messages to the distant lands of the future.
By riding words that are bridled and reined
Man has quickened
The pace of time's slow clocks:
The speed of his reason has cut through material blocks,
Explored recalcitrant mysteries;
With word-armies
Drawn into battle-lines he resists the perpetual assault of imbecility.
But sometimes they slip like robbers into realms of fantasy,
Float on ebbing waters
Of sleep, free of barriers,
Lashing any sort of flotsam and jetsam into metre.
From them, the free-roving mind fashions

Artistic creations
Of a kind that do not conform to an orderly
Universe – whose threads are tenuous, loose, arbitrary,
Like a dozen puppies brawling,
Scrambling at each other's necks to no purpose or meaning:
Each bites another –
They squeal and yelp blue murder,
But their bites and yelps carry no true import of enmity,
Their violence is bombast, empty fury.
In my mind I imagine words thus shot of their meaning,
Hordes of them running amuck all day,
As if in the sky there were nonsense nursery syllables booming –
Horselum, bridelum, ridelum, into the fray.

Notes

In these notes to the poems, I have quoted extensively from Tagore's five main books of English lectures, and from *My Reminiscences*, Surendranath Tagore's translation of the Bengali autobiography that Tagore published in 1912. The following abbreviations are used:

S – *Sādhanā*, 1913
R – *My Reminiscences*, 1917
N – *Nationalism*, 1917
P – *Personality*, 1917
CU – *Creative Unity*, 1922
RM – *The Religion of Man*, 1931

All page references given for the above books are to the original Macmillan editions, except for *The Religion of Man*, which was published by Allen & Unwin.

In limiting my quotations to such a small number of texts, I admit I am making a virtue of necessity: I am not yet in a position to draw on the full range of Tagore's Bengali writings. But since my book is aimed at English readers, and since these six books give a good and complete idea of Tagore's central ideas, it seems sensible to use them.

My aim in these notes is to relate Tagore's poetry to his thought; but I should not wish to suggest that the poems are nothing but vehicles for ideas. Their concrete qualities should speak for themselves.

The subsidiary notes that follow the explanatory comments are on fine points of translation. They are aimed partly at those with a knowledge of Bengali, or one of the other modern Indian languages, or Sanskrit. But to others they may indicate the extent to which I have honoured or betrayed the poems.

All line references are to the translations, not the originals. But I have followed the Bengali lines closely enough for anyone to locate particular phrases without too much difficulty.

Nearly all the poems are ascribed to the book in which they first appeared. Readers consulting the Visva-Bharati edition of Tagore's complete works will sometimes find discrepancies, as poems sometimes appeared again in later books ('Broken Song', for example, was reprinted in the combined volume *kathā skāhinī*, 1903). The edition published by the West Bengal Government in the 1980s restores the poems to their chronological position.

Brahmā, Viṣṇu, Śiva (p. 45)

sṛṣṭi sthiti pralay from *prabhāt-saṅgīt* (Morning Songs), 1883

The poems in this book followed the religious experience described in *R*217: as the sun rose, 'all of a sudden a covering seemed to fall away from my eyes, and I found the world bathed in a wonderful radiance, with waves of beauty and joy swelling on every side'. The vision liberated Tagore from the adolescent egoism, 'the contemplation of my own heart' (*R*200), that had dominated his writing hitherto.

The poem I have chosen was originally much longer: Tagore shortened it when he came to include it in *sañcayitā*, the selected poems that I have used for the first two-thirds of my book. The original title means 'Creation, Preservation, Destruction', the main attributes of the three deities featured in the poem (see Glossary for further information). Tagore's most characteristic addition to the mythology is his image of Viṣṇu as Poet: in l.34 he is called *jagater mahā-bedabyās*, 'the great Vedavyāsa of the world' (Vedavyāsa, often known simply as Vyāsa, was the legendary author of the Mahābhārata, the great primary epic of India); in l.43 the Law that he imposes is called *mahā-chanda mahā-anuprās* ('great metre, great alliteration'). The metaphor recurs in l.78, where the dissolving world is described as *chanda-mukta*, 'free of metre'. ll.44–54 emphasize that beauty can only emerge after the imposition of Law. See *S*98: 'Law is the first step towards freedom, and beauty is the complete liberation which stands on the pedestal of law. Beauty harmonizes in itself the limit and the beyond, the law and the liberty.' *rūp* (l.46,54) means 'form' and 'beauty' in Sanskrit and Bengali.

The poem also shows the influence of science (especially in ll.56–60 and 81–5). Tagore did not believe that science described Reality as he understood it (see notes to 'Deception', 'The Wakening of Śiva', '*The Sick-bed – 21*' and '*On My Birthday – 20*'), but he was always keenly interested in it and felt that India had to learn from the science of the West. Four years before his death he published *biśva-paricay*, an introduction to modern science for Bengali readers.

9 'growing' – *prāṇ-pūrṇa*: 'full of *prāṇ*, life' (and therefore growth).

10 *āśā-pūrṇa atṛptir prāy*: 'like dissatisfaction that is full of hope'.

16 lit., 'from the *gaṅgotrī*-crest of the world'. The Himalayan source of the Ganges (Gaṅgotri) is used here as a metaphor for a Primary Source

27 'conch – *maṅgal-śaṅkha*: 'conch of welfare'. The *Pāñcajanya*, conch of Viṣṇu and his chief incarnation Kṛṣṇa, is important in Indian mythology. See Conch in the Glossary.

44–7 The writing is vague here. Viṣṇu may be floating on the water, or looking into it from the edge of the lake. There is no traditional link between Viṣṇu and the Mānasa lake, and the *ālok-kamal-dal* ('light-lotuses') of 1.47 comes from Tagore's imagination, not mythology.

70 'three eyes' – *tin-kāl-tri-nayan*: 'three-ages-triple-eye', i.e. looking into past, present and future.

Bride (p. 47)

badhū from *mānasī* (The Lady of the Mind), 1890

I have chosen three poems from what is regarded in Bengal as Tagore's first book of genius. It was written over three years, an unusually long time for Tagore. Dissatisfaction with city life was growing in him, and his wife and two young children were subjected to many changes of abode during this period: Darjeeling, Sholapur and Poona in Bombay Presidency, Ghazipur in western U. P., Shelidah in north Bengal, and Santiniketan, where 'Bride' was written. Preference for the rural over the urban became one of Tagore's dominant ideas, inspiring his experiment at Santiniketan. Modern man's alienation from nature 'is the product of the city-wall habit and training of mind' (*S*5; see also *CU*116 and *RM*170 for Tagore's dislike of Calcutta). Tagore's feelings about cities have their roots in his own sense of constriction as a child (see *R*11,45); and this is perhaps why he is able to realize the Bride's unhappiness with such intensity.

'Bride' is also about the devaluation of women, caused by faults in Indian social traditions as well as by modern, urban, male-dominated civilization. In ll.49–50 the Bride is made to feel that she is up for sale, like a garland. But the poem reveals Tagore's loyalty to the positive aspects of Hindu social life: the Bride is prevented by her situation from exercising the qualities of love and devotion that her mother shows (ll.55–62).

The Bride is young, in her teens probably, but not a child. Child-marriage, which Tagore had attacked in a paper on Hindu marriage in 1887, is satirized in another poem in *mānasī*.

The word that I have translated as 'gaiety' in l.54 and 'playing' in l.77 is *khelā*: see notes to the next poem.

3 'shade' – *chāyā sakhī*: the shade that was also *sakhī*, a friend or companion. Some readers say there should be a comma after *chāyā*, making *sakhī* an imaginary confidante to whom the bride is addressing her monologue.

5 'I sit alone with my thoughts' – and also *gṛha-koṇe*: 'in the corner of a room' (cf. l.46).

19 'oleanders' – *karabī*: see Glossary.

35 'open path' – *udār path-ghāṭ*: 'the generous, open-hearted path and steps'.

61 'temple' – *śib-ālay*: 'home of Śiva', Śiva-temple.

Unending Love (p. 49)

ananta prem from *mānasī*, 1890

This poem can be compared with 'Love's Question', but here the lover's hyperbole is presented without irony. It is a lyric poem, not a song, but it takes us into the world of Tagore's songs, in which love between human beings is a manifestation of divine love, and the 'play' (*khelā*, l.13) of lovers a counterpart to the *khelā* of the universe. *khelā* is the interplay between God and his creation; between infinite, eternal Being and finite, mortal Becoming; between Perfection and the desire to become one with that Perfection: 'Brahma is Brahma, he is the infinite ideal of perfection. But we are not what we truly are; we are ever to become true, ever to become Brahma. There is the eternal play of love in the relation between this being and the becoming; and in the depth of this mystery is the source of all truth and beauty that sustains the endless march of creation' (*S*155). *khelā* has a dark side to it, since it separates us from God; and sometimes it stands for the vanity of life (as in l.77 of 'Bride'). But more often it implies creativity: for God can only express his joy through creating finite forms, just as the poet expresses his love through creating poems and songs (see *S*104).

Because *khelā* involves union and separation at the same time, these two feelings are much emphasized in Indian accounts of love. What I have translated as 'meeting' and 'farewell' in l.14 are really the *states* of being together or apart, *milan* and *biraha*.

2 'in life after life' – *janme janme*: 'in birth after birth'. Indian concepts of *karma* and re-birth are involved here.

15 'in shapes' – *sāje*: 'in dress, garb'.

18 'universal life' – *nikhil prāṇer prīti*: 'the delight or gladness (*prīti*) inherent in the universal principle of life (*prāṇ*)'.

The *Meghadūta* (p. 50)

megh-dūt from *mānasī*, 1890

This magnificent poem should be read in conjuction with 'Yakṣa' and the essay on Kālidāsa's *Meghadūta* that I have translated in Appendix A, as well as Kālidāsa's masterpiece itself (see Glossary). Tagore's poem is rhymed in couplets, but with shifting caesura and constant enjambement. The sonorous sinuosity of the verse is what I have tried to capture in my translation. The language is highly Sanskritic: its compounds and mixed metaphors pose great difficulties to the translator. A literal translation of the second sentence of the poem would read: 'Cloud-sonorous stanzas have kept the griefs of all the many separated lovers of the universe in their own dark layers having heaped (them) into cloudy-music.'

In *R*73 Tagore describes the impression made on him by the sound and rhythm of Kālidāsa's poem before he could understand 'a word of Sanskrit'; and we also read of how rainy days had a 'special importance' for him as a child (*R*262). Love of Kālidāsa and love of rain have contributed equally to this poem. Its great theme is *biraha* or *bicched*: yearning, pining, separation: the Yakṣa pining for his beloved; Kālidāsa expressing his own sense of exile (see *RM*166), and thus by extension expressing the *byabadhān* ('gulf', l.116) in the heart of man. Kālidāsa's poetry, in its beauty and artistry, was for Tagore an ideal of perfection somewhat different from the Upaniṣadic ideal he invoked elsewhere – extravagant not chaste, complex not simple. See the essay for the fascination that the names in the poetry had for him. But the ideal had an uneasiness about it, in the image of the Beloved doomed to an eternity of pining amidst the deathless but dead luxuriance of Alakā; and this idea is developed further in 'Yakṣa'. More alive is the beauty of Bengal in the rains: a key-word is *śyām*, which can mean 'black' in Sanskrit, and is a name for Kṛṣṇa, but which in Bengali usually evokes the dark green of wet, tropical vegetation. 'In verdurous Bengal' in l.49 is *śyām-baṅga-deśe*; and 'blue-green shadows' in l.51 are *śyām-chāyā*. Tagore's own *mantra* ('spell', l.106, see Glossary) overlays Kālidāsa's: his poem passes on to its readers the *mukti*, spiritual liberation that Tagore felt when he read Kālidāsa's poem (ll.106–10).

21 'with clothes disordered' – *mlān-beśe*: 'with shabby clothes'.

23 *saṅgīt*, the word for music here, means a union or harmony of songs.

29 'mountains' – *himācal*: the Himalayas.

40–41 lit., 'by swelling the stream of your verse like a rain-filled river'.

66–7 The grammar here seems to suggest that there is only one 'village of Daśārṇa', but Daśārṇa was the name of a region and a people in Ancient India. See Glossary.

70 'jasmine' – *yūthī*: see Glossary.

73 'desperate' – *bikal*: the lotuses are 'crippled' for (want of) the shade of the cloud.

75 'no coyness in their gaze' – *bhrū-bilās śekhe nāi*: 'they have not learnt *bhrū-bilās*, seductive eyebrow movements'.

86–7 lit., 'into darkness so thick it can be pierced by a needle (*sūci-bhedya*), into the main streets, by the light of occasional flashes of lightning'. I have transferred the untranslatable needle-metaphor from the darkness to the lightning.

89–91 See Ganges in the Glossary for the legend alluded to in these lines. Lit., 'There is Kanakhala, where Jāhnavī (Gaṅgā), restless with youth, ignoring the jealous frown of Gaurī (Pārvatī), played with the moonlit matted locks of Dhūrjaṭi (Śiva) with her teasing, surging foam.'

94 *kāmanār mokṣa-dhām*: 'the abode of (spiritual) release from desire'.

The Golden Boat (p. 53)

sonār tarī from *sonār tarī* (The Golden Boat), 1894

In 1890 Tagore's father gave him charge of the family estates, which included land at Shelidah, by the river Padma in north Bengal. As a result, Tagore came into much closer contact with rural, riverine Bengal than he had known hitherto, and the experience inspired poems, short stories and letters. This famous and elusive poem captures much of the atmosphere of Bengal's rivers during the monsoon. The sex of the person in the boat is indeterminate, as Bengali pronouns do not distinguish gender; but Tagore has 'a woman at the helm' in his own translation, so perhaps we should follow him. In l.11 the verb *bāoyā* is used, generally translated as 'to row'; but the boat is big enough to have sails (l.13) and carry a cargo of grain, so it is probably being steered or paddled by a single oar. The river-bank is not precipitous, but a beach shelving down into the water.

Readers will always disagree about the meaning of this poem (and Tagore himself disliked such discussions: poems should *be* not *mean*: see *R*222); but the distinction between self and soul seems to me to lie behind it. Soul is liberated through self-surrender, disinterested love: but there is self-interest in the giving of the harvest by the speaker of the poem, a desire to be rewarded and praised for his efforts (ll.23–4) and a wish for the self to be 'taken aboard' along with what it has given. The result is spiritual failure, a sense of loneliness and alienation. In this mood the *khelā* (l.7) of the swirling floodwaters takes on its negative aspect: the separateness of the created world from its Creator. The image of the village as a painting (l.9) can be compared with the pictorial imagery in 'Railway Station', where there is a similar sense of failure; compare also the story told in *RM*182 of the person who was barred from entering the Garden of Bliss after it was discovered that 'inside his clothes he was secretly trying to smuggle into the garden the self, which only finds its fulfilment by its surrender'.

One can also relate 'The Golden Boat' to the *jīban-debatā* poems, particularly 'Unyielding', which also combines giving and rejection. See notes to 'On the Edge of the Sea'.

2 'sad' – *nāhi bharasā*: 'with no confidence, faith, support, hope'.

4 lit., 'the full river is razor-sharp (in its current) and sharp to the touch'.

13 'he gazes ahead' – *kono dike nāhi cāy*: 'he does not look in any direction'.

23 lit., 'for so long, on the river-bank, that in which I was completely absorbed, forgetful of all other cares'.

28 'rain-sky' – *śrābaṇ-gagan*: 'the Śrābaṇ-sky' (see Glossary).

Broken Song (p. 53)

gān-bhaṅga from *sonār tarī*, 1894

This moving poem expresses some of Tagore's deepest feelings about music, old age and friendship. Its setting is one of the many petty courts that dotted Bengal before the British period. Nineteenth-century Bengalis often felt nostalgia for the apparent indolence, hospitality and tolerance of the Persianized culture of those days, and Tagore was not immune to this (see *R*123), even though this poem shows heartlessness in the midst of that culture. I have translated *rājā* as 'king', though this is probably too elevated a term for Pratāp Rāy, who is no more than a big landowner. Baraj Lāl is shown by his name and his *uṣṇīṣ* ('turban', l.31) to be Hindusthani not Bengali, but the musical fare he has provided over the years seems to be thoroughly Bengali (see Glossary for all unfamiliar terms and names in the poem). Kāśīnāth, though a Bengali by name, may be offering the kind of North Indian vocal music that gives less emphasis to words than in the Bengali tradition and more to virtuoso exposition of a rāga (see *R*205 for the distinctive character of Bengali vocal music, as viewed by Tagore). But the real contrast is one of feeling. Important words in the poem are *prāṇ* (life, vitality), *hṛday* (heart), *sneha* (kindness, love), *prem* (love). Baraj's singing, failing though it is now, had these qualities, appreciated by the king but not by the admirers of Kāśīnāth's cleverer but less heartfelt singing style. True singing was for Tagore the most important of all human arts, taking man closest to the Divine: the unity of a song symbolizes Divine completeness, and the singing of it expresses the unfolding of that completeness through the works of creation (see *S*143 and *P*57). But the main ideal in this poem is the reciprocity of love – love between God and man and love between man and man – symbolized by the perfect sympathy that should be present between singer and audience, and by the images of reciprocity in nature in ll.73–4. Between Pratāp Rāy and Baraj Lāl there is 'perfection of human relationship' (*RM*188); the courtiers, in contrast, show human failure to love.

6 'give frequent gasps of praise' – *saghane bale 'bāhā bāhā'*: 'they repeatedly say "bāh, bāḥ"' (an expression of praise or approval).

11 The two main types of song about Durgā prevalent in Bengal are mentioned in this line, *āgamanī* and *bijayā*. See Durgā in the Glossary.

38 'Superb, bravo' – *āhāhā, bāhā bāhā*: see above.

55 'as he prays to his teacher's name' – *smaraṇ kare guru-debe*: 'as he remembers his *guru-deb*'. A musician's guru is like a close personal deity (*deb*), to be prayed to in times of trouble.

61 'the old' – *sakhī*: 'friend'. His tānpurā is a friend or confidante to him.

64 'Come' – *āis*: Pratāp Rāy uses the most intimate of imperative verb-forms here.

74 'the woods' – *ban-sabhā*: 'the court or assembly of the woods'. The woods are responsive in a way that the king's court (*sabhā*) is not.

76 'where listeners are dumb' – *yekhāne* . . . *bobār sabhā*: 'where there is a court of the dumb (at heart)'.

A Half-acre of Land (p. 55)

dui bighā jami from *citrā* (The Multi-Coloured), 1896

Read at a straightforwardly realistic level, this poem needs little by way of explanation. The title means literally 'two *bighā*s of land' (see Glossary). For *sādhu*, and the double meaning of the word that is exploited ironically at the end of the poem also see Glossary ('the irony of life', l.71, is my own clarifying interpolation). But some of Tagore's distinctive attitudes to nature, asceticism and human relations are implicit in the poem. The famous third stanza, often quoted for its patriotic feeling, can be compared with *R*208, where Tagore writes of his return to Bengal after his abortive voyage to England in 1881 (he set sail with a nephew who quickly began to feel sea-sick and to miss his new wife, so they turned back at Madras): 'This Bengal sky full of light, this south breeze, this flow of the river, this right royal laziness, this broad leisure stretching from horizon to horizon and from green earth to blue sky, all these were to me as food and drink to the hungry and thirsty. Here it felt indeed like a home, and in these I recognized the ministrations of a Mother.' The stanza should be read as a meditation: it begins with *namonamo nama*, the expression of obeisance used to begin the prayers to God and meditations on the harmony of nature which Tagore taught his pupils at Santiniketan (see *S*17 and *P*155). The fact that asceticism does not bring peace to Upen's heart shows Tagore's distrust of those forms of religion that seek to separate God from the world (see *S*129, and his exposition in *P*56 of the verses of the Īśā Upaniṣad in which we are warned that 'the sole pursuit of the infinite' is even more dangerous than exclusive concentration on the finite). The half-acre of land, personified as a mother when she belonged to Upen and as a fallen or kept woman (*kulaṭā*, l.37) after the landlord has turned her into a garden, shows, as in 'Broken Song', two kinds of human relationship. One, based on love, brings heavenly perfection: in l.47 the half-acre is called *kalyāṇ-mayī*, full of the grace and prosperity that is associated with the goddess Lakṣmī, and is described as feeding Upen with *sudhā*, nectar. The other is an unequal relationship of the kind that is defined in *CU*158, in which woman tries to mitigate her state of bondage 'by rendering herself and her home a luxury to man'.

7 'with my hands on my heart' – *bakṣe juṛiyā pāṇi*: 'with my hands folded on my breast', i.e. palms touching in the familiar Indian gesture of supplication or greeting.

10 lit., 'Am I so *lakṣmī-chāṛā* that I must sell my mother because of poverty?' See Lakṣmī in the Glossary.
19 'I roamed the world *sannyāsī-beśe*' – 'dressed as an ascetic'.
20 'places' – *dhām*: this word can connote a holy place, a place of pilgrimage.
21 'in desert' – *bijane*: in places empty of people rather than deserts in the technical sense.
34 'the festival-carriage' – *rath-talā*: the place where the *rath*, the chariot used in the annual Hindu chariot festival, is kept.
35 'granary' – *nandīr golā*: 'Nandī's granary' (the name of the owner).
53 'storm' – *jyaiṣther jhaṛe*: a storm in the month of Jyaiṣṭha (see Glossary).
70 'pukka' – *pākā*: the word really means 'ripe'.

Day's End (p. 57)

dina-śeṣe from *citrā*, 1896

Many of the images and symbols in this poem obsessed Tagore throughout his career. 'Buying and selling' (l.32) often stands for worldly as opposed to spiritual endeavour: compare 'Highest Price' and 'Freedom-bound' l.10, and the references to 'the market' in *N*64 and *P*107. Sunset, strangely beautiful girl, royal buildings, music combine to suggest an ideal world of beauty, drawing the speaker away from worldly concerns. But the mood is equivocal: the impulse to look beyond the world and the wish to stay within it were equal in Tagore. A key-word is *udās*, used in l.25. The word means detached, the state of mind that is necessary for spiritual liberation; but in other contexts Tagore associates it with aloofness, an absence of human feeling (see notes to 'Unyielding', 'Earth', 'In the Eyes of a Peacock' for further mention of the word). The descending darkness in the poem, the stillness, the sleeping birds suggest a defeatist longing for oblivion, the same desire to escape from life that makes a sad conclusion to 'Bride'. The static, luxuriant beauty of the royal city where the traveller wishes to moor can be compared to Alakā in 'The *Meghadūta*' and 'Yakṣa', where the ideal is similarly equivocal.

2,30 *ār beye kāj nāi taraṇī*: 'there is no point in rowing (*beye*) the boat any more'; but 'rowing' suggests a smaller boat than Bengal's river-craft, which do, in any case, often have sails. See notes on 'The Golden Boat'.
15 lit., 'the light of the clouds glitters on a golden trident': presumably there is a Śiva-temple nearby, with its identifying trident; unless the phrase *kanaker triśūle* simply means 'in the form of a golden trident' and describes the shape of the sunlit clouds.
22 the breeze is *atidūr*, 'far-off', rather than the palace.
24 lit., 'The earth before me disappears somewhere, stretches out of sight'; but the meaning is linked to *udās* in the next line.

On the Edge of the Sea (p. 58)

sindhu-pāre from *citrā*, 1896

This strange, uneasy poem is an example of Tagore at his most inspirational: imagination is let loose, unrestrained by moral or religious preoccupations. Tagore's concept of *jīban-debatā* ('life-god') was a flexible one, so that people argue about what he meant by it. In *RM*96 it simply seems to be God, realized in one's own human consciousness: a universal Being 'shaping the universe to its eternal idea', but a personal God too, 'seeking his best expression in all my experiences, uniting them into an ever-widening individuality which is a spiritual work of art'. But in this poem, where the *jīban-debatā* takes on female form, the emphasis is not on a controlling harmony, but a driving destiny forcing the self through experiences whose meaning or logic is by no means clear: the pieces of one's life may be part of a design, but one cannot know the design, one is merely aware of a mysterious compulsion leading one on from one experience or activity to another. The poem can be compared with one I have not translated, *niruddeś yātrā* in *sonār tarī*, in which a beautiful woman guides the poet in a golden boat towards the sunset, but refuses to tell him where she is taking him.

The illusory or magical nature of the experience in the poem is emphasized by certain key-words in the Bengali. In l.22 the speaker mounts the horse *mantra-mugdha acetan-sama*: 'bewitched by a spell [*mantra*: see Glossary] and as if unconscious'; in l.24 everything is *miche*, false, unreal; the things he passes as he rides may all be *maner bhul* (l.44: 'mistakes of the mind'); in l.94 he stands *mohe*, in a state of *moha*, illusion, ignorance, enchantment. All this suggests the *māyā* that in Indian tradition separates mortal existence from God. But the *jīban-debatā* reveals itself in this very *māyā*, and mocks the poet for being surprised. This is the paradox of *khelā*, the inseparable interplay of world and spirit: and *khelā* is used in l.117. Compare 'Last Tryst', where the *jīban-debatā* also appears in a guise opposite to what one might expect.

1 'winter' – *pauṣ*: the month of Pauṣ (see Glossary).

20 'with cold' – not in the original, but the nakedness of the tree is emphasized: it is *pallab-hīn*, 'leafless', and has *nagna-śākhā*, 'naked branches'.

70 'tune' – *tān*: the word is usually applied to the elaborate figurations that decorate tunes in Indian music. The same word is used in l.121.

82 'ritual grasses' – *dhānya-dūrbā*: 'paddy and grass', used as symbols of auspiciousness.

83 'forest-women' – *kirāt-nārīr dal*: 'a group of *kirāt* women' (see Glossary).

106,107 'bed' – *śayan*: 'bedding' rather than a raised bed. I translated the word as 'linen' in l.62.

Love's Question (p. 61)

praṇay-praśna from *kalpanā* (Imagination), 1900

This poem has a double irony: the far-fetched praise the lover gives his beloved is both untrue and true. Love between people is love between God and man in microcosm. Divine joy manifest in the abundance of creation (*S*104) is answered by creative works that are an expression of man's own 'surplus' (*RM*57): extravagant poetic conceits are the counterpart of extravagance in the created world. Beauty in nature and art cannot be accounted for rationally or scientifically, and is therefore 'untrue'; but it is real, an expression of divine or human joy, and therefore 'true'. In *P*34 Tagore writes: 'The poet says of the beloved: "It seems to me that I have gazed at your beauty from the beginning of my existence, that I have kept you in my arms for countless ages, yet it has not been enough for me" . . . Judged from the standpoint of reason these are exaggerations, but from that of the heart, freed from limits of facts, they are true.'

2 'ever-loving friend' – *cira-bhakta*: 'eternal devotee'.
9 'tree of paradise' – *cira-mandār*: 'the eternal *mandāra*-tree' (see Glossary).
15 'the breeze' – *adhīr samīr*: 'the impatient breeze'.
30 hair (*alak*: a tress or fringe of hair) is also mentioned in the Bengali.
33 'infinite Truth' – *asīmer tattva*: 'knowledge of the infinite'.

Snatched by the Gods (p. 62)

debatār grās from *kathā* (Tales), 1900

Many of the poems in the two books of narrative poetry that Tagore wrote between 1897 and 1899 were on patriotic historical subjects, in keeping with the mood of the times. The Sedition Bill of 1898 shocked Tagore into making one of his most dramatic interventions into nationalist politics, reading a paper against the Government at a public meeting in Calcutta and raising funds for the defence of Bal Gangadhar Tilak, who had been arrested. But there is nothing revivalist about 'Snatched by the Gods'. The title, and the word *debatā* wherever it occurs in the poem, poses a translation problem: really only one god is being referred to, probably Varuṇa, the sea-god, god of boatmen. But 'the god' is awkward in English unless it has been specified, and 'God' needs to be preserved for l.47 and l.157 where Mokṣadā is clearly addressing a different sort of god altogether, a supreme yet personal God such as Tagore tried to define in *RM*, representing a much higher morality than the boatmen's god. In l.47 she uses the name *nārāyaṇ*, an epithet meaning 'son of man' (the primeval man, Nara) that is sometimes applied to Viṣṇu but which Tagore defines as 'the supreme Reality of Man, which is divine' (*RM*67); and in l.157

she uses the term *antaryāmī*, which means 'one who is able to know another's *antar*, heart, mind', i.e. the 'Man of my Heart' of *CU*78. To show the difference between the jealous god of the boatmen and the God manifest in Mokṣadā's maternal love is one of the purposes of the poem, and the distinction has to be conveyed somehow in translation.

The language of the poem is highly varied, ranging from the colloquial dialogue of ll.27–69 to the intense rhetoric of ll.81–93. The lines are rhymed in couplets, but run on with tremendous pace. An important word is *sneha*, love, tenderness, used in ll.41 and 49; also in l.87 where Earth is described as *sneha-mayī*, full of love, the counterpart in Nature to human maternal love. Other key-words are *rakṣa*, used in ll.134, 148, 150 and 154 of both 'saving' or keeping a promise and of 'saving' or sparing Rākhāl; and *satya*, used both of the 'truth' that has to be kept with the sea-god in l.155 and the truth of Mokṣadā's feelings in l.159. The conflict between two kinds of 'saving', two kinds of 'truth', parallels the two kinds of god.

8 'Dear Grandfather' – *dādā-ṭhākur*: not really her grandfather or *dādā-maśay*. The term is applied respectfully to a person of age and standing, or to a Brahmin by a non-Brahmin.

17 'with his aunt' – *māsīr kāche*: 'with his *māsī* (maternal aunt)'.

29 'pays respects to' – *praṇamiyā*: 'having done *praṇām* to' (see Glossary).

65 'Annadā' – Maitra actually uses the affectionate term *bhāi*, not her name.

72 'womenfolk' – *kula-nārī*: 'married women, housewives'.

98 'with hope of departure' – *āśār saṃbāde*: 'with a message of hope'; an ironic phrase in view of what follows.

103 'says his prayers' – *debatāre smari*: 'remembering (the god'. See above.

107 'four miles' – *dui kroś*: 'two *kroś*' (a *kroś* is a distance of 8,000 cubits or just over two miles).

New Rain (p. 66)

naba-barṣā from *kṣaṇikā* (The Flitting One), 1900

The poems in this book are marked by intense delight and energy, and an exuberant inventiveness of form. It was the first time that Tagore had used abbreviated, colloquial verb-forms in poetry: this opened up many new rhythmic and stylistic possibilities and was a revolution in Bengali poetry. The book also shows the influence of nursery-rhymes and folk poetry, a growing interest for Tagore: see Appendix B.

Tagore's love of rain has already been noted in connection with 'The *Meghadūta*': here it is the vitality, *prāṇ* (used in ll.4 and 14), of the rain rather than its poignancy that is captured. Newness is stressed throughout: words for 'new' are used more than I have been able to manage in my translation, in ll.7, 13, 17, 24, 38; in l.31 the boat is called *taruṇ*, an untranslatable word meaning new, youthful, fresh, shining. The poem is full of remarkable sound effects: l.6 reads *guruguru megh gumari gumari garaje gagane gagane, garaje gagane*; and l.27 *jharake jharake jhariche bakul*. Many lines are impossible to translate literally: l.28 is (approximately) 'her *ā̃cal* (loose end of the sari) becomes eager in the sky'.

Could the imagery of verses 4 and 6 owe something to 'Moran's Garden', Tagore's brother Jyotirindranath's villa at Chandernagore, described in *R*210? Of the pictures in the sitting-room Tagore writes: 'One of the pictures was of a swing hanging from a branch half hidden in dense foliage, and in the checkered light and shade of this bower two persons were swinging; and there was another of a broad flight of steps leading into some castle-like palace, up and down which men and women in festive garb were going and coming . . .'

8 the original suggests streaming rain rather than rushing flood-water here.

14 lit., 'my life (*prāṇ*) has awoken today, blooming in or with delighted *nīp*-groves'. *kadam* or *kadamba* is the more usual name for this flower. See Glossary.

14 'coolly' – *snigdha*: 'cool', but the Sanskrit root *snih-*, from which the word is derived, also means 'to love': cf. Bengali *sneha*, love, mentioned in my notes to 'Snatched by the Gods'. So 'coolly and lovingly' would be a fuller translation.

24 'jasmine' – *mālatī*: see Glossary.

26 'in the wilderness' – *nirjane*: 'in solitude, in a place where there are no other people'.

29 'hair unplaited' – the Bengali conveys a sense of hair *becoming* unplaited as the girl swings.

The Hero (p. 68)

bīr-puruṣ from *śiśu* (The Child), 1903

Tagore's wife died in 1902, and as a result he had to look after his three youngest children. Soon his daughter Rani fell ill, and Tagore took her to Almora in the hills to try to save her life. 'The Hero' was among the poems that he wrote there to comfort and amuse her and the two youngest children, Mira and Samindra. *śiśu* consists of these, and some earlier poems about children.

Tagore was never happier than when he was 'giving his heart to children' (*R*158), and felt that children have much to teach us. Compare 'Highest Price', 'Grandfather's Holiday' and 'New Birth' ll.24–6. Certain linguistic details in 'The Hero' stress the contrast between the boy's age and the braggadocio of his fantasy. In ll.32–4 he uses 'low-grade' imperative forms such as would never be used by a child to an adult; in ll.36 and 54, on the other hand, he is addressed as *khokā*, a term only used for a small boy. In l.48 his mother takes him in her lap as one would take a small child; and in l.53 he shows an endearing desire to brag to *dādā*, elder brother.

An equivalently tight verse form seemed essential in translation, and I have sometimes had to compress or re-order the lines.

8–9 lit., 'evening comes, the sun is setting,/we seem to have come to an area of open land adjoining a pair of ponds'.

15 The land is covered with *cor-kāṭā*, lit. 'thief-prickle', a plant with burs that stick to the clothes of passers-by.

19 two lines in the original: lit., 'who knows where we are going,/it is hard to see well in the dark'.

21 'what's that lantern?' – *oi-ye kiser ālo*? 'what is that the light of over there?'

22,35 'shouts and yells' – the Bengali gives the actual shouts: *hā̃re re re re re.*

25–7 lit., 'you, in fear, in one corner of the palanquin, are remembering a god (*ṭhākur-debatā*) in your mind'. Only one god is implied: see notes to 'Snatched by the Gods'.

40 'you would faint' – *tomār gā̃ye debe kā̃ṭā*: 'there would be a prickling over your body'.

50–52 lit., 'every day there is so much that happens that is worthless, trivial (*yā-tā*);/Oh why do such (events) not occur truly?'

Death-wedding (p. 69)

maraṇ-milan from *utsarga* (Dedications), 1914

In 1903 Tagore published his poetical works to date, arranged according to theme, and for each section he wrote an introductory poem. These were eventually published as a separate volume in 1914, but in *sañcayitā* they were restored to their chronological position.

'Death Wedding' was first published in the journal *baṅgadarśan* in August–September 1902. There is disagreement about what could have inspired it. It has been related to the ideal of revolutionary martyrdom that was beginning to enter the air of Bengal; or to the death of Swami Vivekananda early in the year. Perhaps it can be taken as a premonition of the deaths of Tagore's wife Mrinalini in 1902, his daughter Rani in 1903, his beloved assistant at Santiniketan the young poet Satischandra Ray in 1904, Tagore's father in 1905 and his younger son Samindra in 1907. The poem is brilliant in structure and conception, but one may find an emptiness in it, as though Tagore yet had to face the full reality of death. In *RM*198 he writes of the four proper stages of life according to Indian tradition: the fourth, the *pravrajyā*, is 'the expectant awaiting of freedom across death . . . Enriched with its experiences, the soul now leaves the narrower life for the universal life, to which it dedicates its accumulated wisdom, and itself enters into relations with the Life Eternal, so that, when finally the decaying body has come to the very end of its tether, the soul views its breaking away quite simply and without regret, in the expectation of its own entry into the Infinite.' To want Death to act according to one's wishes is not compatible with this. Cf. '*The Borderland – 10*' where Tagore is also not ready for death, though for different reasons.

The artifice of the verse and structure of 'Death-wedding' is paralled by an emphasis on form and style in its content. In l.3 Tagore asks whether Death's furtive approach is *praṇayer-i dharan*: 'the (proper) form of love'; and in l.19 he asks, *milaner eki rīti ei*: 'is this the (right) style of union?'. Verse 4 describes Śiva's appearance and trappings; in l.40 there is the auspicious outward sign of Gaurī's happiness – the fluttering left eye; in l.50 Tagore asks to be dressed *naba rakta-basane*, 'in new blood-red robes', suggestive of *śakti* (see Glossary).

1 'Death, Death' – in the original this recurrent phrase is literally 'O Death, O my Death' (*ogo maraṇ, he mor maraṇ*).

32 *babam-babam*: slapping of the cheeks with the fingers is a feature of some of Hinduism's more esoteric or cultic rituals.

35–6 'was this not/A better way of wedding' – I have interpolated these words.

37 'deathly wedding-party's din' – *śmaśān-bāsīr kal-kal*: 'the din of the dwellers in cremation-grounds', i.e. those followers of Śiva that dwell in *śmaśān*, cremation grounds (see Śiva in the Glossary).

63 'Death, Death' – 'O Lord' (*ogo nāth*) precedes the refrain at this point.

66 'infinity' – *akūl*: 'without shore', a more spatial word than 'infinity', so I have inserted 'sea' in l.65.

Arrival (p. 71)

āgaman from *kheyā* (The Ferry), 1906

In this book we see the movement towards simple language, symbolism and preoccupation with religious themes that reaches its culmination in the poems and songs of *gītāñjali* (1910) and *gītimālya* (1914). 'Arrival' was the first poem by Tagore that I tried to translate. The compelling rhythm of the original seemed to me such an important part of its power that I tried to copy it in English. To do this, I had to put in rather more prop-words than I would now favour. The original poem has great concision. In the first two verses, the following words and phrases are my own addition, *metri causa*: l.4 'dark', l.5 'amongst us', l.5 'of Night', l.7 'outer', l.8 'they rattle when it blows', l.10

'peacefulness', l.11 'at the doors'. I have made finite verbs non-finite in ll.3–4 of each verse.

The poem is about the discovery of soul, God ('the King') being identified with soul in Tagore and in Indian tradition generally. It contains the paradox that on the one hand our selves are free to accept or reject soul/God; but on the other hand it will reveal itself anyway. Compare two passages in *S*: on p. 41 Tagore writes of the freedom of the self: 'There our God must win his entrance. There he comes as a guest, not as a king, and therefore he has to wait until he is invited'; but on p. 33 Tagore quotes a conversation with a rural ascetic: '"Why don't you preach your doctrine to all the people of the world?" I asked. "Whoever feels thirsty will of himself come to the river," was his reply. "But then, do you find it so? Are they coming?" The man gave a gentle smile, and with an assurance which had not the least tinge of impatience or anxiety, he said, "They must come, one and all."' The sudden, unexpected discovery that one must go to the river, whether one likes it or not, can be traumatic and humiliating – hence the terror and storminess of Tagore's poem. One of its most remarkable *coups* is the way it moves to general statement in the last verse: here the speaker is not the 'one or two' of the previous verses, but the converted soul itself. Low-grade imperatives and pronouns are used, emphasizing the humbling of the self.

16 *kṣaṇe kṣaṇe cetan kari*: 'becoming spasmodically conscious'.
30 'celebration' – *abhyarthan*: 'reception, greeting, welcome'.
31 'lowly' is my addition. The conch, for all its divine and epic associations, is used in ordinary, simple, domestic worship. See Conch in the Glossary.
32 'King of Night' – *ā̃dhār gharer rājā*: 'king of the dark house'.

Highest Price (p. 72)

caram mūlya from *gītimālya* (String of Songs), 1914

Ancient India, in which kings or rich men could keep slaves, lies behind the symbolism of this poem. The hawker who is speaking does not ask 'Who will buy my wares?' but quite clearly 'Who will buy *me*?', i.e. who will buy me into slavery, so that I no longer have to fend for myself. At the symbolic level the slavery that is being asked for is the complete self-surrender required for the liberation of the soul through love. In *S*115 Tagore writes: 'It is not that we desire freedom alone, we want thraldom as well. It is the high function of love to welcome all limitations and to transcend them. For nothing is more independent than love, and where else, again, shall we find so much of dependence? In love, thraldom is as glorious as freedom.' Love can only be bought by love: the king cannot buy it with power, the rich man cannot buy it with gold, the woman cannot buy it with seduction. Only the child, with his wholly disinterested 'playful face' (*khelār mukhe*, l.30), secures it, releasing the speaker from the burden of self (I have interpolated 'cares' in ll.1 and 28, to bring out this meaning). The ability that children have to find joy in the simplest things is the 'chief lesson' that they have for us (*R*17). In l.18 the speaker walks on *anya-manā*, 'with his mind elsewhere'. This implies not just absent-mindedness but the 'crying for the across' (*S*162) that makes the self ever restless. But the child shows that release from the burden of the self can be found near, not far. Writing in *R*242 of the 'closeness of attention even to trifling things' in his youthful book *chabi o gān* (Pictures and Songs, 1884), Tagore says: 'Whatever my eyes fell upon found a response within me. Like children who can play with sand or stones or shells or whatever they can get (for the spirit of play is within them), so also we, when filled with the song of youth, become aware that the harp of the universe has its variously tuned strings everywhere stretched, and the nearest may serve as well as any other for our accompaniment, there is no need to seek afar.'

'Highest Price' was written in Urbana, U.S.A. Tagore's son Rathindranath, who had just graduated in agricultural science at the University of Illinois and was working on a doctorate, persuaded his father to join him there in October 1912. A month later the English *Gitanjali* was published, and a year later, soon after his return to India, Tagore was awarded the Nobel Prize.

3–5 lit., 'Alas, my days pass in this way – the load on my head becomes an unbearable responsibility, encumbrance'.
9–12 lit., 'Grasping me by the hand he says, "I'll buy you by force." After struggling, the force he had comes to an end.'

12 I have had to omit 'crown on his head' from this line.

1914–1936

The Conch (p. 77)

śaṅkha from *balākā* (Wild Geese), 1916

The numbing series of bereavements, from his wife's death in 1902 to the death of his youngest son Samindra of cholera in 1907, had left Tagore almost entirely alone, as his two surviving daughters were married and Rathindranath was in America. Loneliness and austerity mark the songs and poems of the *gītāñjali* period. In *balākā*, Tagore's creative energies revived, and the book is regarded by many as his finest. 'The Conch' sets the tone: a revived will-power, a determination not to be defeated either by personal suffering or the anguish that the outbreak of the First World War caused Tagore. A new avant-garde magazine, *sabuj patra* (Green Leaves), started in 1914 by Tagore's friend Pramatha Chaudhuri, was also a stimulus: Tagore poured out poems, stories, essays and novels for it.

The conch of Tagore's poem can be identified with the Pāñcajanya, Kṛṣṇa's conch in the Mahābhārata, since the poem is full of the call to spiritual fight that we find in the Bhagavad Gītā, Kṛṣṇa's great song of encouragement to Arjuna inserted into Book VI of the epic. The poem is a call to a self, a people or even a world that have ignored Kṛṣṇa's words, have let his conch – the symbol of the 'ideal of fight' (*RM*85), since heroes in Indian epic rally their troops by blowing conches – lie neglected in the dust. Longing for serenity and longing for action were equal impulses in Tagore, and in keeping with the teachings of the Gītā he aimed to reconcile the two. He saw heroic action as 'the best ideal in the West, the great truth of fight'(*RM*65), whereas 'the life of inner peace and perfection' was associated with India. To combine these 'two guiding spirits', represented by the two sages Viśvāmitra and Vaśiṣṭha in the Rāmāyaṇa (*CU*65), was part of his programme for bringing East and West together. 'Disinterested action' was the key to such a reconciliation: 'According to the Gita, the deeds that are done solely for the sake of self fetter our soul; the disinterested action, performed for the sake of giving up self, is the true sacrifice. For creation itself comes of the self-sacrifice of Brahma, which has no other purpose; and therefore, in our performance of the duty which is self-sacrificing, we realize the spirit of Brahma' (*RM*83). In verse 2 of 'The Conch' the speaker makes the wrong approach to God: his flower-offering and his longing for *śānti-svarga* ('heavenly quiet', l.8) are self-interested. The sudden discovery of moral conscience on seeing the conch has traumatic surprise in it, comparable with 'Arrival': it is the 'second birth', the discovery described in *P*80 that man's 'true life is in the region of what ought to be'. The poem has a wild, gestural quality, but its underlying ideas are perfectly cogent and representative of an important strain in Indian thought.

6 'inspiring conch' – *abhay śaṅkha*: 'the conch that dispels fear'. The phrase is used again in the last line of the poem. *mahā-śaṅkha* ('great conch', l.12) also carries the meaning 'conch which inspires courage'.

14 lit., 'Shall I weave garlands of red *jabā*-flowers? Alas for my *rajanī-gandhā*-flowers' (his 'offering' in l.7). The former are associated with *śakti* (l.36) and with Kālī; the latter are a modern flower with romantic associations. See Glossary.

19–20 lit., 'O touch (me) with the philosopher's stone of youth (*yaubaner-i paraś-maṇi*)./ Let music arise in the tune of rāg Dīpak, (let my) life's delight (be) set ablaze.' See Glossary for the significance of rāg Dīpak.

26 'monsoon showers of arrows' – *śrābaṇ-dhārā-sama bāṇ*: 'arrows like a stream in the month of Śrābaṇ (see Glossary).

35 This line is not wholly clear, because of grammatical ambiguity. The most likely literal interpretation seems to me: 'A victory-drum will sound in my breast in response to your sorrow' (the sorrow or shame of your lying in the dust); but it could mean: 'Your victory-drum will

sound as a result of the sorrow in my breast' (i.e. my sorrow that you should be lying in the dust will inspire me to action).

36 lit., 'I shall give all my power (*śakti*), I shall take (win back) your inspiring conch'.

Shah-Jahan (p. 78)

śā-jāhān from *balākā*, 1916

This poem is in the most characteristic style of the poems in *balākā*. Their verse technique is an extraordinary combination of freedom and discipline: the varying line-lengths, restlessly shifting across the page to make the visual patterns that became one of Tagore's main poetic trade-marks from now on, interact with an infinitely careful placing of words and rhymes. 'Shah-Jahan' is generally rhymed in couplets: I have used half-rhymes, but have let them be paired anywhere in the section in which they occur. The complexity of language, metaphor and thought in the poem poses a great challenge to the translator. The mixture of abstract and concrete ('cheek of time', 1.16; 'whispers in the year of eternity', 1.56) has ample Shakespearean precedent in English, but is not easy in the rigidified language of the present day. The poem contains many difficult lines, but after much work and thought I am convinced that there are no real obscurities or unclarities, if we apply our understanding fully. For a long time I was puzzled by 'the seed' of 1.132. But since the 'deathless plant' into which it grew is quite clearly the Taj Mahal itself, speaking in ll.139–49, and since it was 'shed from the garland of your life' *and* 'blown by your heart's feelings', it must have originated in the Emperor's love and grief – so I have translated it as 'grief's seed'. Ll.64–70 are very difficult, but as so often Tagore's general ideas are of assistance. The beauty of the *cāmelī*-flower in the light of the full moon in 1.67 is *dehahīn*, without body, disembodied, because for Tagore beauty was beyond facts: the *cāmelī*-flower is a fact, but its beauty is a reality beyond fact, just as the continuing presence of Shah-Jahan's beloved beyond death is a reality beyond fact: 'beauty is not a mere fact; it cannot be accounted for, it cannot be surveyed and mapped. It is an expression. Facts are like wine-cups that carry it, they are hidden by it, it overflows them' (*P*34). The passage is evoking things that are perceived but which remain out of physical reach. Ll.68–9 recall the sentence from the Īśā Upaniṣad quoted by Tagore in *P*62: 'Mind comes back baffled and words also.'

The mixture of form and freedom in the verse of the poem is also the key to its meaning – indeed I can think of no other poem in which form is so completely wedded to content. Its most important underlying idea is of life as a force whose forward movement cannot be checked. Whatever evil and suffering there may be in mortal existence, 'life itself is optimistic: it wants to go on' (*S*52). Death does not deny life's onward movement: it confirms it.

The passage describing Tagore's reaction to the death of his sister-in-law in *R*257 is relevant here: Tagore's grief eventually gave way to the realization that 'an unopposed life-force' would be an intolerable burden: if there were no death, life would be 'a stable permanent fixture' – and stability and permanence are the opposite of life's essential quality. In one sense, Shah-Jahan's building of the Taj Mahal shows a failure to understand this: in attempting to immortalize the life of his beloved and his grief at her loss 'in the beauty of serene stone' (l.58) he achieves the opposite, he perpetuates death. But it would be wrong to think that Tagore is writing off the Taj, the *Meghadūta* with which it is compared (l.61) and thus all great art as spiritual failure, a denial of 'life's quick spate' (l.23). For pervading the whole of life and death is Brahman, 'the Infinite, the Perfect, the Eternal' (*P*152). Great art expresses this. In fact great art expresses movement and stability at the same time: the *Meghadūta* does this; the Taj does this – because its architecture expresses movement (l.62) as well as stillness and because it conveys a message of immortality (ll.139–49) as well as mortality; and Tagore's poem does it through its combination of movement and form.

Perhaps it is necessary to have seen the Taj Mahal to appreciate fully a poem which so uniquely captures its beauty and atmosphere. See *P*18 for the contrast Tagore often made between the Moghuls and the British: the Moghuls, though imperialists, 'lived and died in India' and left behind 'their human personality' in their buildings and other works of art. But the British government in India 'is official and therefore an abstraction. It has nothing to express in the true language of art. For law, efficiency and exploitation cannot sing themselves into epic stones.'

27–9 lit., 'as a result of the magical murmur of the south wind, in your garden the buds of spring *mādhabī*-creepers at that moment fill the restless, fleeting *añcal* (sari-end) of the garden'.

33 'jasmine' – *kunda*: see Glossary.

35 the 'later season' is *hemanta*, the season between autumn and winter in Bengal.

39 I have interpolated this line.

47 'formless' – *rūp-hīn*: the word can also mean 'without beauty', making an antithesis with *aparūp*, 'wonderful, very beautiful' in l.45.

49 'forever' – *bāro mās*: 'twelve months', i.e. 'you could not go on weeping for months on end'.

64 'loverless beloved' – *birahiṇī priyā*: 'separated beloved', and therefore full of *biraha*. See notes on 'The *Meghadūta*'.

82 'musicians' – *nahabat*: an orchestra in which the *sānāi*, a reed instrument associated with wedding-festivities, predominates.

89 'incorruptible' – *amalin*: 'spotless, pure white', as is the Taj Mahal.

147 'gate' – *simha-dvār*: 'lion-gate'.

Gift (p. 81)

dān from *balākā*, 1916

This exquisitely delicate love-poem might at first sight seem, like 'Unending Love' or 'Unyielding', to take us into the world of Tagore's songs; but in fact Tagore by a concentration of imagination and feeling is trying to touch realities that lie even beyond song. Normally song was an artistic ideal for him: 'the true poets, they who are seers, seek to express the universe in terms of music' (*S*142); and a flower, particularly a rose, was an image of perfection (cf. '*The Sick-bed – 21*') and an ideal gift: 'Somehow we feel that through a rose the language of love reaches our heart. Do we not carry a rose to our beloved because in it is already embodied a message which, unlike our language of words, cannot be analysed? Through this gift of a rose we utilize a universal language of joy for our own purpose of expression' (*RM*125). Yet neither songs nor roses are sufficient here. What the poet wants to do is present his beloved with the 'perfect gift of joy' (*S*108) that is at the heart of creation itself. Songs and flowers are mortal; but 'the infinite is giving himself out through finitude' (*P*69) perpetually. Because of *māyā*, ignorance, we only perceive this fleetingly – but the divine giving never ceases. At first sight the gifts that the poet wants to give seem *more* transient, *more* fleeting than a song or a flower: but somehow Tagore manages to tell us that it is the perception that is fleeting, not the gift itself. It is hard to say how this is achieved, without detailed recourse to the Bengali words and images. But the key may lie in the many expressions of suddenness and surprise in ll.30–50, and the moments of stasis, suspension that follow each gift (ll.34, 40, 47). In life, surprise is often associated with a sudden discovery of something that was there already, there all the time perhaps, though we were unaware of it; and when we are surprised by joy we are indeed stopped in our tracks, momentarily removed from the temporal to the eternal.

13–14 The original is more definite: 'The evening light (that I have here)? This lamp's light (that I have here) in this lonely, private corner of (my) still, silent house?'

35–6 lit., 'let that path-losing gift be yours'.

41 lit., 'touches a philosopher's stone on your dreams'.

42 'innocent' – *ajānā*: 'unknown, intangible'.

44 'truest treasure' – *āmār yā śreṣṭha-dhan*: 'that which is my highest wealth'.

46–7 'its tune stops us in our tracks' – *pathere śihari diyā sure*: 'having made the path tremble with its melody'.

51 lit., 'Friend, that which you get from there' (the place where the 'truest treasure' is to be found).

Deception (p. 83)

phā̃ki from *palātakā* (The Runaway), 1918

The poems in *palātakā* develop the metrical freedom of *balākā* in the direction of greater closeness to spoken Bengali in both rhythm and diction. The subjects of the poems are also more down-to-earth, close to the world of Tagore's short stories. 'Deception' is rhymed in couplets, but I have not used rhyme or half-rhyme in my translation, as the poem looks forward to the *gadya-kabitā* (prose-poetry, *vers libre*) of Tagore's late books.

'Deception' is a famous poem, not just because it tells a touching story so deftly and well, but because it brings together so many of Tagore's deepest values, ranging from his distrust of orthodox medical treatment (ll.2–5) to his intense admiration for woman's ability to love, an ability so often betrayed and trampled on by men. Tagore felt that modern civilization created war between the sexes 'because man is driven to professionalism, producing wealth for himself and others, continually turning the wheel of power for his own sake or for the sake of the universal officialdom, leaving woman alone to wither and to die or to fight her own battle unaided' (*N*10). As in 'Bride', the traditional Indian joint-family system does not pass without criticism (ll.9–12); but many telling details connect the speaker's moral failure to his modernness. He passes the time at Bilāspur station by reading an English novel, which shows both his educational standing and his boredom with the rural scene that Binu finds so enchanting; l.73 shows him to be an office-worker; his treatment of Rukmiṇī implies not simple caste antagonism but a contempt for poverty and rural backwardness, a bourgeois tendency to judge people according to money. Binu, in contrast, displays human qualities that transcend time and place: her state of mind in ll.15–32 is that which is described in *S*42: her 'spirit has been made one with God'; for her, 'all the conflicts and contradictions of life are reconciled; knowledge, love and action harmonized; pleasure and pain become one in beauty, enjoyment and renunciation equal in goodness'. Her delight in the commonplace in ll.42–8 is that which is described in *P*175, a passage which makes it clear that Tagore felt such perception came more easily to women than to men. Her love and reverence for her husband in ll.109–14 is the 'ultimate perfection of all womanly love' that Tagore found in his English landlady Mrs Scott (*R*166). See *P*169 for the role that Tagore thought women should play in correcting the 'one-sidedness' of modern industrial civilization.

As so often in Tagore's writings, moral values can be linked to artistic ideals. The 'Real' that Binu perceives (and which, in dying, she perhaps teaches her husband to perceive) is the Real that Tagore felt it was the duty of the artist to express: not the reality described by science, but the reality felt by man's combined moral, spiritual and imaginative faculties. See *P*4,50 where Tagore dissociates science from Reality as he understood it, and

*RM*139 where he defines art as 'the response of man's creative soul to the call of the Real'. Binu in her *ānanda*, joy (ll.22, 40) on her first train journey feels that call.

13,16 The allusions in these lines are to the *baraṇ* (welcoming) ritual in which a mother-in-law lifts up an earthenware lamp on a plate and touches the forehead of bride and bridegroom with it, and the *śubha-dṛṣṭi*, the moment in Hindu marriage when the bride is unveiled.

26–7 lit., 'so it seemed that today through her gifts and her thoughts (meditation, *dhyān*) she would have to fill the journey with universal welfare (*kalyāṇ*)'.

48 'what a lovely place to live' – *orā keman sukhe āche*: 'in what happiness they (the stationmaster and his family) live'.

Grandfather's Holiday (p. 86)

ṭhākur-dādār chuṭi from *palātakā*, 1918

In spirit this poem seems to belong more to Tagore's next book, *śiśu bholānāth* (see next page). It is in many ways the very definition of an untranslatable poem, because it hinges on a word – *chuṭi*, repeated in almost every line of the original – for which there is no real equivalent in English. In ordinary spoken Bengali it means 'holiday', anything from a school half-holiday to an extended vacation: but like *khelā* it has much wider, even metaphysical connotations. *chuṭi* is a state of mind – of delight, playfulness, freedom from restrictions – in which there is no difference between work and play. There is no such difference in the creative processes of Nature itself, nor is there in the activity of young children, who are closer to nature than adults. So *chuṭi* is both a state of mind and a universal process going on all around us. Adults, by their inhibitions and their wrong attitude to work, all too often cut themselves off from it. In *S*133 Tagore writes: 'Our day of work is not our day of joy – for that we require a holiday; for miserable that we are, we cannot find our holiday in our work. The river finds its holiday in its outward flow, the fire in its outburst of flame, the scent of the flower in its permeation of the atmosphere, but in our everyday work there is no such holiday for us. It is because we do not let ourselves go, because we do not give ourselves joyously and entirely up to it, that our work overpowers us.'

I have had to translate this poem freely, using different English words for *chuṭi* whenever it occurs. A literal translation of Verse 1 would read: 'Your *chuṭi* is in the blue sky, your *chuṭi* is in the fields,/Your *chuṭi* is in the steps of that bottomless pond,/Your *chuṭi* is at the bottom of tamarind-trees, in the corners of barns,/Your *chuṭi* is in the bushes in the Pārul-ḍāṅgā forest./Your *chuṭi*'s hope trembles in the fields of unripe paddy,/Your *chuṭi*'s happiness dances in the waves of the river.' I did not realize when I first translated the poem that Pārul-ḍāṅgā was a village near Santiniketan; but as it was perhaps named after its *pārul*-bushes, I have left my version alone. I have also not touched my free rendering of the last line of the poem (lit., 'You awake my *chuṭi*, in that is my *jit*, victory'), because the passage from *S* quoted above suggests that 'letting oneself go' was what Tagore had in mind: the 'victory' is the victory over adult inhibition.

Palm-tree (p. 87)

tāl-gāch from *śiśu bholānāth* (The Child Forgetful), 1922

Like *śiśu*, 1903, this is another book in which children and their 'inexpensive power to be happy' (*RM* 173) feature largely. It seems to have given Tagore relief after his exhausting foreign tour of 1920–21, his efforts for Visva-Bharati, and his increasing misgivings about the direction that Gandhi's Swaraj movement was taking. (At a meeting between Tagore and Gandhi in Calcutta in September 1921, Gandhi failed to persuade Tagore to give active support to the movement, and Tagore withdrew to Santiniketan.)

Most Bengali schoolchildren know 'Palm-tree' by heart, and little needs to be said about it. It is both a perfect word-picture of a palm-tree tossing in the wind and a brilliant summary of what Nature meant to Tagore. Though there is restlessness in its content, it conveys balance and peace: the tree, drawn to both sky and earth equally, expresses the balancing of infinite and finite, transcendent and immanent that is the subject of the Īśā Upaniṣad (expounded by Tagore in *P* ch. II) and the object of man's *sādhanā* or spiritual endeavour. We can learn to achieve this balance by observing Nature. Trees were often objects of meditation for Tagore: cf. 'In Praise of Trees', or the passage in *P* 133 describing how the view of the tree tops from the upper terrace of his house at Santiniketan brought peace to his heart after a period of stress and worry over his school.

1 'single-legged giant' – *ek pāye dā̃ṛiye*: 'standing on one leg'.
10 'feathers' – *ḍānā*: 'wings'.
13–14 the original is full of onomatopoeia: *sārādin jhar-jhar thatthar/kā̃pe pātā pattar.*

The Wakening of Śiva (p. 88)

tapobhaṅga from *pūrabī* (Pūrvī – Indian musical rāga), 1925

Most of the poems in this very fine book were written a year or so after 'The Wakening of Śiva', on the ship to South America or in Buenos Aires (see next poem). Though the rāga of the title is associated with evening, and its melancholy mood pervades much of the book's content, 'The Wakening of Śiva' (the Bengali title means 'Breaking of Penance') is a passionate paean to the spirit of youthfulness, still exuberantly alive in the 61-year-old poet's creative powers, and ever active in the processes of Nature. It is perhaps the most complex and challenging of all the poems I have translated, in its extravagantly Sanskritic language, its use of classical literature and myth, and its intricacy of thought, feeling and structure. The entries on Śiva, Kāma and Kālidāsa in the Glossary should help the non-Indian reader with its images and allusions: but the poem has many difficulties even for those who are familiar with its literary and mythological background.

In a manner that is characteristic of Indian mythology and religion itself – in which deities can undergo constant metamorphosis and worshippers can identify themselves with or act out the divine – Tagore constantly changes the roles he plays in his own poem. The 'past days' that are the subject of many of the sentences in verses 1–3 are his own days of youthful poetic exuberance, and Śiva's days in his active, creative phase; so Śiva is the poet himself when we get to verses 6–7, his ascetic phase being associated with advancing years and dormant creativity; in ll.71–2 Tagore is separate again, preparing to welcome the end of Śiva's trance; in verses 10–11 he is Kāma, waking Śiva – but in ll.86–8 he is separate from Kāma, though supplying him with passion; in the last two verses he is the archetypal poet, a member of Śiva and Umā's wedding procession, celebrating 'the eternal wedding of love'(*CU*52: Tagore writes here of Kālidāsa's *Kumāra-sambhava*, the poem which lies behind 'The Wakening of Śiva' and which we know from *R*75 and 110 had a formative influence on Tagore).

These bewildering shifts are a vital part of the 'extravagance' that is at the heart of the poem's purpose and meaning, just as constant changes of costume define extravagance in drama or life. Asceticism was not attractive to Tagore. He associated it with the kind of religion that separates God from the world (see *S*129) or which seeks 'the utter extinction of the individual separateness' (*RM*202) through mystical communion rather than realization through love, creativity and action. He also associated it with intellect divorced from feeling, with science as opposed to poetry. See *N*34, where he writes: 'Our intellect is an ascetic who wears no clothes, takes no food, knows no sleep, has no wishes, feels no love or hatred or pity for human limitations, who only reasons, unmoved, through the vicissitudes of life. It burrows to the roots of things, because it has no personal concern with the thing itself.' Poetry, on the other hand, expresses everything that cannot be described by intellect, cannot be reduced to law: extravagance of language and imagery matches the extravagance of colour, form, scent, sound in Nature itself. In *RM*155 Tagore writes of the flowers, leaves and fruits of a tree that 'their exuberance is not a malady of exaggeration, but a blessing'. The poet's exuberance is also a blessing, 'heaven's conspiracy' (l.74) against all that is repressed, logical, rule-bound.

But neither Nature nor poetry can do without Law (see notes to 'Brahmā, Viṣṇu, Śiva'), and like 'Palm-tree', though on a larger scale, 'The Wakening of Śiva' achieves a remarkable balance: Śiva's periods of asceticism are part of the essential law or rhythm of life. In *N*51 Tagore writes: 'In the rhythm of life, pauses there must be for the renewal of life. Life in its activity is ever spending itself, burning all its fuel. This extravagance cannot go on indefinitely, but is always followed by a passive stage, when all expenditure is stopped and all adventures abandoned in favour of rest and slow recuperation.' Verses 7–8 show the necessity of Śiva's quiescent phase and the latency of the active phase within it. The word *līlā* (ll.37, 54) expresses this rhythm or law of alternating activity and passivity: it also expresses the interaction of law and freedom, intellect and feeling that such alternations imply. A further meaning is found in ll.38–40, perhaps the most difficult in the poem: literal translation is impossible, but the 'world-poem' of *S*99 is in them, Underlying Form and free, fluctuous Expression of that Form irreducibly combined. Like *khelā*, the basic meaning of *līlā* is play, sport: but it is a much more elevated word, even harder to define, and I have left it untranslated. Perhaps the very rhythm and structure of 'The Wakening of Śiva', even in translation, will best convey its meaning.

6 'post-monsoon' – *āśviner*: 'of (the month of) Āśvin' (see Glossary).

8 'harsh' – *nirmam*: the word can mean 'heartless, cruel', but also 'selfless', as befits Śiva in his ascetic phase.

20–21 lit., 'they ('the days' described in verse 2) brought the mantras of your meditation to the shore of the outside, to the scent of flowers in the fun of the aimless south wind'. Śiva's creative energy, directed inwards during his ascetic phase, was thus redirected into the external beauties of Nature.

22 'oleanders' – *karabikā*: see Glossary.

28 The word used is *aiśvarya*, 'superhuman power'. In Indian philosophic tradition eight kinds of *aiśvarya* are distinguished, and Śiva possesses all of them.

36–7 lit., 'In the light of the moon on your (Śiva's) forehead, with eyes dreaming of paradise,/ I saw the *līlā* of eternal newness filling my heart.'

45 'lie forgotten' – *luṇṭhita*: 'rolling about (in the dust)'. The mixture of metaphors becomes too rich for English.

62 The original has *cañcal muhūrta*, '*restless* moments', but I have tried to convey this with the word 'energy' in l.63.

71 'fossilized' – the word used is *sthabir*, which means 'decrepit', but is also a term for a kind of Buddhist ascetic.

95 'your consort's rāga' – *bhairabī*: rāg Bhairavī. See Glossary.

99 'what I am' – *mor sāj*: 'my dress, guise, manner, appearance'.

Guest (p. 91)

atithi from *pūrabī*, 1925

This poem was written in November 1924, in Buenos Aires, for the feminist and writer Victoria Ocampo. Tagore had originally accepted an invitation to attend the centenary celebrations of the independence of the Republic of Peru, but he fell ill *en route* and never got further than Buenos Aires. The seven weeks that Tagore spent in the villa that Victoria Ocampo found for him at San Isidro were, however, a time of great peace and happiness for him. Tagore's father Debendranath used to point out the stars to the eleven-year-old Tagore on their trip to the Himalayas in 1873: 'As dusk came on the stars blazed out wonderfully through the clear mountain atmosphere, and my father showed me the constellations or treated me to an astronomical discourse' (*R*93). By linking the music of the stars to human love, Tagore manages to convey his sense of a Personality at the heart of the universe, his insistence that the universe can only be understood in human terms (see *RM*, especially chapters I and VII and the conversation with Einstein in Appendix II). The poem also conveys, in a way that is much harder to define, reciprocity of love: the stars' love and the lady's love are explicit: the poet's answering love implicit but equally strong. The message in ll.8 and 12 in the Bengali is simply 'We/I know you, know you' (or perhaps 'know that we/I know you'). My alteration was originally perhaps dictated by rhythm and half-rhyme. But on reflection I am content with it: 'ours' and 'mine' imply a return of love on the part of the poet, a return that the original communicates through its verbal music and the nuances of its words, but which perhaps needs to be made more explicit in translation. Without such a sense of love returned, the poem is incomplete. See *CU*80, where Tagore writes: 'God's will, in giving his love, finds its completeness in man's will returning that love. Therefore Humanity is a necessary factor in the perfecting of the divine truth. The Infinite, for its self-expression, comes down into the manifoldness of the Finite; and the Finite, for its self-realization, must rise into the unity of the Infinite. Then only is the Cycle of Truth complete.'

6–7 lit., 'a message of light came into my life (*prāṇ*) harmoniously from on high'.

9–10 lit., 'the day that Earth took (you) into her lap from the lap of darkness'.

In Praise of Trees (p. 91)

bṛkṣa-bandanā from *bana-bāṇī* (The Message of the Forest), 1931

This book brought together a number of poems and songs about trees, some of which were written in connection with the annual Tree-Planting Festival that Tagore instituted in 1928 at Santiniketan. 'In Praise of Trees' was written in 1926. It is a meditation rather than a description, and the word for meditation, *dhyān*, is used in l.64 (lit., 'By the power of meditation I have gone into your midst. I have known . . .'). Trees are often associated with meditation in Tagore's writings and Indian tradition generally, for the sages who wrote the Upaniṣads and other great spiritual texts were forest-dwellers, and the forest *āśram*, in which a sage would train his disciples in meditation and self-realization, was the original idea behind the experiment at Santiniketan (see *CU*46 and *P*127). But the originality of the poem is that it is not an expression of 'secluded communion' (*S*129) with God revealed through Nature: it is as much concerned with humanity as with trees, with art and action as with Nature or mysticism. Its purpose is to show that humanity and Nature are inseparably linked. Its vision of the triumphant march of life is reminiscent of a passage in *N*65 in which Tagore hails the human defiance of limitations that he saw as Europe's most positive contribution to the world; and even more of a passage in *P*29 on the triumphant march of art: 'Thus art is signalling man's conquest of the world by its symbols of beauty, springing up in spots which were barren of all voice and colours. It is supplying man with his banners, under which he marches against the inane and the inert . . . For the one effort of man's personality is to transform everything with which he has any true concern into the human. And art is like the spread of vegetation, to show how far man has reclaimed the desert for his own.' Ll.53–67, on the other hand, are much more Indian, evocative of the serenity sought by the forest sages. What Tagore is after, as so often, is a balance between these two impulses – the European and the Indian, the active and the meditative: he is suggesting that trees can show us that the two *can* be reconciled, valour can be restrained with patience, creative power can be peaceful (ll.54–6). The key-words in the poem are *prāṇ*, life, used in ll.1, 61, 76; *śakti*, power, in l.73; and *tej*, power or fire, in ll.68 and 77: and its dominant ideal is that of Natural and Human *prāṇ*, *śakti* or *tej* acting in harmony. Tagore has taken the view of the forest-sages that 'the perfect relation with this world is the relation of union' (*CU*46) and given it a much more active and dynamic form, allowing for activism, art, even science as expressions of that relation.

bana-bāṇī was dedicated to Tagore's friend the plant-physiologist J. C. Bose, who did pioneering work on the life-reactions of plants. The blending of science and poetry in, for example, ll.35–53 is comparable to passages in 'Brahmā, Viṣṇu, Śiva' and 'Earth.'

7 'by mixed magic' – *miśra-mantre*: 'with mixed mantras'.

16–25 The rather obscure imagery of these lines appears to come from Tagore's imagination, rather than mythology. The relationship between Earth and Spirit is seen in human terms, which is in keeping with the poem as a whole.

34 'code' – *panthā*: '(religious) path or system'.

42 'prismatic tune' – *gāner indra-dhanu*: 'a rainbow of songs'.
48 'celestial' – *indrer*. 'Indra's'.
49 'shattering *līlā-nṛtye*: 'with the dance of their *līlā* (see Notes to 'The Wakening of Śiva').
57 'to learn the art of peace' – *śānti-dīkṣā labhibāre*: 'to be initiated into peace'. *dīkṣā* is religious initiation.
65–6 There is ritual imagery here, of the *homāgni*, the sacred fire used in Hindu ceremonies, and of the *yajña* (sacrifice) of creation in the sun's fire.

Last Honey (p. 93)

śeṣ madhu from *mahuā*, 1929

In 1928 a group of admirers in Calcutta asked Tagore for an anthology of his love poems, for use as a presentation at weddings. The request stimulated Tagore into writing an entirely new collection, which he named after the *mahuā*-flower (see Glossary).

The book is particularly admired in Bengal for its sensuousness, its musicality of imagery and verse, its resurgent youthfulness combined with maturity of vision. I have not attempted to translate the love-poems in the book; but 'Last Honey' is typical of it in other ways. The 'end of the year' – the Bengali year, that is, which ends in mid-April – evokes Tagore's own advancing age, and in each verse there are images of death, barrenness or departure. But the poem is not depressed or pessimistic: there is vigour in its deft verse structure; the passing of spring brings sudden, short-lived abundance and delight. There is an implied link with Tagore's own creativity: the passing of his youth has produced a sudden fecundity – he must make the most of it. But it would be wrong to liken its mood to European *carpe diem*: the spring breeze is a *sannyāsī* (ascetic, l.1), willingly renouncing the world for spiritual gain. See *RM*198 on the Four Stages of Life: 'Last Honey' could be described as a poem of the Third Stage, in which 'the decline of the bodily powers must be taken as a warning that it is coming to its natural end. This must not be taken dismally as a notice of dismissal to one still eager to stick to his post but joyfully as maturity may be accepted as the stage of fulfilment.' On the other hand, we have seen in previous poems – 'A Half-acre of Land', 'The Wakening of Śiva' – that Tagore had mixed feelings about renunciation; hence the strange, ambiguous, bitter-sweet tone of this beautiful poem.

4 lit., 'the tired languorous earth spreads out her *añcal* (loose end of the sari) beneath the trees'.
6 'lays its welcoming bed' – *ray āsan pete*: 'remains having laid out (its) seat'. *āsan* means anything for sitting on, not necessarily a raised seat; but *āsan pātā* is also an idiom meaning to offer hospitality.

9–10 lit., 'I seem to hear in the forest-branches the flute of the end of the day being played; smear today (your) wings with memory-laden fragrant pollen'.

15–16 lit., 'I know that the *dolan-cā̃pā* buds trembling in the Caitra breeze will bloom today in the fierce heat and sun of Baiśākh. You will now finish all that they have to give.' The original thus speaks of the immediate *flowering* of the *dolan-cā̃pā* buds with the onset of summer; but the general drift of the poem suggests that the heat will quickly wither them – hence my translation.

20 The year or Caitra is described here as *maraṇer svayambarā*, 'one who has herself chosen death as a bridegroom'. In ancient India, *svayaṃ-vara* was the election of a husband by a high-born girl at a public assembly of suitors.

Sea-maiden (p. 94)

sāgarikā from *mahuā*, 1929

This poem was written on a tour of Malaya and the Dutch East Indies in 1927. It was published in a slightly longer form in the journal *prabāsī*, with the title *bālī*. It is generally assumed to be an allegory on the Indian relationship with South-East Asia. Ll.1–40 evoke the golden days of Indian influence on Bali. The poet speaks for India personified as Kāma (see Glossary): he arouses the sea-maiden (Bali) to love and to the worship of Śiva. The relationship between them becomes the counterpart to the divine love of Śiva and Pārvatī (which is also manifest in the beauties and the balancing of opposite forces in Nature – ll.19–20, 39–40). Ll.41–6 describe the breaking off of that relationship through the 'shipwreck' of Indian civilization – its long centuries of decline and stagnation. In ll.47–68 Tagore speaks for modern India, 'broken in fortune' (l.47): the vīṇā of l.67 may possibly associate him with Nārada, divine inventor of the instrument; but it is frequently just a symbol of Tagore's own poetic calling (cf. '*The Borderland – 10*' or 'Unyielding'. Sarasvatī, goddess of the arts, carries a vīṇā). By this stage in his career, Tagore could think of himself as India's ambassador to the world. He sees in Balinese religion, music and dance many legacies of its earlier contact with India, and asks whether the 'sea-maiden' still recognizes him.

Beyond this basic allegoric structure, the images of the poem should not be given too precise a significance. Each of them has a long history in Tagore's poetry and song, reading and experience. The sea-maiden has something of the mermaid about her at the beginning; later, something of the Hindu Bride image that is behind so many of Tagore's ideal females (see *R*101).

9 'majestically' – *rāj-beśī*: 'in royal attire'.

16 'jasmine' – *yūthī*: see Glossary.

19–20 lit., 'light filled the sky, revealing Pārvatī smiling at the face of Dhūrjaṭī (Śiva)'.

Question (p. 96)

praśna from *pariśeṣ* (The End), 1932

Tagore quite wrongly imagined that this would be his last book of verse. The political background to it was sombre: 'Question' was written just after the arrest of Gandhi following the failure of the Second Round Table Conference in London. A Tagore Festival, organized in Calcutta at the end of 1931, was cut short by the news. But it would be wrong to link this grand, impassioned poem too closely to any one time or people. The youthful terrorists who had been periodically active in Bengal for the last twenty years may be behind ll.11–12; but youthful torment at injustice and futile or misguided attempts to remedy it are as perennial as the contradiction described in ll.5–6. The vulnerable, bewildered human being in Tagore was increasingly to be the subject of his late poetry; but he never lapsed into self-pity. The precision and vigour of the rhythm and phrasing of this poem belie its content. A famous reading of it by Tagore himself on record conveys strength not weakness, courage not despair. There is even a note of wryness in his voice.

12 'dashing their heads against stone' is a metaphor for fruitless effort in Bengali, like English 'beating one's head against a brick wall'.

Flute-music (p. 96)

bā̃śi from *punaśca* (The Postscript), 1932

In the passage on the progress of art in *P*29, quoted in my notes to 'In Praise of Trees', Tagore writes: 'The classical literature of the ancient time was only peopled by saints and kings and heroes. It threw no light upon men who loved and suffered in obscurity. But as the illumination of man's personality throws its light upon a wider space, penetrating into hidden corners, the world of art also crosses its frontiers and extends its boundaries into unexplored regions.' 'Flute-music' is a prime example of Tagore's tireless effort throughout his life to extend his artistic range; the humdrum background, the ordinariness of the speaker of the poem are matched by the informal diction and the abandonment of rhyme. But in technique it is not quite the *gadya-kabitā* (prose-poetry) of most of the poems that Tagore wrote over the next four years: there is great concentration in the short lines and laconic phrasing. The achievement of the poem is to show that deep human feeling and spiritual or artistic perception can co-exist with urban squalor. Tagore himself had an urban childhood – privileged maybe, but cramped and confined in other ways: and Haripada's discovery of perfect beauty in Kāntabābu's amateurish playing is akin to

Tagore's own youthful 'vision' from his brother's Sudder Street house, described in *R*217, and his discovery that, far from being confined to the Himalayas, 'He who is the Giver can vouchsafe a vision of the eternal universe in the dingiest of lanes, and in a moment of time.' The maturity of the poem lies in its ironies (in ll.27–35, for example), and its closeness to the ridiculous. But it never *becomes* ridiculous: even Kāntabābu, a failed Romantic perfectly sketched in five lines, is redeemed by the impression his music makes on Haripada the clerk.

4 'dẹcaying' – *lonā-dharā*: 'full of *lonā*', which is dry rot or wet rot due to excess salt in mortar or bricks.

7–8 The reference is to the crude, often gilt paper markers bearing the symbol of a mill stuck on the end of a bale of cloth.

30 The 'auspicious moment' (*lagna*) for a Hindu wedding has to be fixed astrologically: the speaker says ironically that the auspiciousness was proved by the fact that he ran away.

47 A typical Vaiṣṇava name is given: 'like Gopīkānta Gōsāi's mind'. See Glossary.

58 It has been suggested to me that Tagore meant 'clarinet' rather than cornet. It would not be easy to play Indian rāgas on a cornet.

78–81 The Dhaleśvarī river (see Glossary); the *tamāl*-trees, and the Dacca sari (a handwoven sari such as would be worn at a wedding) all evoke Haripada's East Bengali origins.

Unyielding (p. 98)

udāsīn from *bithikā* (The Avenue), 1935

The mystery and the questioning that dominate this book appear lightly and gracefully in this poem, but its implications darken on close examination. The title means 'detached, indifferent', but it is one of the most elusive of Indian words (*udās* and *udāsīn* are the same: see notes to 'Day's End'). For those whose aim is to liberate the soul 'from the bond of personality which keeps it in an ever-revealing circle of limitation' (*RM*202) it is an ideal state of existence: but Tagore never subscribed to so absolute an ideal. He was a dualist, whose ideal was 'a fulfilment in love within the range of our limitation which accepts all sufferings and yet rises above them' (*RM*203). So far him *audāsya*, indifference (used in l.22) was an equivocal state, serene maybe, but exclusive of human feeling and personal relationship. This is what we have in this poem. One can take it to be simply an account of unrequited love; or one can read it as a *jīban-debatā* poem (see notes to 'The Golden Boat', 'On the Edge of the Sea', 'Last Tryst'). Tagore wrote many songs in which that complex amalgam of God, Nature and (usually female) personality that he called his *jīban-debatā* remains aloof, unresponsive to his gifts or questions. Perhaps here, as in 'The

Golden Boat', this is because the speaker remains self-interested: he is proud of his artistry (verse 3), wants to be applauded for it.

7 'perfectness' – *pūrṇatā*: 'fullness, completeness, ripeness'.
20 'right time' – *lagna*: 'auspicious moment'.
27 lit., 'that there was still some rhythm (*chanda*) in your anklets'.
28 'moon' – *malin śaśī*: 'dull, glum, sorrowful moon'.
30–31 lit., 'Did my vīṇā's lament give you some companionship, raise waves on the shore of sleep?'

Earth (p. 99)

pṛthibī from *patra-puṭ* (Cup made of Leaves), 1936

This majestic poem sets the tone for the book in which it occurs. The poems are largely about the natural world, and manage by their scale and sweep to articulate natural processes more powerfully than any poetry Tagore had written since *balākā*. Rich, Sanskritic diction is combined with the free, metreless verse technique that Tagore had developed primarily for more domestic subject matter.

'Earth' is a disquieting poem, because the unity and harmony that Tagore felt were inherent in the natural world (see *S*6 or *CU*4) appear here in such a harsh and inhuman form. The poem is poles apart from the 'harmony of the stars' of 'Guest'. Compare it with a passage in *S*96: 'We have what we call in Sanskrit *dvandva*, a series of opposites in Creation; such as the positive pole and the negative, the centripetal force and the centrifugal, attraction and repulsion . . . There is a bond of harmony between our two eyes, which makes them act in unison. Likewise there is an unbreakable continuity of relation in the physical world between heat and cold, light and darkness, motion and rest . . . That is why these opposites do not bring confusion in the universe, but harmony.' *dvandva* is the main theme of 'Earth', but it is a balance of conflict, of power, not a serene harmony. The word occurs in l.6, with the adjective *duḥsaha*, unbearable, unendurable. The poem up to l.43 might appear to be an essentially scientific view of Earth, hence its callousness (see notes to 'The Wakening of Śiva', 'Deception', '*The Sick-bed – 21*'), for though it uses mythological symbolism, its view of the earth's development seems to owe something to Darwin and Freud. But by the end of the poem one is convinced that it is a complete picture of Reality as Tagore understood it. In *P*4 he writes: 'The world of science is not a world of reality, it is an abstract world of force.' But all the elements of reality that Tagore felt were beyond the reach of science are present in the poem: *prāṇ*, the life-force, in l.25; *śānti*, peace, in l.31; beauty and abundance in l.56; *ānanda*, joy, in l.60; love in l.71. All the poem does is take us deeper into that Reality, show us the struggle and conflict on which its harmony is based. The key-line of the poem is l.85: the poet says that he has not come before Earth today *Kono moha niye*, 'with any illusion'. The ruthless vision of personal extinction in ll.94–5 is a consequence of this realism. One can take this as undermining the philosophy of *S* or *RM* if one likes, but what meaning does the 'true value' of l.88 or the 'scrap of success' of l.92 have without that philosophy? The poem is about Earth not Brahman, and though Brahman may be immanent in the earth, he is not Earth itself. It is Earth who is *udāsīn* (l.96), not necessarily God.

1,98 'homage' – *pranati*: '*praṇām*'. See Glossary.
17 lit., 'the victory-gate (*jay-toraṇ*) of civilization rises on the foundation of your cruelty'.
19,26 Demons/Gods: the grammar seems to suggest a singular Demon and God, but I have taken this as a 'generic singular' (as in English 'The snake is a dangerous animal').
31 'dispensing peace from her chalice' – *māthāy niye śānti-ghaṭ*: 'carrying a pitcher of peace on her head'.
33 'primal barbarity' – the original is more concrete: *ādim barbar*, 'the primeval savage'.
58 lit., 'where the happy morning sun rubs out the dew-drops every day by brushing them with its sunbeam-scarf'.
60 lit., 'this unspoken message: "I am joyful"'.
71 'rhapsodies and soliloquies of love' – *biraha-milaner svagata-pralāp*: 'the self-absorbed delirium of separateness and union'.
79–81 These lines evoke quite precisely the stratification of earth's history in its soil.
93 'sign' – *tilak*: Hindu sectarian mark, painted or printed on the forehead.

Africa (p. 102)

āphrikā from *patra-puṭ*, second edition, 1938

There are at least four versions of this poem, including two texts in 'rhymeless metrical' verse before Tagore arrived at his final free version. I have followed the text (originally published in the journal *prabāsī* in 1936) that appears in the current standard *sañcayitā*, on the editors' assurance that it was 'the poet's final version'. But the text in the second edition of *patra-puṭ* (the poem did not appear in the first edition) does contain one significant difference: in l.44, instead of *yugānter kabi*, 'poet of the end of the age', it prints *yugāntarer kabi*, 'poet of the beginning of the age, the new age'.

'Africa' can be linked to Tagore's shock at Mussolini's invasion of Ethiopia in 1935, but its scope is much wider. An interest in primitive cultures – in Africa, South America and Melanesia – had been growing in Tagore for some time, and tribal art influenced his paintings. This poem does not romanticize or idealize African native culture: it depicts pre-civilized savagery, the dark continent (ll.8–9). Passages in *RM* make it clear that for Tagore the tragedy of imperialism in Africa was that natural development towards civilization had been thwarted. Tribal rituals, dances, warpaint might be savage: but they express dissatisfaction with human limitations, sublimation of the individual into a larger community, an embryonic sense of a transcendent power: 'However crude all this may be, it proves that Man has a feeling that he is truly represented in something which exceeds himself. He is aware that he is not imperfect, but incomplete. He knows that in himself some meaning has yet to be realized' (*RM*59). In primitive religion he 'tried to gain a perfect communion with the mysterious magic of Nature's forces through his own power of magic' (*RM*74: cf. ll.10–14 in the poem). In other words, tribal culture contains the seeds of higher culture and religion. Imperialism is the true barbarity, because it stamps out human potential. It is self-destructive as well as destructive. In *CU*103 Tagore writes: 'The blindness of contempt is more hopeless than the blindness of ignorance; for contempt kills the light which ignorance merely leaves unignited.' The poem ends with a terrifying and ever more pertinent vision of the consequences of 'the blindness of contempt', of modern civilization killing its own light.

10–19 Strictly, all the tenses in these lines are past continuous, implying that Africa *was doing* all the things described at the time of the arrival of her European colonists.

11 lit., 'you were gathering the secrets of the impenetrable'.

14 'worked spells' – *mantra jāgācchila*: 'was awaking mantras'.

14 'unconscious' – *cetanātīt*: 'beyond consciousness'. This compound may be a straight translation of Freudian 'unconscious'; or it may carry the meaning: 'mind that has not yet developed full consciousness; half-consciousness'.

19 The metaphor is of Śiva's *tāṇḍava* dance of destruction, and the frenetic drumming that accompanies it.

1937–1941

The Borderland – 9 (p. 107)

Poem No. 9 from *prāntik* (The Borderland), 1938

In September 1937 Tagore suddenly fell seriously ill. Although he recovered, his years of touring were at an end. His last foreign tour had been in 1932 – to Iran and Iraq; but he had followed it with tours of India and Ceylon with a troupe from Visva-Bharati, staging his dance-dramas to raise funds for the university.

The untitled poems in 'The Borderland' were written as he convalesced from the illness. They are all in tightly controlled, unrhymed verse, with equality of line-length. Through symbolism, imagery and rhythm they communicate with uncanny power states of consciousness beyond or beneath the normal. The phrase in the first line of Poem No. 9 describes the atmosphere of the book as a whole: *abasanna cetanār go-dhūli-belāy*, 'in the cow-dust-time (dusk) of exhausted consciousness' – the borderland between life and death.

This poem is a kind of diminuendo and crescendo combined. On the one hand, the gradual ebbing of consciousness towards a state of fusion 'with endless night', *antahīn tamisrāy*, l.15; on the other a steady mounting movement towards the climactic quotation from the Īśā Upaniṣad: 'O Sun, withdraw thy rays, reveal thy exceeding beauty to me and let me realize that the Person who is there is the One who I am' (*RM*115; see also *P*72). Tagore always translated *puruṣ* as Person, and I have followed him in l.19. *kalyāṇatama*, the superlative adjective used in l.18, conveys goodness, health, grace, as well as kindness and beauty.

4 lit., 'its life-long store of memories under a painted cover'.

7–8 The sounds could include bells, chants, conches being blown.

14 'particles' – *bindu*: 'drops'.

16 'at the altar of the stars' – *nakṣatra-bedīr tale*: 'at the bottom of the *bedī* of the stars'. A *bedī* is a low platform on which an image of a deity might be mounted.

The Borderland – 10 (p. 107)

Poem No. 10 from *prāntik*, 1938

This poem is certainly not easy to understand in Bengali, but some of its paradoxes are elucidated by the great abundance of synonyms that Indian languages have. In l.3 Tagore uses one word for light, *alo*(*k*), and in l.5 another, *jyoti*. Ll.4–5 are literally 'the light (*ālok*) that is the light (*jyoti*) of the universal light (*jyoti*)'. Tagore is distinguishing between light as the opposite of dark and light as a metaphor for the primary energy of the universe. There is the same contrast in ll.6–8: 'hymn to light' (*ālok*)/'realm of light' (*jyoti*). *jyoti* is indeed a more elevated word than *ālo*, an Upaniṣadic word, with radiance or halo in it.

The poem is about spiritual unreadiness for death. One can take it to imply that Tagore has not yet reached that state of total serenity described in *S*21 as having been achieved by 'the Rishis of India'. He writes of them: 'They did not recognize any essential opposition between life and death, and they said with absolute assurance, "It is life that is death" . . . They knew that mere appearance and disappearance are on the surface, like waves on the sea, but life which is permanent knows no decay or diminution.' This is the 'serene image of the terrible' of l.14 of the poem. But such complete 'liberation of consciousness' (*S*20) was in many ways alien to Tagore, alien to his humanism and his belief in realization through action and love. In *S*123 he writes of Man's need constantly to defy death and transience by creating noble works: 'This *mahatī vinashṭiḥ – this great destruction* he cannot bear, and accordingly he toils and suffers in order that he may gain in stature by transcending his present, in order to become that which he is not.' And in *P*64, after quoting again from the Īśā Upaniṣad, he writes: 'Only by living life fully can you outgrow it. When the fruit has served its full term, drawing its juice from the branch as it dances with the wind and matures in the sun, then it feels in its core the call of the beyond and becomes ready for its career of a wider life.' This is the key to the meaning of ll.15–19. Meditation is not the only way to prepare for death: there is the way of work, creativity, the human counterpart to the creative *ānanda*, joy (l.17) of the universe itself (see *S*104).

10 'to the theatre of physical existence' – *jībaner raṅga-bhūme*: 'to the playground of life', *jīban* being understood as material, physical existence, and *raṅga-bhūmi* being the familiar Indian concept of the world as an arena for the *khelā* or *līlā* of different forces.

11 'spirit' – the word used is *caram*, the Ultimate, the reality described in ll.3–5.

13 'a rāga of silent wrath' – *niḥśabda bhairab naba-rāge*: *bhairab* means terrifying, awesome; is a name for Śiva in his awesome aspect; and is the name of a musical rāga. The phrase could mean 'in a silent new Bhairav rāga'. See Glossary.

Leaving Home (p. 108)

ghar-chāṛā from *sẽjuti* (The Evening Lamp), 1938

Life's approaching end dominates the poems in this volume, but in 'Leaving Home' the theme is not stated explicitly. Indeed I find this apparently straightforward poem remarkable for what it leaves unsaid, unresolved, indeterminate. Even its main character seems to exist outside the poem, though it describes his actions and feelings. Wider knowledge of Tagore would lead one to see in the poem certain characteristic antitheses: between an inhuman world of professional duty (l.6) and a human world of comfort and relationship (ll.7,55); between the callous alarm-clock and taxi, and the 'play of life', *prāṇ-līlā*, recalled in ll.42–52; between darkness and light. Darkness itself is not attractive in the poem: it is associated with meaninglessness (l.21), uncertainty (l.35), suppression of *saṃsār* (l.42), which is human, social, domestic life. It is redeemed by the starlight of ll.61–3. This is the 'poetry of the stars' described in *P*59: 'the silent meeting of soul with soul, at the confluence of the light and the dark, where the infinite prints its kiss on the forehead of the finite, where we can hear the music of the Great I AM pealing from the grand organ of creation through its countless reeds in endless harmony'. The image of the morning-star gives the poem connotations of spiritual as well as physical journeying – though again, nothing is explicit. Its realistic details, its combination of mystery and ordinariness, uncertainty and calm, show the inseparability of worldly and spiritual life. *RM*108 provides further insight into the poem: 'In the night we stumble over things and become acutely conscious of their individual separateness. But the day reveals the great unity which embraces them. The man whose inner vision is bathed in an illumination of his consciousness at once realizes the spiritual unity reigning supreme over all differences.' In ll.8–21 we have the 'individual separateness' of objects in the night; in ll.42–52 we have inner, daylight vision.

8 'all' – *gṛha-sajjā yata*: 'all the household effects, accoutrements'.
14 'spattered' – *dāg-dharā*: 'marked', i.e. with the silvering worn away, 'foxed'.
24 'aloof' – *udāsīn*: see notes to 'Unyielding'.
53 'weed' – *pānā*: see Glossary.
60 'dark' – *nibiṛ-ā̃dhār-ḍhālā*: 'poured over with dense darkness'.

In the Eyes of a Peacock (p. 109)

mayūrer dṛṣṭi from *ākāś-pradīp* (The Lamp in the Sky), 1939

This book consists mainly of poems of reminiscence or reflection on a life's work. Although Tagore's personal feelings are seldom absent from his poetry, it is not often that he writes as directly and naturally about a real-life experience as in 'In the Eyes of a Peacock'. It paints a vivid picture of the 78-year-old poet enjoying what leisure his fame and responsibilities allowed him, and enjoying the company of the girl called 'Sunayanī' in the poem. I have been given two suggestions as to her identity: either she is Maitraye Devi, author of a well-known book of reminiscences (see p. 168), who was about twenty-five when the poem was written; or she is Nandini, adopted daughter of Tagore's son Rathindranath, and therefore likely to address Tagore as *dādā-maśay* (Grandfather, l.49).

Early morning was always Tagore's favourite time of day. In *RM*99 he describes how even as a child he would rush out at dawn into the garden of the Jorasanko house to 'drink in at a draught the overflowing light and peace of those silent hours'. The key-word of the poem is once again *udāsīn*, indifferent, l.20, or *audasīnya*, indifference, l.26; or associated words like *bairāgya*, apathy towards worldly interests, l.42. Like 'Earth', the poem presents a vision of personal littleness and extinction in the face of the vast, impersonal forces of Nature. But it is transmuted into a much calmer, mellower form: the ruthless vastness of Earth is reduced to a peacock's stare. This mellowness makes the poem less disturbing than 'Earth'. But there is further reason: whereas the 'true value' that Tagore hoped to achieve in his life was left bafflingly undefined in that poem, here both his own poetic endeavours and the 'poet of Mohenjodaro' are given sudden value and meaning by the spark of love (l.67). How this happens is a mystery, but it is an experience common to most people at times in their lives. All Tagore's religious ideas have their roots in simple, common human experience. The potential for the miracle was already there in ll.1–39, which evoke peace and beauty as well as *audasīnya*. In *R*216 Tagore writes that when he was able to put his own self in the background, he 'could see the world in its own true aspect. And that aspect has nothing of triviality in it, it is full of beauty and joy.' By seeing his own writings as nothing more than 'autumnal flocks of insects' (l.45), Tagore has already surrendered self: Sunayanī completes a circle he has already half-drawn for himself. 'Love is what brings together and inseparably connects both the act of abandoning and that of receiving' (*S*114).

19 lit., 'with the meaningless restlessness of its vitality (*prāṇ*)'.
45 lit., 'like the flocks of insects at the *dīpābalī* of Śiva'. This is a reference to the insects that cluster round the lamps put out during the autumn festival of Diwali (see Glossary).
51,52 Sunayanī means 'lovely-eyed'. Tagore puns on the verb *śunā*, to listen.
76–8 In Hindu mythology the sun sets behind a mountain called *astācal* and rises above a mountain called *udayācal*; these words are used in the normal Bengali expressions for sunset and sunrise, and are exploited in these lines. Lit., 'Poet of Mohenjodaro, your evening star has crossed the *astācal* and has climbed to the crest of my life's *udayācal*.'

New Birth (p. 111)

naba-jātak from ***naba-jātak*** (The Newly Born), 1940

Tagore wrote this book in horror and agony at a world plunging itself into war again, and this short opening poem sets the tone: deep gloom combined with hope against hope of a new dawn, a new civilization to come. Sometimes that hope and faith is defiant: here it is as vulnerable and yet as indestructible as the 'message of reassurance' that each new-born child seems to bring into the world. Many passages in Tagore's English prose writings can be quoted in relation to this poem. See *CU*26, where he writes in hope of 'a new age . . . the sudden guest who comes as the messenger of emancipation'; *CU*52 on Kālidāsa's *Kumāra-sambhava*, relevant to the 'birth of the hero' hoped for in ll.11–13; *CU*129 on Christ; and *P*104: 'Yes, the divine in man [cf. l.9] is not afraid of success, or of organization; it does not believe in the precautions of prudence and dimensions of power. Its strength is not in the muscle or the machine, neither in cleverness of policy nor in callousness of conscience; it is in its spirit of perfection. The today scoffs at it, but it has the eternity of tomorrow on its side. In appearance it is helpless like a babe, but its tears of suffering in the night set in motion all the unseen powers of heaven, the Mother in all creation is awakened.'

1 *nabīn āgantuk*: lit., 'New Comer, New Arrival'; unfortunately the first is awkward as two words in English, and the second is sentimental.

5–6 lit., 'What seat (*āsan*) has the playground of life (*jībaner raṅga-bhūmi*) spread out for you?'

Flying Man (p.112)

pakṣi-mānab from *naba-jātak*, 1940

Another poem of horror and frail hope. Its theme is likely to strike a chord in any sensitive observer of the modern world, and has no doubt inspired many unpublished poems by unknown poets. Tagore was never afraid to write poems on subjects that poets more worldly than he would leave to the naïve amateur.

Tagore's feeling for the sky is attested in numerous poems (cf. 'Palm-tree'). In *RM*92 he associates it with freedom and human aspiration, and writes of how he has always been 'inspired by the tropical sky with its suggestion of an uttermost Beyond'. 'Flying Man' is as much about the Bengal sky as about birds or aeroplanes: about the *prāṇ*, life (l.10), expressed in its clouds and winds, and the peace of its vast expanses (l.16). The aeroplane is nothing less than a symbol of the entire nationalist, mechanical, self-seeking civilization that appeared to be meeting its nemesis at the time of writing and which Tagore felt was essentially at odds with the *prāṇ-deb*, life-divinity (l.25). See *N*43,60 and above all the passionate rhetoric of *N*92, which I have quoted in the Introduction to this book (p. 29).

I wanted in my translation to equal the powerful, rhymed, three-lined verses of the original, and have therefore had to deal freely with its syntax in places; but the Bengali syntax is sometimes rather imprecise, guided as much by rhythmic effects as by meaning.

Tagore had flown to Iran in 1932, and had reported ill of the experience in his diary of the tour. He wrote prophetically of the appalling detachment from moral involvement that aeroplanes would bring to warfare.

1 'Satanic machine' – *yantra-dānab*: 'mechanical demon'.

10–12 lit., 'Their *līlā* is bound to the rhythm of the wind; their life (*prāṇ*) and their songs are tuned to the music of the sky.'

28–30 lit., 'Proclaiming its incompatibility with the sky, it roars with a harsh voice, shattering the winds.'

35–6 lit., 'Disturbance (like) impending thunder does not obey any barrier anywhere.'

37–9 lit., 'Hatred and envy, lighting the flame of death, spread universal horror through great destruction in the skies.'

43 'at the end of this history' – *e itihāser śeṣ adhyāy-tale*: 'at the bottom of the last chapter of this history'. The end of an era is implied, not the end of the world.

Railway Station (p. 113)

iṣṭeśan from *naba-jātak*, 1940

It is easy to misjudge this poem, to see its insights as superficial or facile. But when we put it in the context of Tagore's general ideas its purpose becomes clear: the dissatisfaction it may leave in its readers is an important part of its meaning.

The core of the poem lies in the vision of the coming and going of the station as nothing more than *calacchabi* (1.12) or *calti chabi* (1.49), 'moving pictures': i.e. an insubstantial, unreal, arbitrary sequence of painted images. We often find in Tagore's writing that painting is associated with the unreal. In 'The Golden Boat' I noted that the image of the village as a painting helped to contribute to the mood of alienation – world and self separated from the reality of God and soul. In 'Across the Sea' the mysterious, unreal horse stands 'motionless like an image in a picture' (l.14). On the opening page of *R*, Tagore distinguishes between the 'set of pictures' that memory paints and Life itself. What we have in 'Railway Station' is a vision of life with its essential reality left out – hence its tone of alienation, pointlessness, ennui (the two opening lines convey not any real love or involvement but boredom: the speaker has nothing better to do than come to the station morning and evening). We could call the absent reality God or Brahman and leave it at that. But some passages from Tagore's prose shed further light. In *RM*154 he writes: 'What is evident in this world is the endless procession of moving things; but what is to be realized is the supreme Truth by which the human world is permeated. We must never forget today that a mere movement is not valuable in itself, that it may be a sign of a dangerous form of inertia.' Inertia is indeed the mood of 'Railway Station', though it appears to be about movement. In *S*99 Tagore compares the rhythm, expansion, contraction, movement and pause of 'the world-poem' to a railway station: 'but the station platform is not our own home' – and we will only feel at home if we are aware of the underlying unity or perfection that the rhythm expresses. In *N*147 he writes of the 'suppression of higher humanity in crowd minds': in 'Railway Station' we see people as crowds, individuality suppressed. Thus *khelā* in this poem (l.29) appears in its negative aspect, the meaningless play of the world when we separate it from God (see notes to 'Unending Love', 'The Golden Boat'). The poem gives us an image and definition of spiritual failure.

4–5 The words for flow-tide (*ujān*) and ebb-tide (*bhāṭā*) – as in the big rivers of Bengal – are applied to the up and down trains.

12–15 lit., 'This image of pictures moving brings to (my) mind a language of perpetual coming together and perpetual forgetting, nothing but coming and going.'

19–20 lit., 'Behind this (phenomenon) lies the urgency of joys and sorrows, losses and gains agitating them violently.' I have had to interpret these lines somewhat to make them fit with what precedes them.

23 i.e., no one can bear to wait to let others on first.

50–51 My translation is elliptical here. Lit., 'Morning and evening I watch the moving pictures of life, with these I remain alone in the coming and going of the station.'

Freedom-bound (p. 115)

mukta-pathe from *sānāi*, 1940

sānāi, named after the reed instrument that is particularly associated with weddings in India, is a quieter book than *naba-jātak*, with the poet more at ease with himself. Many of the poems were written in the hills – in Almora and Kalimpong, or at Mongpu, where Tagore enjoyed peace and happiness as the guest of Maitraye Devi and her family. (An English translation of her reminiscences, *Tagore by Fireside*, was published in Calcutta in 1961.) But we shall see in 'Bombshell' and 'Last Tryst' that dark notes were not absent completely.

'Freedom-bound', like 'Railway Station', has more to it than first appears. It is an unusual poem for Tagore, but at the same time very characteristic. The title means 'on the path to *mukti*, freedom'. In *CU*201 Tagore defines *mukti* as 'the one abiding ideal in the religious life of India . . . the deliverance of man's soul through its union in *ananda* with the universe'. For Tagore this ideal was dualistic (see notes to 'Unyielding'): utter extinction of the self was not attractive to him, because it was incompatible with Love. The *mukti* of 'Freedom-bound' is *mukti* through love, a liberation that is emphasized by the unconventionality of that love and by the gypsy-beloved's free-roving nature. A friend of mine criticized my English title for its 'Empsonian ambiguity'; but curiously enough its ambiguity, which had not occurred to me until he pointed it out, is in perfect keeping with Tagore's conception of love. See *S*115 where Tagore writes: 'Bondage and liberation are not antagonistic in love. For love is most free and at the same time most bound'; and in *RM*190, Tagore quotes a Baul song (see Glossary) which sings of the ultimacy of love, a state from which there can in fact be no *mukti*: 'It goes on blossoming for ages, the soul-lotus, in which I am bound, as well as thou, without escape. There is no end to the opening of its petals, and the honey in it has so much sweetness that thou, like an enchanted bee, canst never desert it, and therefore thou art bound, and I am, and *mukti* is nowhere.'

Might that honey-image lie behind the 'lotus honey' carried by the gypsy-woman in 'Freedom-bound'? Certainly the Baul sect had a great influence on the heterodox, fetterless, itinerant characters that crop up frequently in Tagore's writing. For further possible influences, see the description of the wandering mad woman in *CU*77, of 'Peari, the old scullery-maid' in *R*262, and a recollection of a childish escapade in *R*48.

3–4 'scourge of all proprieties' – *bhadra-niyam-bhaṅga*: 'breaker of polite rules' – not quite so strongly put as in my translation.

9–10 Not easy lines to translate literally, but perhaps: 'the respectable people of the village, who are always out for a hard bargain'. Buying and selling, 'the noise of the markets' (*P*107) is often an image of worldliness and materialism in Tagore.

13 'form' – the word *rūp* also means beauty.

18 *tumi pathik-badhū*: 'you traveller-bride'.

22 *bhāber sahaj khelā*: 'the simple play of feeling'. *bhāb*, feeling, also means 'loving rapport', a mutuality and equality of affection.

39–40 lit., 'I lose the way to the Brahmins' houses when I see you'; but the lines have to be taken metaphorically.

43 'hem' – *ā̃cal*: the loose end of the sari.

Yakṣa (p. 116)

yakṣa from *sānāi*, 1940

This poem should be read in conjunction with 'The *Meghadūta*', and Tagore's essay on Kālidāsa's masterpiece which I have included in Appendix A. It is peculiarly difficult to translate. I found myself defeated in any attempt to match the rhymes of the Bengali with English rhymes or half-rhymes. The poem is essentially and deliberately paradoxical. In ll.1–10 we have the paradoxical union of joy and longing, beauty and pain in the Yakṣa's yearning for his beloved, which Tagore tries to match in his imagery of rain that is 'heart-rending' and 'shadow-cast' but beautiful as well. In ll.15–16 there is a complex image involving a *ṭīkā*, which is a commentary on another classic poem: the *ṭīkā* is defined as being written in *mandākrānta* metre, the metre of Kālidāsa's *Meghadūta*; so the *Meghadūta*, though a poem in its own right and not a *ṭīkā*, in another sense *is* a *ṭīkā* in which joy comments on sorrow (lit., 'This world (universe) is its poem: in its *mandākrānta* metre a distant presage of joy writes a commentary on a vast backdrop of sorrow'). In ll.19–30 we have the paradox that though the Yakṣa's Beloved, pining in Alakā, represents an ideal, it is a sterile ideal, its very perfection is inarticulate, its immortality (l.30) is a grief greater than any mortal grief. The poem thus has three main ideas: the combination of joy and sorrow in the Yakṣa's yearning; the link made between that combination and the 'fire of creation' itself; and the view that the Yakṣa's state of imperfect yearning for perfection is preferable to the perfection itself. These three main ideas take us into the very heart of Tagore's religious and artistic thought. In *CU*35, in the chapter on the Creative Ideal, Tagore writes: 'this world is a creation . . . in its centre there is a living idea which reveals itself in an eternal symphony, played on innumerable instruments, all keeping perfect time.' This 'living idea' can be identified with the Yakṣa's ideal, with the Beloved in Alakā, with the 'joy' of ll.6 and 16; but the revelation of the idea through time and space, the unrolling of the world-poem, involves separation from that ideal, the pain of yearning for it. Joy and pain are thus an inextricable reflection of the creative *khelā* of the universe (the word is not used in the poem, but the idea is there): 'The sacrifice which is at the heart of creation is both joy and pain at the same moment' (*CU*40). Each needs the other. Hence the paradox that the immortal Beloved/Alakā ideal, which ought to be unalloyed joy, would actually be more unbearable than mortality, since it lacks the power to express itself through pain and yearning (at the end of my Introduction, p.38, I described the ideal as 'equivocal': here we see why). And hence Tagore's dualism; for perfection unable to enter into a relationship with imperfection would be torment indeed ('the terrible weight of an unopposed life-force' of *R*259). Thus in l.31 the Yakṣa beats at his Beloved's door *prabhu-bare*, 'by the boon or grace of God'. The Yakṣa is advantaged by his very mortality: his freedom to yearn is a gift from God.

10 'accompanies' – *pade pade . . . mele*: 'matches its steps to, flies in harmony with'. The sentence also includes *pathe pathe*: 'from one (flight) path to another'.

14 lit., 'to close the gap with perfection (between itself and perfection)'.

23 she is worn out with waiting *āgantuk pantha-lāgi*: 'for the coming traveller'.

Last Tryst (p. 117)

śeṣ abhisār from *sānāi*, 1940

Baffling though this poem is, I have no doubt that it is a *jīban-debatā* poem, and should be related to 'On the Edge of the Sea'. The 'coming storm' of l.2 could be associated with contemporary world events, or with the approach of death ('a season new to me', l.36). But the purpose of the poem is to reveal the mysterious, potent workings of the *jīban-debatā* through all experience, including death. In youth (l.15) it prompted poems of joy; now its appearance and promptings are different – but it is still the same *jīban-debatā*, still the poet's strange guide and bride.

I do not believe it is really possible in the last analysis to separate the *jīban-debatā* from God or Brahman himself: what the concept stands for is the mystery of the way in which God reveals himself in human life and experience. In l.19 the word which I have translated as 'indescribably lovely' is *anirbacanīya*, 'inexpressible'. In *RM*186 Tagore uses the word to describe the Supreme Unity, or God, and translates it as 'ineffable'. The strange destiny or unity guiding his life, the unity of a work of art or of Brahman himself – all these are essentially the same for Tagore, and are 'ineffable'. In *CU*17 he writes that in Art 'we forget the claims of necessity, the thrift of usefulness, – the spires of our temples try to kiss the stars and the notes of our music to fathom the depth of the ineffable'. The ineffable works through everything – pain, death, even a whole world 'broken into chaos'. The moral problems that arise from such thinking did not escape Tagore (in *RM*107 he admitted: 'Frankly, I acknowledge that I cannot satisfactorily answer any questions about evil'); but his deepest inner experience demanded it. His views on the problem of evil in *S* ch. III were true to his real feelings, and to the mainstream of Indian religious thought.

13–14 'in the guise of a storm' – ***duryoge bhūmikāy***: the words could also mean 'as presage or earnest of a bad or dangerous time', or simply 'with a storm (in the background)'.

19 'jasmine' – ***yūthikā***: see Glossary.

25–7 lit., 'What signs (*iṅgit*) the briefly shining flame of lightning reveals in your face! How novel its language!'

41 'palace of silence' – ***nīraber sabhāṅgan-tale***: 'in this (royal) courtyard of silence'.

Injury (p. 118)

apaghāt from *sānāi*, 1940

The title of the poem is hard to translate precisely into English: it means a sudden blow that is accidental but also somehow fated. Though written at Kalimpong, the mention of Nadiyā in l.4 places the poem in north Bengal. Modest and commonplace though it is, only Tagore could have written it, with the security of its rural scene deftly evoked by seemingly casual detail, and the intrusion of pain at the horrors of the world in the last two lines (the Russians attacked Finland in November 1939, seizing territory and setting up a puppet government). The poem is a comment on a world made smaller by modern communications; but it also presents a more perennial conflict. On the one hand we have the workings of a harmonious universe through the rhythms of human social life and the interplay of man and Nature (the *prāṇ-līlā* described in ll.42–52 of 'Leaving Home'); on the other we have human actions and sufferings at odds with that harmony (ll.28–9). In *R*219 Tagore's maturing consciousness sees in the movements of passers-by 'that amazingly beautiful greater dance which goes on at this very moment throughout the world of men'. The dance includes 'two smiling youths nonchalantly going their way, the arm of one on the other's shoulder' that are like the 'two friends' in 'Injury'. How is one to reconcile the coexistence of this dance of humanity with the constant interruptions and injuries suffered by it? The *koel*-bird in l.27 seems to express the uneasiness of the paradox.

16 There are grammatical indications that the friends are male.
25 'balm' – *neśākhāni*: 'the intoxication', but *bhā̃ṭi*-flowers have medicinal qualities. See Glossary.

The Sick-bed – 6 (p. 119)

Poem No. 6 in *rog-śayyāy*, 1940

The poems in Tagore's last four books are nearly all unrhymed and free in rhythm, with a straight margin. All ostentatious artistry is stripped away: the language is unadorned – sometimes austere, sometimes conversational. The poet speaks in his own undisguised voice: there are no masks or disguises. Tagore went on writing almost to his last hour, dictating poems when he became too weak to write.

The illness that resulted in the poems in *rog-śayyāy* and its sequel *ārogya* had struck Tagore at Kalimpong in September 1940. He was taken to Calcutta, where he was nursed for two months. '*The Sick-Bed – 6*' was written in Calcutta, in Jorosanko, the Tagore family home. The 'day-break sparrow' is a symbol of many things: of the pure spirit of life, *prāṇ* (used in l.54); of freedom from restriction and convention; of the spirit of whimsy and playfulness that dominates Tagore's late books of nonsense-rhymes for children and which clearly brought him relief from anxiety (see notes to '*On My Birthday – 20*'); of amateurism; of light. The last two are especially important. No one was more dedicated to work than Tagore, but professionalism, as defined in his prose writings, he disliked. See *CU*145 where he writes of the rigidity, specialization and power-hunger that goes with professionalism, or *N*10 where he writes of how women suffer 'because man is driven to professionalism, producing wealth for himself and others, continually turning the wheel of power for his own sake or for the sake of the universal officialdom'. Conventional education merely prepared people for professions: Tagore tried in his own educational theory and practice to correct this tendency. The sparrow is gloriously amateur. It is also associated with dawn, with light: the whole poem leads up to what is really a prayer for light (ll.53–8), an expression in the simplest possible terms of the Gāyatrī, the Vedic prayer for self-realization that Tagore, as a Brahmin, was taught at his sacred-thread ceremony (see *R*72 and *RM*92), and which he used as a mantra throughout his life. The sparrow brings the 'assurance' that comes each day with the dawn light (*S*89): it shows that it is available to all, for free – 'We do not have to run to the grocer's shop for our morning light; we open our eyes and there it is . . .' (*S*148). You do not have to be Kālidāsa, or Rabindranath Tagore. We are all, potentially, 'children of light' (*P*31).

11 lit., 'they get *bakśiś* from the poets'.

14 *ostādi*, 'musical mastery', is used in the original here: 'he displays such *ostādi* that . . .' Cf. 'Broken Song', where the old singer Baraj Lāl is addressed as *ustād* by Pratāp Rāy (see Glossary).

15 'applause' – *bāhabā*: the standard expression of appreciation and admiration (*bāḥ*!). Cf. notes to 'Broken Song'.

29–30 The word used in the original, *bāynā*, means advance money paid under a contract: the sparrow is not employed as a professional dancer by the Spring.

The Sick-bed – 21 (p. 121)

Poem No. 21 in *rog-śayyāy*, 1940

Soon after writing the last poem, Tagore was allowed back to Santiniketan; this poem was written there at the end of November 1940.

I have already referred in my notes to 'The Wakening of Siva', 'Deception' and 'Earth' to Tagore's views on the limitations of a purely scientific picture of the world (not that he was opposed to science: he was always keenly interested in it); at first reading, this poem would seem to be on this theme. The scientific account of the universe (ll.8–13) excludes the beauty of the rose, and because of this breaks up the unity of reality into constituent elements. See *P*50 on the 'fatal touch' of science; and *RM*125 where he uses 'that mystery-play, the rose' as an example of the unity and beauty that science ignores. But usually in such passages Tagore speaks of the 'impersonality' of science, as opposed both to the individual human personality that perceives 'the reality of the world' and 'that central personality, in relation to which the world is a world' (*P*50). But is the vision of universe as rose in ll.20–30 a personal one? Human personality is strangely absent both from the seer and the seen – it is not at all like Binu's vision of 'universal grace' in 'Deception', or 'the harmony of the stars', linked to human love, in 'Guest'.

It seems to me that there are two possible ways of reading this poem. One is to see its vision of the universe as personalized by the fact that the rose has been put by Tagore's bedside by a loving hand. See my notes to 'Gift' and the passage from *RM*125 about 'the language of love' expressed in a rose. The other is to see the poem as closer to transcendentalism than to the dualism of the Religion of Man. In *RM*191 Tagore distinguishes his religion from 'the tendency of the Indian mind ... towards that transcendentalism which does not hold religion to be ultimate but rather to be a means to a further end. This end consists in the perfect liberation of the individual in the universal spirit across the furthest limits of humanity itself. Such an extreme form of mysticism may be explained to my Western readers by its analogy in science. For science may truly be described as mysticism in the realm of material knowledge.' Science, by going beyond the world of personality and appearances, brings a 'freedom of spirit' similar to that sought by Indian mystics through the ages: both science and mysticism can produce 'the purest feeling of disinterested delight'. Such a feeling is not present in '*The Sick-Bed – 21*', for Tagore is not a mystic: rather there is humble wonder at a universe which may indeed be as impersonal and amoral as scientists and mystics perceive it to be, but which is nevertheless sublimely beautiful in that very impersonality. The poem seems at first to be about the limitations of science; but by the end, if we follow this second interpretation, it is about the poetry of science.

4 'through cyclic time' – *yug-yugānter ābartane*: 'through the whirl or revolution of age after age'. Hindu perception of the cyclic nature of time and world-history and Western evolutionary theory seem to be combined in this phrase.

5 'final beauty' – *saundaryer pariṇāme*: 'to the end-state of beauty'.

19 lit., 'I, a poet, do not know debate, argument (*tarka*)'.

Recovery – 10 (p. 121)

Poem No. 10 from *ārogya*, 1941

This poem was written in February 1941. In 'Injury' the paradox of two antagonistic realities in the world – the dance of human life and the constant shocks and injuries to that dance – was presented without any attempt at resolution. In this poem, Tagore resolves the paradox by associating the former with ordinary people through the ages, and the latter with rulers, states and power. It is a distinction that one can feel particularly acutely in India, where the massive rural population carries on with their ancient way of life regardless of who may be in power over them and with very little sense of belonging to a nation, and where many empires have risen and fallen. An important word in the poem is *jāl*, net or web, which is used in ll.13 and 27: it is often in Tagore's writing associated with what is illusory or transitory (cf. 'Across the Sea', l.87, where the 'ancient Brahmin' draws a *rekhār jāl*, 'a network of lines'), and here Pāṭhān, Moghul and British empires are seen, for all their cruelty and exploitation, as nothing more than *jāl, māyā*, compared to the reality and continuity of the life and work of the common people of India. The poem is convincing, as its plain phrases build up to the climax of ll.55–9, and Tagore's feeling for the common people of India was genuine too, proved by years of effort at Santiniketan and Sriniketan and many short stories and poems. His hatred of nationalism had its roots in it, for anyone who knows India knows that there is indeed an 'India devoid of all politics, the India of no nations' (*N*7). But the poem is not propaganda against empires and states, rather a poignant profession of faith in their ultimate irrelevance. See the rhetoric of *N*46, a similar profession of faith, written during an earlier World War.

29–30 lit., 'will not leave the slightest trace on the courses of the planets'.
36 *mānuṣer nitya prayojane*: 'by man's eternal necessities'.
57–9 lit., 'Sorrow and joy, day and night, raise the sonorous sound of the great mantra of Life (*jībaner mahā-mantra-dhvani*)'.

Recovery – 14 (p. 123)

Poem No. 14 in *ārogya*, 1941

For eight months Tagore lived an invalid existence in Uttarāyaṇ, his house at Santiniketan. A local pariah dog became a welcome visitor and inspired this poem, written in December 1940. It reconfirms the Religion of Man, and though definition or description of that religion remains difficult, the image of the 'faithful dog' helps to convey it to one's feelings and imagination. In *RM*143 Tagore writes: 'From the time when Man became truly conscious of his own self he also became conscious of a mysterious spirit of unity which found its manifestation through him in his society . . . Somehow Man has felt that this comprehensive spirit of unity has a divine character which could claim the sacrifice of all that is individual in him, that in it dwells his highest meaning transcending his limited self, representing his best freedom.' Tagore goes on to refer to *dharma*, the Sanskrit word that sometimes has to be translated as 'religion', sometimes as 'justice', sometimes as 'duty to one's caste or station in life', but which Tagore saw as above all 'the virtue of a thing, the essential quality of it, for instance heat is the essential quality of fire, though in certain of its stages it may be absent' (*RM*144). The essential quality or *dharma* of man is thus revealed in self-sacrifice, subordination of individual desires to the needs and ideals of humanity as a whole. The dog's devotion directs the poet to that *dharma*, that *sampūrṇa mānuṣ* (l.10), that 'truth of the Supreme Man' (*RM*144). The poem does not explicitly go further, to Tagore's identification of human personality with the supreme personality governing the universe; but the full range of Tagore's religion is implicit in ll.14–15 (in *P*21 Tagore points to a translation difficulty here: 'the English word "consciousness" has not yet outgrown the cocoon stage of its scholastic inertia, therefore it is seldom used in poetry; whereas its Indian synonym "cetana" is a vital word and is of constant poetical use'); and the last line cannot be understood without it. The word that I have translated as 'meaning', following Tagore's phrase 'highest meaning' in the quotation from *RM*143 above, is *paricay*, which normally means 'acquaintance' or 'particulars about one's identity' – name, address and so on. Tagore is saying that the dog directs us to what human personality makes us acquainted with in the universe: i.e. it is through human personality, consciousness, love, self-sacrifice, creativity that we become acquainted with the personality of God himself. Thus 'the truth of the Universe is human truth' (*RM*222: conversation with Einstein). Human *dharma* is the *dharma* of the universe as a whole.

Dharma and canine fidelity are linked in a famous passage near the end of the Mahābhārata, when Yudhiṣṭhira, eldest of the five Pāṇḍava brothers, refuses to enter heaven without his dog Dhruba. Eventually the dog is allowed in, and turns out to be the god Dharma.

17 'humility' – *dīnatā*: the word means need, indigence, as well as humbleness.

19 lit., 'I cannot think what worth'; but the phrase is elliptical: it means 'having thought, I cannot see any limit to the worth'.

23 'in the universe' – *sṛṣṭi-mājhe*: 'in Creation, the created universe'.

On My Birthday – 20 (p. 124)

Poem No. 20 from *janma-dine*, 1941

Tagore's penultimate book includes some poems written before *rog-śayyāy* and *ārogya*. This remarkable poem dates from September 1940, just before Tagore fell ill. It is rhymed, but rhythm is free and lines varied in length. It is linked to the world of Tagore's paintings and to his late books of nonsense verse (*khāp-chāṛā*, 1937; *chaṛār chabi*, 1937; *se*, 1937; *galpasalpa*, 1941), and his late book of childhood reminiscence *chele-belā* (Boyhood Days), 1940. But I hope I may be forgiven for ending my selection with a poem in which exuberant imaginative creativity rather than wisdom is to the fore (see Introduction, p. 34, for my reasons for not translating any poems from Tagore's last book, *śeṣ lekhā* (Last Writings), 1941).

There are paradoxes in Tagore's thoughts about Law and about Mind, and they lie behind this poem. On the one hand, Law is an essential aspect of creation, of human artistic creation as much as Creation itself (cf. the central section of 'Brahmā, Viṣṇu, Śiva' in which Viṣṇu 'binds with his mace/All things to Law' – ll.40–41). Equally, Mind and Intellect are essential to the progress of man. But in both law and mind there are inherent dangers, of the abstract as opposed to the real, of a purely scientific view of the world rather than a moral or imaginative one, of the tyranny of scientific or political organization. In *N*34–46 Tagore writes of this, seeing the nation state (at the time of writing reaching its nemesis in the First World War) as the end-product of a process that does indeed start with the organization of reality in human language: 'The grammarian walks straight through all poetry and goes to the root of words without obstruction, because he is seeking not reality but law. When he finds the law, he is able to teach people how to master words. This is a power, – the power which fulfils some special usefulness, some particular need of man . . . This satisfaction of man's needs is a great thing. It gives him freedom in the material world . . . He can do things in a shorter time and occupies a larger space with more thoroughness of advantage . . . This progress of power attains more and more rapidity of pace. And, for the reason that it is a detached part of man, it soon outruns the complete humanity. The moral man remains behind, because it has to deal with the whole reality, not merely with the law of things, which is impersonal and therefore abstract.' Ll.26–35 should be read in the light of this, and the attraction of nursery and nonsense poetry as a reflection of Nature and consciousness undistorted by law stems from Tagore's doubts about language and the intellect. These doubts have a long history. In *R*222 Tagore writes of how the very meaning of words can interfere with poetry as an image of reality: 'That words have meanings is just the difficulty. That is why the poet has to turn and twist them in metre and verse, so that the meaning may be held somewhat in check, and the feeling allowed a chance to express itself.' Reality – especially the natural world – he tended to compare to music: see *S*142 when he writes in a vein very similar to ll.21–5 of '*On My Birthday – 20*', and says that 'the true poets . . . seek to express the universe in terms of music'.

The fantasy that Tagore voices in the poem is of language breaking its own constraints and thus coming close to music – as the meaningless jingles of nursery rhymes approach music. In *R*5 (and in the piece I have translated in Appendix B), he refers to the first line of poetry that made an impression on him, the nursery jingle: *bṛṣṭi paṛe ṭāpur-ṭupur, nadī ela bāṇ*, and implies that its appeal was essentially rhythmic and musical. '*On My Birthday – 20*' ends with another nonsense 'touchstone', the opening line of another Bengali nursery rhyme: *āgḍum bāgḍum ghoṛāḍum sāje*. In his book *lok-sāhitya* (Folk Literature – see Appendix B), Tagore says that the first part of the poem seems to be a description of a wedding procession, but of the first line itself he says: 'I do not know whether it has any clear meaning or not'. The meaninglessness is what is important (my own translation of the line was influenced by the resemblance of two of its words to the words for 'horse' and 'bridle').

But is the reality that nursery rhymes capture and which is reflected in the unconscious really totally arbitrary, lawless? No, because it is the stuff of Nature, the harmonious 'world-song' (*S*143), the miraculous blend of law and freedom, being and becoming, unity and diversity, infinite and finite that is the *khelā* of the universe itself. '*On My Birthday – 20*' is an attempt, not uncommon in twentieth-century art, to pierce through the order that our intellects impose on reality to some deeper order beyond, to 'the eternal law of harmony which is everywhere' (*S*141). Nothing is entirely free of it. Even nonsense rhymes have metre (l.39).

16 'mindless' – *manohīn*: 'without mind', i.e. at a stage of human development prior to the emergence of mind and consciousness.

13–14 lit., 'we who were born children of the earth's breathed-out wind's original music'.

22 *sṛṣṭir dhvanir mantra*: 'the mantras of the sounds of Creation'.

24 'approaching' – *digante*: 'on the horizon'. The 'sound' is probably wind, rather than thunder.

25 lit., 'that which awakes the huge delirium of dawn at the end of the night'.

27 'in complex webs of order' – *jaṭil niyam-sūtra-jāle*: 'in nets of threads of complex rule', i.e. rules of semantics and grammar. See notes to '*Recovery – 10*' for comment on *jāl*.

32 'material blocks' – *jaṛer acal bādhā*: 'unmoving barriers of matter'.

33 lit., 'roamed through their hard-to-penetrate invisible mystery-worlds'.

34 'word-armies' – the word for the epic armies of the Mahābhārata (*akṣauhinī*) is used here.

47 lit., 'they set up with their terrible noise a storm or roaring'.

49 lit., 'only their sound, only their postures have become maddened'. The word for 'posture' (*bhaṅgī*) was used in l.12.

*

Of the above poems, Tagore himself did translations of the following (with one exception, page references are to the standard Macmillan edition of his *Collected Poems and Plays*):

The Golden Boat	*The Fugitive* I.17 (p. 412)
Day's End	*The Fugitive* I.3 (p. 406)
Love's Question	*The Gardener* 32 (p. 112)
The Hero	*The Crescent Moon* (p. 78)
Death-wedding	*The Gardener* 81 (p. 144)
Arrival	*Gitanjali* 51 (p. 24)
Highest Price	*The Crescent Moon* (p. 86)
The Conch	*Fruit-Gathering* 35 (p. 191)
Shah-Jahan	*Lover's Gift* 1 (p. 7 in the original edition; not included in the *Collected Poems and Plays*)
Gift	*Lover's Gift* 2 (p. 255)

Grandfather's Holiday	*The Fugitive* III.12 (p. 433)
Guest	No. 72 in the 2nd edition of *Poems*, a collection published by Visva-Bharati in 1943
Question	*The Fugitive* (p. 450)
Africa	No. 98 in the 1st Edition of *Poems*, 1942

Appendix A

The following essay on Kālidāsa's *Meghadūta* was written in 1890, some eighteen months after the poem in *mānasī*, and was published in *prācīn sāhitya* (Ancient Literature), 1907.

Not merely a temporal but an eternal gulf seems to separate us from the great slice of ancient India – stretching from the Rāmagiri to the Himalayas – through which life's stream flowed in the form of the *mandākrānta*[1] metre of the *Meghadūta*. That Daśārṇa in whose woods hedges of *ketakī*-flowers blossomed, whose house-crows busied themselves with nest-building in village-shrines on the eve of the new year, in whose bordering *jambu*-groves fruit ripened almost to the darkness of black clouds, where has it gone? And the old villagers of Avantī telling stories of Udayana and Vāsavadattā, where are they? And what of Ujjayinī on the banks of the Śiprā? Certainly it had immense beauty, immense wealth, but our memories are not loaded with detailed descriptions of it: we can get a whiff of the incense of the townswomen's hairdressing wafting from the windows of its palaces; we can have a sense in our minds of the empty streets of the huge, deserted city and its great stillness when the doves were asleep on its pinnacles in the dark night; we can see faintly like a slim shadow the lonely Beloved[2] pacing with anxious steps and quaking heart through the darkness of the empty corridors of that shuttered, sleeping palace; and we long to be able to place just a little light – like the thread of gold in a whetstone – near her feet.

How beautiful are the names of the rivers and mountains and cities of that stretch of ancient India! Avantī, Vidiśā, Ujjayinī; Vindhya, Kailāsa, Devagiri; Revā, Śiprā, Vetravatī. There is such beauty and dignity and purity in the names. The times seem to have deteriorated since then: in their language, manners and mentality there seems to be an ageing, a corruption. The names we use have deteriorated accordingly. I feel that if only there were still some path by which we could return to Avantī and Vidiśā, or the banks of the Revā, Śiprā or Nirvindhyā rivers, then we would gain deliverance from the mean and ugly clamour all around us today.

Therefore the Yakṣa's cloud as it flies above mountains and rivers and cities is accompanied by the reader's long sigh of distress at separation. We are cut

1. See notes to 'Yakṣa' (p. 169).
2. The Beloved is called an *abhisāriṇī*, one who waits for a tryst. The word immediately reminds Bengali readers of Rādhā pining for Kṛṣṇa. See *Vaiṣṇava* in the Glossary.

off from the poet's India, from its village women whose love-softened eyes were innocent of seductive eyebrow movements, and from its townswomen whose alluring glances darted up like swarms of bees from heavily-lashed dark eyes versed in such movements. We cannot send a messenger other than the poet's cloud to anyone there now.

I remember that some English poet has written that men are like separate small islands, with a sea of innumerable salt-tears dividing them. When we look at each other from a long way off, then we feel that once we lived in a single great country; but now through somebody's curse the grief of separation foams up between us. When we look from this sea-girdled petty present towards the shore of that past stretch of land described by the poet, then we feel as if a link ought to have stayed between us and the garland-making women who gathered flowers in the *yūthī*-groves on the banks of the Śiprā river, the old men in the courtyards of Avantī who told stories of Udayana, and the travelling exiles who pined for their own wives whenever they saw the first clouds of Áṣāṛh. There is a profound human unity connecting us, but a cruel temporal gulf. Through the grace of the poet, that past time has reached its fullest expression in the city of Alakā in all its immeasurable beauty; we send our own imaginary *Meghadūta* there from our present, alienated, mortal world.

But it is not just a matter of past and present: in each of us there is an unfathomable sense of separation. That Person with whom we long to be united dwells on the unreachable shore of her own Mānasa lake; only our Imagination can be dispatched there; there is no way in which we can arrive there corporeally. Here I am and there you are; there is an infinite gulf between us – who can cross it? Who can gain a sight of that most beloved, indestructible Being dwelling at the centre of infinity? Today in our confusion of mind and body, light and dark, in the hurtling stream of life and death, we can catch a slender scent of her only through language, feeling, intimation. If a southern breeze comes to me from you, this is my good fortune, and the most that anyone can expect in this cut-off world.

bhittvā sadhyaḥ kisalaya-puṭān deva-dāru-drumāṇāṃ
ye tat-kṣīra-sruti-surabhayo dakṣiṇena pravṛttāḥ
āliṅgyante guṇavati mayā te tuṣārādri-vātāḥ
pūrvaṃ spṛṣṭaṃ yadi kila bhaved aṅgam ebhis taveti[3]

3. Kālidāsa's *Meghadūta* II.44

O my perfect one, those winds
off the Himalayas that suddenly open
the budding deodar shoots and now blow
southward scented with the ooze of their resin,
I hug close to myself, thinking
maybe they have touched your body.

(trans. Leonard Nathan, University of California Press, 1976)

Alluding to these words of eternal separation, a Vaiṣṇava poet sang: *dūhu kole dūhu kā̃de biccheda bhābiyā.*[4]

We are each of us standing alone on a deserted mountain-top looking northwards: before us, sky and cloud and the lovely natural sight of Revā and Śiprā and Avantī and Ujjayinī – a picture of extravagant joy, beauty and delight that reminds us that it will not allow us to approach: it excites us with yearning, unceasingly. Such is the distance between us two Beings.

But I feel as though at one time we were together in one mental realm[5] from which we have been exiled. Thus the Vaiṣṇava poet writes: *hiyāra bhitara haite ke kaila bāhira.*[6] Why did this happen? That Person who was part of my mind, why is she outside it now? I know that your place is not there! Balarām Dās says: *tẽi balarāmer pahu cita nahe sthira.*[7] Beings who were once united in one all-pervading single mind are all outside it today. So when we and that Person look at each other our hearts cannot be still: they are afflicted with *viraha*,[8] anxious with longing. We try in our hearts to become one again, but the immensity of Earth intervenes.

O pining Yakṣa in your deserted mountain turret, who can reassure you that in a wonderfully beautiful world, on a night of full autumn moonlight, you will be united eternally with the Person you embrace in your dreams, to whom you send your message on a cloud. I know, I know that you would not find any difference between matter[9] and consciousness, if only the distinction between truth and imagination could disappear.

4. 'They weep in each other's arms when they think of separation.'

5. *mānasa-lok*: 'mind-world'. Tagore may be punning here with the Mānasa lake on whose shore the Beloved dwells.

6. 'Who brought (you) out from inside the heart?'

7. 'Because of that, the heart of Balarām's lord (Kṛṣṇa) is restless.'

8. See notes to 'The *Meghadūta*' (p. 131).

9. *acetan*: 'non-conscious, inanimate', perhaps corresponding with 'Earth' above. We are bound to earth and to material existence, however far consciousness and imagination may strive to reach.

Appendix B

The first two chapters of *lok-sāhitya* (Folk Literature), 1907, consist of a collection of Bengali nursery rhymes, with comments by Tagore. The translation below is of the beginning of Chapter I.

For some time I have been engaged in collecting all the Bengali rhymes that women currently use to divert their children. These rhymes may indeed have special value in the determination of the history of our language and society, but it is the simple, natural, poetic quality in them that has made them especially attractive to me.

I am fearful of making my simple likes or dislikes my critical starting-off point, because those who are expert critics condemn such writing as egoism.

I would humbly submit to those who make this judgement that there is no conceit in such egoism, rather the reverse. Those who are proper critics carry a pair of scales; they ascribe to literary works a fixed weight by weighing them against certain fixed maxims; whatever composition is before them, they can give it an appropriate number and stamp.

But those who through ignorance and inexperience are unable to determine weight in this way have to base their criticism on pleasure or displeasure; so for them it is arrogant to introduce gospel truth into the discussion of literature. They find it better to say which piece of writing they like or dislike than to say which is good or bad.

If anyone asks me who wants to hear such things, my reply is that everyone comes to hear them in literature itself. The word 'criticism' is reserved for literary criticism, but most literature is nothing but a criticism of nature and human life. When a poet expresses his own joy or grief or surprise concerning nature, mankind or events, and tries to convey his feelings through passion and literary skill alone to another mind, no one condemns him. And all the reader does is to see, equally egotistically, 'whether the poet's words agree with my way of thinking or not'. So if the critic of poetry is also prepared to abandon logical argument and value-judgement and present to his readers the feeling of a reader, then it is not right to find fault with him.

In particular, what I have sat down to communicate today will have to contain some autobiography. It is impossible for me to distinguish the aesthetic delight that I find in nursery rhymes from my own childhood memories. The present writer does not have the analytic power required to decide how much the sweetness of these rhymes is based on my own infant memories and how much on eternal literary excellence. It is best to admit this at the outset.

'The rain falls pitter-patter, the river has overflowed.'[1] This nursery rhyme was like a magic spell to me in childhood, and I still cannot forget its enchantment. I am unable to appreciate clearly the sweetness and appropriateness of nursery rhymes unless I remember that spellbound state of mind. I cannot understand why so many poems great and small, so much philosophical and moral discussion, such intense human endeavour, such sweated exertion should vanish every day into futile oblivion, while all these incongruous, nonsensical arbitrary verses remain perpetually current in popular memory.

There is a timelessness in all these nursery rhymes. They never carry any indication of who wrote them, and no one ever thinks to ask on which day or in which year they were written. Because of this inherent timelessness, even if they were written in our own day they are ancient, and even if they were written thousands of years ago they are new.

If you look closely, you see that there is nothing as ancient as infancy. Adults have been changed in many different ways by place, time, education and custom, but infants are the same today as they were a hundred thousand years ago. Unchanging ancientness is born into human homes again and again in the form of a baby, yet the freshness, beauty, innocence and sweetness it had at the beginning of history is the same today. The reason for this eternal newness is that infants are the creations of Nature. But adults are to a very great extent man's own making. In the same way, nursery rhymes are infant-literature; they are born spontaneously and naturally in the human mind.

There is a special significance in saying that they are born spontaneously. In their natural state, our minds are filled with images and echoes of the universe wandering about in a broken, disconnected way. They can take on a variety of shapes, and can suddenly shift from one subject to another. Just as the wind contains dust from the road, flower-pollen, countless odours, various sounds, stray leaves, drops of water, vapours from the earth – all the strange, uprooted, aerial bits and pieces of this swirling, churned-up world wandering around without meaning – so too our minds. There too in the ceaseless stream of consciousness many colours, scents and sounds, puffs of fancy, snatches of thought, broken pieces of language – all the many hundreds of abandoned, forgotten, detached materials of our experiential world – float about aimlessly and inconsequentially.

When we aim our thoughts consciously in some particular direction, then all this humming activity suddenly stops, the web of particles flies away, the entire shadowy mirage is removed in a trice, our imagination and intelligence concentrate themselves into a unity, and proceed intently. The substance that we call Mind possesses such superior mastery that when it wakes and asserts itself then most of our inner and outer world is overwhelmed by its influence:

1. *bṛṣṭi paṛe ṭāpur-ṭupur, nade ela bāṇ*: Tagore used to call this rhyme *āmār śaiśaber megh-dūt*, 'my childhood Meghadūta'.

under its discipline, rule, language, and by the commands of its servants, the whole world is reduced. Think of all the thousands of kinds of small and large noises that are perpetually sounding – bird-calls, rustling leaves, gurgling waters, the mingled noises of human habitations – and think of all the shaking, stirring, coming, going, the restless stream of mortal existence playing and swirling on and on: yet what a tiny part of it do we notice. The main reason for this is that, like a fisherman, our mind is able to throw only a single net and take up only that little bit that is caught in one throw: all the rest eludes it. When it sees, then it does not hear well; when it hears, then it does not see well; and when it thinks, then it does not see or hear well. It is able to a great degree to exclude all unnecessary materials from the path of its attention. This power is the chief thing that preserves its supremacy even in the midst of the boundless variety of the world. In the Purāṇas[2] one can read that in ancient times certain great souls were able to achieve the power to live or die at will. Our mind has power to be blind or deaf at will, and because we have to use that power at every step, most of the world from the time we are born to the time we die carries on outside our consciousness. The mind takes up what it prepares for itself; it perceives whatever is formed by its own needs and nature; with what is happening or developing all around it – even in its own inner regions – it is not much concerned.

If the reflected stream of all the dream-like shadows and sounds that wander about like endlessly-forming clouds in the sky of our mind in its simple state, sometimes combining, sometimes separating, going through various shapes and colours, moving at the chance dictate of invisible winds, could be projected on to some non-conscious screen,[3] then we would see a considerable resemblance between that projection and these rhymes that we are discussing. These rhymes are nothing but the shadows of our ever-changing inner sky; they are like shadows projected on to the clear waters of a lake by clouds playing in the heavens. That is why I said that they are born spontaneously.

Before I quote some nursery rhymes here by way of illustration, I must beg for my readers' indulgence. Firstly, how can the sound of the affectionate, sweet, natural voice that always went with these rhymes issue from the pen of a man like me, sober, old and conscious of my position? My readers must recall to mind from their own homes, from their own childhood memories, that soothing sweetness of voice. What magic spell do I possess to bring before my readers the love, the music, the evening lamp-lit pictures of beauty that are forever intimately associated with it? I trust that the spell will lie in the rhymes themselves.

2. Hindu myths.

3. Writing in the very early days of the cinema, Tagore may be striving here for a Bengali expression for a cinema-screen (*acetan paṭ*: 'non-conscious, inanimate screen'). Present-day Bengali would simply use the English word 'screen'.

Secondly, to place all these homely, unkempt, unsophisticated nursery rhymes[4] in the middle of a guarded and conventional literary essay is to do them some unfairness – like putting an ordinary housewife in the witness-box of a court of law for cross-examination. But I have no choice. Courts have to work according to the rules of courts; essays have to be written according to the rules of writing essays. Some cruelty is unavoidable.

4. *meyeli charā*: 'rhymes such as women (*meye*) use'. *meyeli* is hard to translate: it is neither 'womanish', nor 'womanly', nor 'effeminate'.

Glossary

This Glossary is not a complete index, but I have given page references to the items included. It gives only the basic information required for this book. The most convenient source of further information is Benjamin Walker's *Hindu World*, London, 1968. For musical rāgas, I have used Walter Kaufman's *The Rāgas of North India*, Indiana, 1968: but I have also been greatly helped on musical matters by Jonathan Katz, of the Indian Institute, Oxford. My thanks to him and to Dr Jim Robinson, who kindly checked the mythological items; on names of flowers and trees, I should like to acknowledge the special assistance given me by Mrs Sujata Chaudhuri of Calcutta.

Aghrāṇ (108)
Bengali month (strictly *agrahāyaṇ*), mid-November to mid-December; part of the season between autumn and winter known as *hemanta*.

Ākanda (93)
Flower, growing on a small tree; light mauvish-green calyx, small mauve bud-like petals. In the right conditions it can bloom from February to October.

Akbar (98)
The third Moghul Emperor, from 1556 to 1605, and the real founder of the Moghul dynasty and empire. He strove for conciliation between Hindus and Muslims and tried to promulgate a new, universalist religion. He built the magnificent new city of Fatehpur Sikri near Agra, but after 1588 he ceased to use it as a capital and it became deserted.

Alakā (38, 52, 116, 131, 135, 169, 170, 181)
Capital city and paradise of Kubera, chief of the Yakṣas. Because by Kālidāsa's time Kubera was also lord of riches, Alakā was regarded as the wealthiest of the many paradisical *loka*s (regions) of Hindu cosmology.

Āmrakūṭa (51)
Mountain in the Vindhya range.

Ārākān (86)
Coastal region of Burma, on the east side of the Bay of Bengal. For the station-master in 'Deception', it is Timbuctoo.

Āṣāṛh (50, 51, 118)
Bengali month, mid-June to mid-July; the rainy season in Bengal.

Āśvin (87, 152)
Bengali month, mid-September to mid-October; autumn in Bengal.

Avantī (51, 180, 181, 182)
Region of central India, whose capital was Ujjayinī. Both region and city are now known as Ujjain.

Baiśākh (94, 98, 101)
First month of the Bengali year, mid-April to mid-May; summer in Bengal.

Bakul (58, 67, 73)
Small creamy-white star-like flower, growing on a large tree. It is sweet-scented, can bloom from February to July, and is celebrated in poetry.

Balarām Dās (182)
A Bengali Vaiṣṇava poet of the sixteenth century.

Bāul (168, 169)
Name of a heterodox religious sect in Bengal. Their faith belongs to a mystical tradition known as *sahajīyā* (*sahaj* means 'simple, direct'), and the Bāul relationship with God is direct and personal, bypassing all scripture, ritual or priestcraft. They are not ascetics or celibates, but have traditionally led a wandering life, singing songs for a living. Tagore was much influenced by their religion, their freedom from convention, and their devotional songs. The Pauṣ Melā (a fair held in the month of Pauṣ), when Baul singers congregate, is an important event in the Santiniketan calendar.

Bhairav (163)
Musical rāga, performed in the morning. Bhairava is a name of Śiva in his terrifying aspect, and the rāga is serious and even awesome in character.

Bhairavī (152)
A morning rāga, traditionally often performed at the end of a concert. Bhairavī is one of the names of Śiva's consort, and the rāga is named after her. It is calm and pensive in mood.

Bhāṭi (119, 172)
White flower with dark red spots, growing in bunches on a bush. It has a strong, sweet smell, and can bloom from January to April. The plant is supposed to have medicinal properties, especially good for skin ailments.

Bhūpālī (54)
Pentatonic rāga, sung in the first part of the night. It is simple in structure, dignified and calm.

Bighā (84, 134)
Unit of land measurement, roughly equal to a third of an acre.

Bilāspur (83, 85, 148)
Town in Madhya Pradesh, Central India.

Brahmā (45)
Creator and first god of the triad of classical Hinduism. He was popular at one time, but is now worshipped much less than the great gods Viṣṇu and Śiva. He is depicted as red in colour, with four faces and four arms. The 'fire-matted hair' that Tagore gives him in 'Brahmā, Viṣṇu, Śiva' does not feature in the traditional iconography of Brahmā.

Brahman (17, 24, 37, 130, 144, 160, 167, 170, 171)
The absolute, eternal and universal God or Spirit of the Upaniṣads, corresponding to the *ātman* or Soul in man. 'Brahman' is the stem-form of the word, and is used by most modern writers. Tagore, however, frequently writes 'Brahma' in his English lectures, the neuter nominative form, not to be confused with Brahmā, the masculine nominative.

Brahmāvarta (52)
One of the ancient names used for the territory settled by the Indo-Aryans: originally the land between the Ganges and the Jumna.

Brahmin (60, 62, 63, 64, 65, 66, 169, 172, 174)
Name of the first of the four main Hindu castes. Strictly it should be 'brāhmaṇ'; but it is conventionally spelt 'brahmin' to distinguish it from Brahman (the Supreme Spirit) and the Brāhmaṇas, sacred scriptures used by Brahmins, who are hereditary priests.

Caitra (88, 93, 94, 110, 119, 156)
The last month of the Bengali year, mid-March to mid-April; spring in Bengal.

Cāmelī (79, 145)
Strictly, the Spanish jasmine; small white flower growing in clusters on a creeper. It is sweetly scented, and can bloom from February to July. But the name is commonly given to the jasmine or *jātī* (q.v.).

Cā̃pā (campā, campak) (94)
The Champak tree; its elongated golden-yellow flowers bloom in summer and are compared by poets to beautiful tapering fingers.

Conch (45, 60, 70, 71, 72, 77, 128, 144)
Shell that (perforated at one end) can be blown like a horn. In the Mahābhārata, each hero has a conch which he blows in battle and which often has a name. The most important conch in Hindu mythology is the Pāñcajanya, which was once inhabited by a demon killed by Viṣṇu, and which is therefore associated with Viṣṇu and his chief incarnation Kṛṣṇa (see notes

to 'The Conch', p. 144). Śiva also carries a conch, along with his trident and drum. Because of these divine associations, conches are blown in temple worship and on festive occasions such as the arrival of a bride or bridegroom. In Tagore's poetry the conch can be an emblem of destructive power, or victory, or celebration.

Cūrṇī (64)
River of West Bengal, joining the Hooghly from the east, south of Rānāghāṭ.

Daśārṇa (51, 131, 180)
Name of a people and a region somewhere in North or Central India, mentioned in Kālidāsa's *Meghadūta*.

Devagiri (180)
Name of a mountain mentioned in Kālidāsa's *Meghadūta*.

Dhaleśvarī (97, 98, 158)
River in Assam, east of the Silhyet district of present-day Bangladesh.

Dhūrjati (131, 157)
Name of Śiva: 'having heavy matted locks'.

Dīpak (144)
Musical rāga. Ancient musicians are said to have kindled flame by the performance of this rāga: there is a story of the great sixteenth-century musician Tānsen lighting up all the candles in Akbar's palace when he sang it once. There is therefore superstition attached to it, and many musicians shy away from performing it or even mentioning its name.

Diwali (dīpālī, dīpāvalī, dīpānvitā) (165)
Late autumn Festival of Lamps (*dīpa*), when lights are put outside houses or floated on rivers in honour of Lakṣmī in many parts of India, but in Bengal usually in honour of Kālī (whence the festival is often known as Kālī-pūjā).

Dolan-cā̃pā (94, 156)
White or cream-yellow flower, growing on a small bush. It is sweet-scented and blooms in spring.

Durgā (54, 64, 133)
The form of Śiva's *śakti* or consort that is most popular in Bengal. Bengal's main religious festival, Durgā-pūjā, held in October/November, goes back to Rāma's worship of Durgā for victory over the demon king Rāvana, as mentioned in the medieval Bengali version of the Rāmāyana. The festival starts with her supposed coming from her husband's home to her parental home, and ends with her tearful return to her husband on the day known as *bijayā*

daśamī ('the Victorious Tenth'). Two types of song are sung through the autumn in connection with these events: *āgamanī*, welcoming Durgā's arrival at her parents' home, and *bijayā*, songs of sorrow at her departure. (See Pārvatī for Durgā's parentage.)

Gaṇeśa (96)
Elephant-headed god, son of Śiva and Pārvatī, bringer of good luck, including good luck in business or shop-keeping.

Ganges (Gaṅgā) (50, 52, 88, 128, 131)
Sacred river of North India; eldest daughter of Himavat (see 'Himālaya'). Originally a heavenly river, she was brought down to earth by the prayers of the saint Bhagīratha; but Śiva, to save the earth from the shock of her fall, caught the river on his matted hair, and checked her course. Pārvatī, Śiva's wife, was jealous of her sister Gaṅgā for being allowed to play with Śiva's hair.

Gaurī (70, 131)
Another name for Durgā or Pārvatī: the 'Golden One'.

Ghāt (107)
A mooring-place; or steps leading down to a tank or river where people can bathe or wash clothes.

Himālaya (86, 88, 131, 153, 180, 181)
The great northern mountain range of the Indian sub-continent, the Himalayas. The name means 'abode of snow'. In Hindu mythology, Himālaya (or Himavat) is the husband of Menakā and father of Pārvatī and Gaṅgā (see **Ganges**).

Hindusthānī (84, 133)
Someone from Hindi-speaking North India, as opposed to Bengal.

Holi (54)
Hindu spring and fertility festival, characterized by the joyous throwing of coloured powders and sprinkling of coloured liquids at people.

Indra (89, 113, 155)
King of the gods in the Ṛg-veda, most ancient of Indian texts; the Indian Jupiter, lord of the sky whose thunderbolt conquers demons. In Kālidāsa's *Kumāra-sambhava* he sends Kāma to try to break Śiva's penance (see **Kālidāsa**).

Jabā (68, 144)
Hibiscus; it grows on a bushy plant, is bell-shaped, and is generally scarlet, though other colours are found. It can bloom nearly all the year round, and one of its varieties is used in the worship of Kālī.

Jāhnavī (131)
Name of Gaṅgā (the Ganges): 'daughter of Jahnu' after a sage of that name who was disturbed by the river and drank her up in anger; but who later relented and allowed her to flow from his ear.

Jambu (51, 180)
Large tree that sheds its leaves in January/February, has fragrant white flowers in March-May, and purplish-black astringent fruit in June/July. Fruit, bark and seeds have medicinal properties; tussore silk-worms are fed on the leaves.

Jārul (119)
Pride of India; deciduous tree, whose leaves fall in February/March after turning red. It has showy mauve or pink flowers growing in clusters, and green fruit turning to woody-brown and not eaten. Its wood is valuable, and its bark, leaves and fruits have medicinal properties.

Jātī (94)
Jasmine; its small star-shaped white or yellow flowers, growing on a shrub, are especially sweet-scented at night, and are profuse in spring and summer. An extract from the flowers is used to make medicines and perfumed hair-oil. The *jātī* is also commonly known as *cāmelī* (q.v.).

Jayadeva (51)
Sanskrit poet of the early twelfth century A.D., born in Bengal. His best known work is the *Gīta-govinda*, 'Song of the Cowherd', a voluptuous poetic drama about Rādhā and Kṛṣṇa.

Jīban-debatā (7, 8, 61)
See Introduction pp. 24, 35, 38, and notes to 'The Golden Boat', 'On the Edge of the Sea', 'Unyielding' and 'Last Tryst' (pp. 132, 136, 158, 170).

Jumna (Yamunā) (80)
River of North India, one of the 'holy triad' (Gaṅgā, Yamunā and Sarasvatī). Delhi is on its banks, and the Taj Mahal at Agra.

Jyaiṣṭha (135)
Second month of the Bengali year, mid-May to mid-June; high summer in Bengal.

Kacu (116)
The taro, a coarse herbaceous plant cultivated for its tubers; also the dasheen, ornamental varieties of which are planted in gardens (and known in India as Bleeding Heart).

Kadam/Kadamba (67, 139)
Flower growing on a large tree, with tiny florets set on a yellow-orange ball.

It is sweet-scented, grows in the rainy season, is associated with Kṛṣṇa and is therefore celebrated in Vaiṣṇava poetry.

Kāfī (54)
Musical rāga, spelt *kāphi* in Bengali (the name is Persian). It is mostly used in lighter forms of composition such as *ṭhumrī*.

Kailāsa (180)
A great Himalayan peak, said to be the abode of Śiva as well as the site of the Yakṣa city of Alakā.

Kālī (144)
The most frightening of the forms of Śiva's *śakti* or consort, with an important cult in Bengal centred in the Kalighat Temple in Calcutta. Tagore attacked Kālī-worship in his play *bisarjan* (Sacrifice), 1890.

Kālidāsa (38, 120, 130, 131, 151, 165, 169, 173, 180)
Greatest poet and dramatist of Sanskrit literature, who lived some time between A.D. 350 and 600. Little is known about him: he is traditionally supposed to have been the most brilliant of the 'nine gems' of literature at the court of Vikramāditya in Ujjain. The works of Kālidāsa that had the greatest influence on Tagore were the *Meghadūta* (Cloud-Messenger) and the *Kumāra-sambhava* (Kumāra's Occasioning, usually known as 'The Birth of the War-god'). The *Meghadūta* is in the form of a message from an exiled Yakṣa in Central India to his pining Beloved in the Yakṣa city of Alakā on Mount Kailāsa, sent on a cloud. The poem gives a bird's eye view of India as the Yakṣa imagines the cloud's progress northwards. The romanticism and yearning of the poem, rather than its worldliness and wit, were what appealed to Tagore. The *Kumāra-sambhava* is based on a major Hindu myth: the gods, in terror of the demon Tāraka, are told by Brahmā that the demon can only be destroyed by the son of Śiva begotten on Pārvatī. Śiva is at the time engaged in deep meditation, so Indra, chief of the gods, persuades Kāma, the god of Love, to smite Śiva with love for Pārvatī. Kāma's first attempt fails: Śiva, discharges a flame from his third eye and burns Kāma to ashes. Later Śiva relents, restores Kāma, and marries Pārvatī (Umā). In the seventh canto of the poem the wedding is flamboyantly described, with the *saptarṣi*, the Seven Sages of Ancient India, in attendance.

Kāma (90, 151, 156)
Indian god of Love, husband of Rati. His bow is made of sugar-cane strung with a row of bees, and his arrows are flowers. He emerged from the primeval chaos, and has no parents. For the story of how he was sent as 'Indra's messenger' to try to break Śiva's penance, so that the universe could be saved from the demon Tāraka, see **Kālidāsa**.

Kanakhala (52, 131)
Mountain, near to which the flow of the Ganges was checked by Śiva's hair. See Ganges.

Kāñcan (88)
White, pinkish-mauve or yellow flower growing on a small tree, lightly scented, growing more or less round the year.

Karabī/Karabikā (129, 152)
Oleander; white, dark pink or red flower, growing in bunches on a large shrub. It has a faint, pleasant smell and blooms throughout the year.

Ketakī (51, 67, 180)
Screw-pine; long spiked leaves covering floral stalks whose pollen is used as a flavouring for *pān* (q.v.), drinks, etc. It is strongly scented, and blooms in the rainy season.

Khasrubāg (86)
Name of a palace at Rampur in Uttar Pradesh; but Tagore may not have had a precise place in mind when he used the name in 'Deception'.

Kiṃśuk (88)
Flame of the Forest; tree with bright orange-red flowers like a parrot's beak, growing in clusters. It is not scented, but flowers profusely in spring, and is associated with spring festivals.

Kirāt (136)
An ancient forest people living in the eastern Himalayas. The name has come to mean simply 'aboriginal' (*ādi-bāsī*) or 'tribal' in Tagore.

Koel (kokil) (47, 119, 172)
A bird that is frequently called 'cuckoo' by translators but which is actually different from either the European cuckoo or the Indian cuckoo, though it belongs to the same order. Its call is much more strident and high-pitched than the cuckoo's note.

Kṛṣṇa (54, 128, 131, 144, 180, 182)
Celebrated incarnation of Viṣṇu and hero of Hindu mythology. In Bengal he is associated with Vaiṣṇavism and the countless medieval Bengali lyrics that celebrate the love of Kṛṣṇa and Rādhā; and with his upbringing in Vraja on the banks of the Jumna in the company of cowherds and milkmaids. Both traditions appear in the *Gīta-govinda* of Jayadeva, Bengal's greatest Sanskrit poet. Kṛṣṇa is dark in complexion and is sometimes called *Śyām* ('black' or 'dark blue or green').

Kumāra-sambhava (151, 165)
See **Kālidāsa**.

Kunda (146)
Small white flower growing on a small shrub, unscented, blooming especially profusely in spring. Poets liken the flower to beautiful teeth.

Kuṛci (110)
White-flowering tree; its whitish timber is used for woodcuts and engraving.

Kurukṣetra (52)
Plain near Delhi, celebrated as the site of the great battle between the Kauravas and Pandavas in the Mahābhārata.

Lakṣmī (46, 52, 85, 134, 135)
Goddess of fortune and beauty, wife of Viṣnu. She is associated with prosperity, goodness and happiness, and with the lotus, which she carries in her hand. *lakṣmī* is an adjective meaning well-behaved and good-natured in Bengali; and *lakṣmī-chāṛā* means 'good-for-nothing'.

Lāṭhi (68)
A stick or staff for fighting with; policeman's baton in modern usage.

Līlā (88, 89, 155, 163, 166, 171)
See notes to 'The Wakening of Śiva', p. 152.

Mādhabī (78, 90, 146)
Creeper with bunches of light-red, pink or (rarely) light-yellow flowers, with a faint, very pleasant smell. It blooms from February to September.

Mahuā (155)
Indian Butter tree: its transparent, light-cream flowers exude a scent of honey, bloom from February to April, and yield a spirit drunk freely by Santhals and other aboriginal groups. Its seeds are crushed for oil (hence its English name), and its sap is used as a cure for rheumatism. Its green, juicy berries are also intoxicating, and are liked by birds and animals.

Makara (94, 95)
Mythical sea-monster, representing the Capricorn of the Hindu zodiac, with head and forelegs of a deer, and body and tail of a fish. It figures on the banner of Kāma, god of Love.

Mālatī (139)
Creeper with white flowers growing in cascading bunches, beautifully perfumed. It blooms from June to August, and is celebrated in poetry.

Mānasa Lake (46, 52, 129, 181, 182)
Sacred lake in the Himalayas, near Mount Kailāsa. The Yakṣa city of Alakā and the abode where the Yakṣa's Beloved pines for him in Kālidāsa's *Meghadūta* are on its shore.

Mandāra (137)
Coral tree: with beautiful clusters of coral-red flowers that blossom when the leaves are shed. It is also regarded as one of the seven trees of *svarga-loka*, most popular of the paradises of Hindu cosmology.

Mantra (60, 88, 131, 136, 152, 154, 161, 172, 175, 178)
This term was originally restricted to the metrical psalms of praise in Vedic literature; but it came to mean any sacred verse of scripture or any spell or formula used in worship, prayer or ritual. The most famous mantra of all is the Gāyatrī, a verse from the Ṛg-veda that all Brahmins are supposed to repeat mentally morning and evening. The importance of mantras to India's many esoteric and mystical cults gives the word connotations of magic as well as prayer.

Meghadūta (50, 51, 79, 130, 146, 169, 180, 181, 184)
See **Kālidāsa**.

Moghul (122, 146, 174)
Muslim dynasty founded by Babur in 1526, which ruled much of India until European adventurism and internal weaknesses began to break up the Moghul empire in the eighteenth century.

Mohenjodaro (110, 111, 165)
A site in Sind, Pakistan, which has given its name to a prehistoric civilization that flourished in the Indus Valley from about 2500 to 1500 B.C.

Mūltān (54)
Musical rāga, usually known as Mūltānī. It is quiet, loving and associated with late afternoon.

Nadiyā (Nabadwīp) (118)
Town and district in West Bengal; a major cultural and religious centre in the Bengali middle ages.

Nirvindhyā (51, 180)
A river flowing north from the Vindhya mountains in Central India.

Oṛiyā (57)
A native of the state of Orissa, south of Bengal.

Pān (54)
Leaf of the betel pepper plant, commonly chewed in India together with betel-nut (which comes from a different plant, the betel palm) and shell lime, with spices added to taste.

Pānā (164)
A pond-weed. Some varieties, such as the Water Hyacinth, have flowers; some are dried and used as a fertilizer.

Pārul (86, 150)
Large brick-red bell-shaped flowers on a small tree, sweet-scented, blooming from April to June.

Pārvatī (94, 95, 131, 156, 157)
Consort of Śiva. She was born of a union between Himavat (see **Himālaya**) and the nymph Menakā, and her name therefore means 'daughter of the mountain'. She tends to appear in Tagore's writings as Śiva's *śakti* manifest in Nature.

Pāṭhān (122, 174)
The tribesmen inhabiting the 'North-West Frontier' region between present-day Pakistan and Afghanistan. The term was sometimes applied to the Delhi sultans (1206–1526), though most of the dynasties of the sultanate were of Turkish origin.

Pauṣ (136)
Bengali winter month, mid-December to mid-January; time of the most important Melā or fair held at Santiniketan (see **Bāul**).

Phālgun (101)
Bengali month, mid-February to mid-March; the first part of spring.

Pinākа (46)
The name of Śiva's bow (though some say it is the name of his trident).

Praṇām (138, 160)
Act of obeisance. Before a deity, one touches the ground with one's forehead; with a respected person, one touches the feet and then one's forehead ('taking the dust' of his or her feet).

Pūjā (94, 108)
General word for most forms of ceremonial worship, from a simple daily offering to a deity to a full-scale religious festival such as Bengal's Durgā-pūjā. It is probably derived from a verb meaning 'smear, put on sticky substances, daub', since a major part of pūjā is the marking or daubing of the image of the deity with various liquids, powders and oily substances (usually red or yellow).

Pūrvī (58, 150)
Musical rāga. It is quiet and serious, and is performed at sunset.

Rādhā (180)
A celebrated cowherdess beloved of Kṛṣṇa; she features greatly in Jayadeva's *Gīta-govinda*, and in the numerous *pada*s (lyric songs) of Bengali Vaiṣṇavism. She became the archetypal Bengali *birahiṇī* (woman separated from and pining for the one she loves).

Rāga (54, 58, 90, 98, 107, 133, 152, 158, 163)
The most important term and element in Indian music. It is derived from the Sanskrit word *raṅga*, 'colour'. Modern Indian languages generally drop the final 'a' in pronunciation, so I have written rāg Pūrvī, rāg Kāfi etc. in my translations. A rāga is a group of notes on which a musical composition or improvisation may be based, and carries a distinguishing name. Traditionally each rāga is associated with a particular mood, time of day, season, etc.; and conservative musicians will only reluctantly perform a rāga at the wrong time. There have been several different systems of classifying rāgas according to a limited number of parent scales. Tagore, when he refers to rāgas in his poems, usually observes another classification which became popular in North India: in this, some of the rāgas are called *rāginīs* (feminine rāgas), subordinated to a small number of male rāgas. The distinction is not often maintained in current speech.

Rajanī-gandhā (144)
Small lily-like bulbiferous plant, with white flowers growing along a long stalk. Its name means 'night-scented', and it is used in bouquets at weddings or to decorate the bridal bed.

Rājbaṃśī (119)
A subdivision of the Māl caste of Bengal: the Māls are supposed to have been aboriginal, non-Aryan cultivators, later absorbed into the lower Hindu castes. But the term Rājbaṃśī or Rajbanshi is not precise, has been claimed by other tribal groups (it literally means 'of royal lineage') and can simply mean 'low-caste'.

Rāmagiri (180)
'Rāma's mountain' in Central India, where Rāma, hero of the Sanskrit epic the Rāmāyaṇa, began a fourteen-year period of exile.

Revā (51, 180, 182)
Sacred river flowing westwards from Mount Āmrakūṭa in the Vindhya mountains.

Rūpnārāyaṇ (65)
A river of West Bengal, a tributary of the Hooghly, joining it from the west near its mouth It is fully tidal, and a danger when in flood to the navigation of the Hooghly.

Sādhu (56, 57, 134)
Term for an ascetic or *sannyāsī*; but also a term for a merchant, trader or money-lender – or simply a prosperous and respected man.

Śahānā (54)
Musical rāga, usually known as Śahānā-kānaḍā. It is solemn, and is sung in the third quarter of the night.

Sajne (93)
Tree with small white flowers growing in clusters, flowering from March to April and faintly perfumed.

Śakti (141, 144, 145, 154)
The energy or active power of a deity personified as his wife. The *śakti* or consort of a god can take many forms; thus Durgā, Kālī and Pārvatī are all *śakti*s of Śiva. The word can also simply mean 'power, strength, might'.

Sannyāsī (121, 135, 155)
An ascetic or monk or religious mendicant.

Sealdah Station (97)
The main railway terminus in North Calcutta.

Sẽuti (88)
A sort of dog-rose; white, with a single row of petals.

Shah-Jahan (78, 145, 146)
Fifth Moghul Emperor, from 1628 to 1658, famous for the Peacock Throne he built for himself and for the magnificent buildings of his capital, Agra. The Taj Mahal, a tomb for his wife Mumtaz Mahal, took over twenty years to build.

Siddha (51)
Name of a class of semi-divine beings who dwell high up, in mountains or in the sky between earth and sun.

Sindhu-Bārõyā (98)
Musical rāga, favoured by Tagore and the Vishnupuri group of musicians; a version of the light rāga Bārvā.

Śiprā (51, 180, 181, 182)
River on whose banks Ujjayinī is situated.

Śiśu (84)
Tree, whose off-white flowers bloom in the rainy season. Its wood is used for making furniture. Known as the Shisham tree in North and Central India.

Śiuli (86)
Night jasmine: small white flowers with orange stalks, blossoming at night and dropping in showers by early morning. It is sweet-scented, and blooms from September to November.

Śiva (46, 47, 52, 58, 70, 89, 90, 94, 95, 129, 131, 135, 141, 151, 152, 156, 157, 161, 163, 165)
Third god of the Hindu triad, and the richest and most contradictory of the three. He is frequently referred to as 'The Destroyer' (as opposed to Brahmā

the Creator and Viṣṇu the Preserver), and in this capacity has a fearsome aspect – with a serpent and necklace of skulls round his neck, a central eye that can shoot out flame, and a train of attendant demons who frequent cremation-grounds. His dance, the *tāṇḍava*, destroys the world, and in this form he is known as Naṭa-rāj, Lord of the Dance. But he is also associated with fertility, the Liṅga or Phallus being the main form in which he is worshipped in Śiva-temples; and the unity of Śiva and his *śakti* or consort (Pārvatī, Durgā, Kālī) represents the perfect balancing of opposing forces in Nature. Śiva's periods of activity and creativity are interrupted by spells of deep meditation or penance: in this form he is 'The Great Ascetic', ash-smeared, bark-clad, destroyer of the god of Love Kāma with a glance of fire from his eye. Śiva's hair is matted together and coiled up above his forehead; on the top of it he bears the Ganges (q.v.). He holds in his eight hands a trident called *triśūla*, whose three prongs denote his creative, destructive and regenerative powers, a drum (*ḍamaru*), a bow (*pināka*), and a horn (usually a conch). He is accompanied by the bull Nandin. He has over a thousand names and epithets.

Śrābaṇ (124, 132, 144)
Bengali month, mid-July to mid-August; second of the two rainy months.

Tāla (95)
Term for the metrical cycles used in Indian music. Originally it meant 'hand-clap', which probably indicates that the rhythm of the music was punctuated by hand-claps, as it still is in South India.

Tamāl (51, 98, 158)
Medium-sized hardy tree with dark-green leaves, and blackish bark and timber. Because of its dark colour it is often compared to Kṛṣṇa.

Tānpurā (54, 55, 133)
Simple stringed instrument that maintains the 'drone' in Indian music, i.e. the tonic and another medial note (usually the fifth or fourth). It normally has four strings.

Udayana (180, 181)
Legendary King of Vatsa, whose romance with Vāsavadattā, treated many times in story and drama, was popular with the people of Avantī (Ujjain).

Ujjayinī (Ujjain) (50, 51, 180, 182)
Capital city of Avantī; one of the Seven Sacred Cities of the Hindus; where Kālidāsa is supposed to have received patronage.

Umā (90, 151)
Name of Śiva's *śakti* or consort; she appears under this name in Kālidāsa's ***Kumāra-sambhava.***

Ustād (54, 173)
A Persian and Urdu term for a master-craftsman or teacher, often applied to distinguished musicians in North India; comparable to 'Maestro'.

Vaiṣṇava (97, 158, 180, 182)
A follower of Vaiṣṇavism, a religion based on intense personal devotion to Viṣṇu and his incarnations Rāma and Kṛṣṇa and their consorts. It was the main religion of medieval Bengal, and inspired numerous songs and manuals on the love of Rādhā and Kṛṣṇa. Pious Vaiṣṇavas are supposed to weep at the mention of Rādhā's name (q.v.).

Vāsavadattā (180)
See **Udayana**.

Vetravatī (51, 180)
River flowing from the Vindhya mountains to the Jumna.

Vidiśā (180)
The capital city of Daśārṇa.

Vikramāditya (120)
Legendary king of Ujjain; Kālidāsa is supposed to have been one of the 'nine gems' of literature who graced his fabulous court.

Vīṇā (60, 61, 90, 95, 99, 107, 156, 159)
Generic term for a number of stringed instruments, now applied to those of the lute-type. The vīṇā is supposed to have been invented by Nārada, chief of the Gandharvas or heavenly musicians, and mythical author of some of the hymns of the Ṛg-veda.

Vindhya (51, 180)
Name of a mountain range across the middle of India.

Viṣṇu (45, 46, 128, 129, 138, 176)
Second god of the Hindu triad, known as 'the Preserver'; he is not such a powerful presence as Śiva in Tagore's poetry, though many Hindus acknowledge him as supreme deity. He has four arms, carries a *gadā* (club or mace), a conch called Pāñcajanya (see **Conch**), a *cakra* or discus (Viṣṇu's sun-symbol), a lotus, a bow and a sword, and has a famous jewel on his breast called Kaustubha. Lakṣmī, goddess of prosperity, is the most important of his wives; Kṛṣṇa his most celebrated incarnation.

Yakṣa (116, 117, 169, 170, 180, 182)
Name of a class of semi-divine beings attendant on Kubera, god of wealth, whose home was Alakā. In Tagore's writings Yaksas take on a distinctly mortal character.

Yaman-Kalyāṇ (54)
Musical rāga, sung in the first quarter of the night, often at the beginning of a concert. It is a soothing, luck-bringing and benedictory rāga, distinguished by a sharpened fourth.

Yūthī / Yūthikā (131, 156, 171, 181)
A kind of jasmine-creeper, with small white flowers, sweetly scented, especially profuse in summer.

Zamindār (56, 84)
Persian term for a landowner that became standard in Bengal.

THE STORY OF PENGUIN CLASSICS

Before 1946 ...'Classics' are mainly the domain of academics and students, without readable editions for everyone else. This all changes when a little-known classicist, E. V. Rieu, presents Penguin founder Allen Lane with the translation of Homer's *Odyssey* that he has been working on and reading to his wife Nelly in his spare time.

1946 *The Odyssey* becomes the first Penguin Classic published, and promptly sells three million copies. Suddenly, classic books are no longer for the privileged few.

1950s Rieu, now series editor, turns to professional writers for the best modern, readable translations, including Dorothy L. Sayers's *Inferno* and Robert Graves's *The Twelve Caesars*, which revives the salacious original.

1960s The Classics are given the distinctive black jackets that have remained a constant throughout the series's various looks. Rieu retires in 1964, hailing the Penguin Classics list as 'the greatest educative force of the 20th century'.

1970s A new generation of translators arrives to swell the Penguin Classics ranks, and the list grows to encompass more philosophy, religion, science, history and politics.

1980s The Penguin American Library joins the Classics stable, with titles such as *The Last of the Mohicans* safeguarded. Penguin Classics now offers the most comprehensive library of world literature available.

1990s The launch of Penguin Audiobooks brings the classics to a listening audience for the first time, and in 1999 the launch of the Penguin Classics website takes them online to a larger global readership than ever before.

The 21st Century Penguin Classics are rejacketed for the first time in nearly twenty years. This world famous series now consists of more than 1300 titles, making the widest range of the best books ever written available to millions – and constantly redefining the meaning of what makes a 'classic'.

The Odyssey continues ...